How and Why to Build a Wine Cellar

RICHARD M. GOLD, PH. D.

The Wine Appreciation Guild
San Francisco

Other Books by
The Wine Appreciation Guild

This book is dedicated to all of the wine buffs who have been enticed into the collection of fine wines only to discover that they have no suitable storage facility.

I thank Neil Carlson, Marie E. Desch, Erez Klein, Paul Provost, Richard Rubin, Robert C. Shepard, and Steve Weisler for critiquing drafts.

How and Why to Build a Wine Cellar, Fourth Edition

Text copyright © 2007 Richard M. Gold, Ph.D.

First published in 1983, How and Why to Build a Passive Wine Cellar
Second Edition published 1985, How and Why to Build a Wine Cellar. Reprinted 1986–93
Third Edition published 1996. Reprinted 2002

The Wine Appreciation Guild
360 Swift Avenue
South San Francisco, CA 94080
(650) 866-3020
www.wineappreciation.com

Library of Congress Cataloging-in-Publication Data

Gold, Richard M.
How and why to build a wine cellar / Richard M. Gold. — 4th ed.
p. cm.
Includes index.
ISBN-13: 978-1-891267-00-0
ISBN-10: 1-891267-00-0
1. Wine cellars. 2. Wine and wine making. I. Wine Appreciation Guild
(San Francisco, Calif.) II. Title.
TP548.G56 2006
641.2'2—dc22
2006030560

TABLE OF CONTENTS

Section 1

****

INTRODUCTION TO WINE CELLARING

Chapter 1

****

A TALE OF TWO WINE CELLARS

This book was written in response to frustrations I experienced while building my own wine cellar. I'd read an article by Terry Robards in the Sunday New York Times (he was their wine consultant at the time) that described home wine cellar construction as the most casual of undertakings. Frank Prial, Robards' replacement at the Times, was equally causal about wine storage. Prial went so far as to recommend the garage as a good place to store wine (4/24/85, page C11). Most garages vie with uninsulated attics for my 5-star Award as the Worst Possible Place to Store Wine.

My home has a basement, and I have reasonably good aim with a hammer. After watching a carpenter build a stud wall, I confidently set aside a weekend for wine cellar construction. At that time it seemed unconscionable to hire a carpenter for such self-indulgence. Doing the work myself made the project morally acceptable, and promised to be fun as well. My advisor on the project worked behind the counter at the lumber yard. He meant well. I selected a convenient spot in the center of my basement near the furnace and laid out a generous 6' by 8' (1.8 by 2.4 m) room. Utilizing the techniques I had recently observed, I put up a 2 x 4 stud wall, stuffed it with 3 1/2" of fiberglass insulation, covered it with drywall, and installed a narrow pre-hung hollow core door.

Since wine cellars have been around for a lot longer than air conditioners, I spurned mechanical cooling. When I finished wine

4

cellar #1 in February, 1979, its temperature was an ideal 55°F (13°C). Following the purchasing advice of my loquacious wine merchant, I began to collect the then highly regarded but now maligned '75 Bordeaux which had recently been released.

The following summer my cellar's temperature rose to nearly 70°F (21°C). I hurriedly chopped a hole in the wine cellar wall and installed a small (5000 BTU) window-type air conditioner to move heat from the wine cellar into the adjacent basement. My troubles, unfortunately, were just beginning. As soon as the temperature got down to 60°F (15°C), the coils of the air conditioner iced up, preventing further airflow. Room air conditioners are not designed to operate at such low temperatures. By directing the cold-air stream from the air conditioner at a wall-mounted supplementary air conditioning thermostat, I was able to get it to run in 30 second bursts, which prevented further ice-ups. The following year I tacked two inches (R-10) of polystyrene to the outside of my wine cellar, but the air conditioner, although it ran less frequently, was still needed.

For the next two years I gave up summer vacations for fear that the air conditioner would ice up again or that a fuse would blow while I was away. I had also neglected to mount the air conditioner high enough to permit gravity powered removal of the condensate via a hose. I did not trust my neighbor to remember to empty the pan full of water that the air conditioner deposited every summer day. I never revealed to my family that my once casual interest in wine now required daily attention. Wine cellar #1 was, in retrospect, under-insulated, under-sized, under-vapor barriered, and inappropriately sited. My 75's would probably not be drinkable for 10 years. Something had to be done.

While collecting wines for a vertical tasting, I visited two home wine cellars that maintained reasonable temperatures without air conditioning. Having run out of excuses by which to deflect my family's requests for a week-long trip to the ocean, and space for my continuing acquisitions, I embarked upon the construction of wine cellar #2. This time I proceeded more cautiously.

Books on underground home construction, soil physics, super-insulation, and solar heating provided valuable suggestions. My new wine cellar was more appropriately sited in a corner of my basement (chapter 6); considerably larger to accommodate my growing stock (chapter 11); and super-insulated (chapter 7) with R-36 interior walls, an R-55 ceiling (chapter 13), and an R-36 door (chapter 14). Despite my greater sophistication this second time around, I had neglected humidity control. Come spring my wooden shelves turned snow white with mold and my wine bottle labels began to decompose. I finally cured the mold epidemic with a polyethylene vapor barrier placed against the interior surface of the concrete foundation walls that made up two sides of my wine cellar (chapter 8).

Soon thereafter, summer heat revealed the need for insulation on the outside surface of the two wine cellar walls that faced the elements. On August 2, 1982 my cellar temperature reached 65°F (18°C) and I panicked. One weekend of digging later, I had installed a two foot (.6 m) wide by 4" (10 cm) thick exterior skirt of extruded polystyrene insulation with a horizontal extension (chapter 7). The very next day my cellar temperature began to fall (figure 6-2). This left me with sufficient time and experience to write this book so that, unlike me, you can build a successful wine cellar on your first attempt.

Despite the relative success of my labors, I was not comfortable with the annual temperature oscillation between 44°F (7°C) and 66°F (19°C). My apprehension was justified by the discovery of excessive ullage (air) in some of the bottles subjected to this large temperature oscillation. The only uninsulated surface that remained was on the interior of the exterior walls. In retrospect, super-insulation of the ceiling and interior walls – which faced spaces with relatively constant temperatures – but not of the exterior walls – which faced the elements – was responsible for the large annual temperature swings.

I installed 1" (2.5 cm) of R-8 Thermax (Hi-R) against the interior surface of the exterior walls. This raised the winter low from 44 to 49.5°F (7 to 9.7°C), while lowering the summer peak from 66 to 64.5°F (19 to 18°C). Unfortunately, no one warned me that Thermax swells as it absorbs moisture in a damp basement, so I installed it snugly. A stack of crates restrained the bulge.

Impressed with the 30% reduction in the annual temperature oscillation, but still shocked by the ullage, I added, in May, 1985, 2" of extruded polystyrene on the interior surface of the exterior walls. This brought the total there to R-18. This final layer of insulation raised the winter low from 49.5 to 51°F (9.7 to 10.5°C), and lowered the summer high from 64.5 to 64°F. The previously applied polyethylene vapor barrier on all the walls kept the humidity below the 80% mold threshold during the spring, but the midwinter humidity now fell to 60%. This low humidity presaged additional ullage. I tried to raise the humidity with pans of water, but ran out of floor space without budging my hygrometer. To moisten the air I invented an unpatentable passive humidifier, which consists of a highly placed basin of water with a towel wick draped over the side. The following year I substituted a humidistat regulated ultrasonic humidifier, which handled the job far more elegantly – until the day it forgot to shut itself off. The basin and towel approach is adequate and safer.

Section One of this book explains why you need a home wine cellar. Section Two provides the rudiments of the physics of temperature, insulation, and moisture that are directly applicable to wine cellar siting and performance and explores the refrigeration option. Section Three details actual construction.

The pleasures to be derived from personally driving the nails transcend the mere dollars saved by not hiring a carpenter, and labor costs saved at construction can be invested in liquid treasure. Should you disdain manual labor, or be infirm, lazy, or short of time, then this book will enable you to knowledgeably instruct and supervise the efforts of your carpenter. A third alternative, for those who have the time but are not sure which end of a nail goes into the wood, is to arrange to work as your carpenter's helper, which reduces cost, provides exercise, and keeps you handy should the carpenter require supervision.

Most of my recommendations come from first-hand experience. Others are untried, but seem theoretically sound. The untested notions are clearly identified. Let me know how my suggestions work out for you, and please pass along any useful hints or goofs that I may have overlooked. My predilection to tinker and suggestions from readers may generate additional ideas that come too late for inclusion in this edition, so email me, GoldDesch@aol.com, or the publisher, info@WineAppreciation.com, if you have specific problems or suggestions.

Construction of a proper cellar, however critical, is pointless if you fail to stock it with suitable beverage. Section Four will help you select the best wines and will help you to keep track of them. Section Five addresses the next phase – wine consumption. Beginners desirous of forming a wine tasting society should profit from the practical advice of one who formed a small tasting group without stealing the mailing list from a major wine shop. Finally, Section Five also contains material that didn't fit anywhere else – travel, illness, and discretion. Don't neglect the medical advice. It might just give your gut a fighting chance to keep pace with your palate.

Chapter 2

****

THREE WINE CELLAR FANTASIES

#1 - The Exotic Wine Cellar Fantasy

In the first fantasy, you inherit your wealthy grandfather's mansion. It comes with a 10-foot (3M) below grade, 3,000-bottle, passive wine cellar. The temperature cycles modestly between a winter low of 50°F (10°C), and a summer high of 59°F (15°C). The relative humidity cycles with equal modesty between 70 and 80%.

Your grandfather selected wisely. You invite your friends to dine, and casually open the '45, '59, '82 and '89 Haut Brion for side by side comparison. Remarkably huge penetrating aromas of smoked nuts, tobacco, coffee, tar and raspberries followed by layer upon layer of fat, supple, jammy fruit, voluptuous texture, and sweet, long, heady finishes evolve over an hour of sniffing and sipping. The wines exceed even the expectations created by Robert Parker's exaltations in The Wine Advocate. Over a series of elegant dinner parties you astound, delight, and thoroughly impress your friends and acquaintances, while sampling the greatest wines ever made. With bottles that your grandfather set aside for the purpose, you host vertical and horizontal tasting extravaganzas attended by the wine elite and glowingly chronicled in the Wine Spectator and The Wine Advocate.

With the proceeds from the sale at auction of a modest selection of your oldest wines you replenish the cellar with the newly release 2005, thus preparing your cellar for your middle age and for your own grandchildren. Your cellar gains reputation as a reliable source of those properly stored mature wines that we have all read about, but which your local wine merchant is not likely to offer for sale. You are besieged by invitations to private tastings *chez* wine gurus at the far corners of the world.

#2 - The Practical Wine Cellar Fantasy

The second wine cellar fantasy is for those with more eclectic interests – people who have no time to pursue wine fame. In this fantasy your lavish pre-wine lifestyle continues as before, but in addition you acquire the sophistication with which to carry your side of the conversation whenever fine wine is served or discussed. You personally construct a modest super-insulated home wine cellar. Upon returning home from busy days at the office, you select fully mature wine to fit the occasion, complement the food, and impress your guests, your spouse, and yourself.

Your personal wine cellar fantasy, be it as grand as the first example, as modest as the second, or somewhere in between, can be made into reality, and without a castle cellar or a rich enophilic grandfather.

#3 - The Garage Will Do Fantasy

Many, including Frank Prial and several of my dear friends, are possessed of the delusion that a typical basement, closet, unheated summer cottage, or dog kennel can serve, unmodified, for wine storage. Pursuant to this fantasy you select a convenient spot away from vibration on the unused side of your two car garage; erect, for security, an uninsulated wall with an uninsulated hollow core door; hang a light, and decorate the walls with branded end panels from Bordeaux crates.

You then invest heavily in the great 2005 Bordeaux. You sample the wines on arrival, perhaps at a grand home tasting. Satisfied that the rave reviews of the wines are justified and confident in the casual storage advice of the experts, you exert great self control and allow the wines to rest unconsumed in the original cases in your unheated and uninsulated aboveground garage. Mercifully, your garage, being attached to the house, does not get cold enough to freeze the wine in winter, and the summer heat is not high enough to expel the corks.

After five years of benign neglect you decide to begin consuming a few of your now presumably slightly matured treasures. You invite the boss to dinner. A few days before the gala you retrieve and stand, to let the sediment settle, a bottle of the Cos and one of the Pichon Lalande.

You note with dismay that the ullage in these eight year old wines is at mid shoulder. It should take 50 years to produce that must ullage, not eight. At the dinner party the guests politely neglect to comment on the wines. You privately note the brown edges and the cardboardy taste. The next day you examine your cache and discover that the ullage is rampant and, furthermore, that the lowermost crates are filled with mold that has destroyed the labels. You then offer your entire collection back to the reputable wine merchant from whom you purchased them. After sampling a few bottles he apologetically declines your offer due to the excessive ullage, ruined labels, and awful taste. To reinstate your former high regard of his purchasing advice, he opens a bottle of Cos that came over in the same shipping container as yours, but which has since resided in his store's excellent cellar. The wine is phenomenal.

The blame for the demise of your wines rests squarely on you and those who advised garage storage. Garages are for cars, not for wine. You fire off an angry letter to Frank Prial. His reply might point out that he had not meant just any garage. He might go on to note that if your particular garage was merely attached to your house, not ten feet beneath it, as some are in New York City, and therefore did not remain cool year round, then you should never have stored your wine there.

The temperature and humidity that are critical for the storage of fine wine rarely come automatically. Wine that has been casually stored in a homeowner's garage or dining room fares no better than that which has been professionally neglected.

Chapter 3

✦✦✦✦✦✦✦✦✦✦✦✦✦✦✦✦✦✦✦✦✦✦✦

THE WINE CELLAR MASTER'S TAX ADVANTAGES

The tax laws of the United States smile favorably upon wine cellaring.

Tax-Free Value Added

If properly cellared, the best of the 1982 Bordeaux have increased 50 fold in value since they were first sold as futures. The Pichon-Lalande that was $10 a bottle on futures went for $200 a decade later and $500 ten years after that – if you could find it. When I opened and enjoyed this beauty I paid absolutely no federal, state or city income or sales tax on its added value. The tax savings alone exceeded the entire 1983 futures price, even if I were to factor in inflation and lost annual bank interest. To add insult to injury, if I had put the initial cost of the '82 Bordeaux futures into the bank, I would have been fully taxed on the modest interest, including the part that represents keeping up with inflation. This would have left me with insufficient capital in my hypothetical account to buy the '82s had I passed them up in 1983 – if I could find them and could be certain that they had been cellared properly.

Tax-Free Wine Sales

The preceding refers only to the saved retail cost of the mature dinner wine that I didn't buy because I already owned it. To get real cash for wine requires a willing and able buyer. If you, as a private party, sell mature wine to a friend, the transaction would violate liquor control laws in most states, and failure to declare your profit on the sale would be income tax fraud. Yet, some private enophiles do illegally sell wine for tax free profit to individuals, restaurants, and wine shops.

Tax-Deductible Charitable Donations

Give your overvalued and underachieving '66 Petrus away for auction sale at a hospital or educational TV fund raiser. You can quite legally claim the full current retail value as a charitable tax deduction. If the donated bottles are to be consumed at a charity dinner, you might also get a free meal, a taste of your wine, and your picture in the paper.

Your Tax-Free Cellar-Construction Salary

In addition to the tax advantages when cellaring wine, there are also tax advantages that accompany wine cellar construction. When you sell the home that you live in you can defer paying any tax on the profit that you make on the sale. You do this by buying, within a set time, currently 24 months, a new home that costs as much or more than the one you're selling. When you retire and sell your last home, after age 55, the federal government generously offers a once-in-a-lifetime income tax forgiveness on up to $500,000 of profit.

The homeowner's tax break extends to the increase in the selling price that's attributable to the value added by your wine cellar. That profit is your tax-free salary for building the cellar. You can repeat the process of cellar construction followed by tax-free profit each time you relocate. There's no guarantee that you can get a better price for your home because it has a wine cellar, but I would wager a bottle of '95 Chateau Musar red that there will be a buyer with an unfulfilled wine cellar fantasy out there when your wine-cellared home comes onto the market.

To bolster the resale value of your wine cellar, maintain and post clear temperature and humidity records showing the annual maxima and minima. Records will also enhance the resale credentials of your wine.

Chapter 4 ***** WINE REQUIRES...

The adequacy of storage is frequently discussed at tastings that feature mature wines. When the '45 Lafite or the '74 Mayacamas is flabby, should we blame the storage and shun the provider's shop or private cellar, or should we conclude that no wine can live forever, regardless of storage?

Every time I discuss wine storage with collectors, some of whom own thousands of bottles of very serious wine, I am astonished anew by the diversity of strongly held but naive notions about wine storage. For example, at a midwinter tasting at my home I proudly displayed the basin and towel wine cellar humidifier that I had just invented. It had elevated my wine cellar's humidity from 60 to 75%. One guest who had been storing classified Bordeaux for decades commented that I was making my cellar too humid.

Another close associate proofread the entire first edition of this book and then proceeded to build a cellar that almost precisely conformed to inadequate cellar #1 as described in chapter one. Collectors with diametrically opposed views on wine storage cannot all be correct.

Most fine red wine is released for sale to the public three years after the harvest, and the best soon sell out. Some stock is held back by established wineries in so-called libraries, or in distribution channels, and some retailers and investors buy in quantity, but by and large the best all but disappear from retail shelves years before they're ready to drink. The wine gluts that one reads about affect wines of lower quality or from off years. Most wine shops have inadequate capital and inadequate environmentally controlled storage to enable them to properly store significant supplies for the many years needed for classic vintages. Even shops that buy in quantity tend to sell out as growing interest outstrips sales expectations. Such are the current economics of the wine industry. Just try to find properly cellared '61, '82, or '90 Bordeaux.

Since relatively few enophiles have proper wine cellars, most potentially great wine is either drunk before its time, or is subjected to abominable storage in dining rooms, closets, furnace rooms or garages. Don't pay premium prices for immature wines for which you have no adequate storage. As with malnourished children, those wines will never realize their potential.

When inviting guests to tastings there are certain individuals I'm reluctant to include, fearing the offered contribution of an ill-stored wine. I know the wine is likely to show poorly. I'm reluctant to offend the misguided cellar master, but as host I have my reputation to uphold. There are others whom I call first, partly to plug holes in the tasting list from their well regulated cellars. Once the wines are assembled, I call my list of cellarless enophiles and then those with disreputable cellars until the seats are filled. When offered a wine from a questionable facility I can honestly protest that I've already assembled the wines.

Ideal wine storage conditions

The one requisite that has general consensus among wine authorities is that the ideal storage temperature is 55°F (13°C). Concerning the permissible deviation from this standard, and the penalty thereof, advice runs the gamut from "no deviation" to "anything between 40 and 75°F (4 and 24°C) is acceptable if you'll be drinking the wine within 20 years". Some stipulate a range of 45 to 65°F (7 to 18°C), or an even more stringent 50 to 59°F (10 to 15°C). Within these ranges one is typically advised to avoid rapid or frequent temperature oscillation, but a single annual temperature oscillation between the permitted extremes is said to be either of no concern or even to be preferred for ideal maturation.

There's been no test of these guidelines - such as assigning half a case of '90 Cheval Blanc to storage conditions "A" and the other half to conditions "B", and periodically submitting the wines to a distinguished tasting panel as they age.

Enophiles who adhere to the constant temperature school install air conditioning or purchase factory assembled refrigerated chambers. The various types are discussed in Chapter nine. If such a cellar is not well insulated, then a single midsummer mechanical or electrical failure could endanger the entire collection. Others are willing to accept, or even prefer, the modest annual temperature oscillation found in a well-insulated, passive (no air conditioner) cellar.

Expansive effects of warming bottled wine

A wine bottle and its contents expand and contract at different rates in response to temperature. Assuming constant pressure, temperature increases expand water (or wine) seven times as much as they expand glass. This means that when temperatures rise, bottled wine expands seven times more than its container.

The relatively tiny air space in a bottle of wine also responds to temperature shifts. If given room to expand, temperature increases would expand air 32 times more than they affect water, and 188 times more than glass. This expansion, if realized, would push wine (or oxygen-free ullage gas if the bottle were upright) out past the cork, or, in some cases, eject it. If wine is expelled past the cork it evaporates into the room, leaving behind a revealing dried out, grape-colored stain. When the bottle cools its contents contract more than it does. The vacuum that develops could suck air through or past the cork into the bottle, or could implode the cork. Any air that enters the bottle contains 20% oxygen, which reacts chemically with the wine. Frequent additions of oxygen will age wine prematurely.

Let me illustrate the magnitude of these effects. When there's no ullage, an 18°F (10°C) temperature rise from 50 to 68°F (10 to 20°C) expands the liquid contents by .044 ounce (1.3 ml, 4 mm neck height, or 26 drops) in excess of bottle expansion. (10 mm of height in the neck of a standard bottle has the capacity of just under 3 ml.)

When a moderate 2.5 cm (1/4 oz or 7.5 ml) of ullage is present the total potential expansion of the contents increases by 30%.

The preceding considerations presume that air and wine move through or around a cork in response to pressure changes. If this did not occur, then temperature oscillations might be of no concern. If the cork seal resists the pressures and the bottle does not burst or implode, then the ullage (volume of gas) in the bottle is compressed when the wine expands as the bottle warms. Conversely, the ullage expands as the wine bottle cools. The ullage absorbs all the pressure because gas is exponentially more squeezable than liquid. The ullage cushions the expansion and contraction of the wine. Greater ullage makes a better cushion, which reduces the internal pressure changes as the bottle warms and cools.

Corks resist modest pressure changes but not extreme pressure changes. It follows that bottles with high fills are the most sensitive to temperature change. The surprising conclusion is that young well-filled bottles may be more sensitive to the effects of temperature oscillation than are mature wines that have acquired additional ullage. This suggests that if you own more wine than your refrigerated cabinet can hold, you should give the constant temperature to the 2005's, not the '61's! On the other hand, the old corks may not be as resistant as the new ones. Temperature sensitivity of the wine per se is another albeit critical matter.

In order to determine whether the annual temperature oscillation of my passive cellar would cause ullage by expelling a small amount of wine each summer, I conducted the following experiment. During the winter of 1985 I measured the ullage in seven bottles of 1978 Mt. Veeder Cabernet Sauvignon (Sidehill Ranch) selected from one case. Not willing to wait ten years for ten annual temperature cycles, I shuttled four of the bottles between my midwinter cellar at its annual low of 50°F (10°C) and my dining room, which averaged 64°F (18°C) during this period. The other three bottles remained on their sides in the cellar.

Two of the traveling bottles were kept upright each time they went upstairs so that air would be pushed against the cork as the contents expanded. The other two were kept on their sides when upstairs, ensuring that wine contacted the cork. Every two days the ullage was measured and the traveling bottles migrated, from cellar to dining room or from dining room to cellar. Finally, one of the constantly cellared bottles was placed in the dining room, on its side, for one continuous 20 day period that equaled the total time that the traveling bottles had been there.

I hypothesized that the bottles that warmed on their sides might lose wine that was forced through or around the cork with each warming, to be replaced with air during cooling, while for the bottles that warmed upright only air would move. If true, this would suggest that constant-temperature storage produces less ullage than seasonal oscillation, and that thermal oscillation during upright storage prevents ullage but admits damaging oxygen that would be revealed by tasting.

Much to my relief, despite ten warming and cooling cycles the horizontally warmed bottles lost a total of only 1.5 mm (1/16") more wine than did the vertically warmed bottles, as measured in the neck. The vertically warmed bottles lost no more than the constant temperature control bottles. The loss to the horizontally stored traveling bottles averaged a mere 0.15 mm (1/160") per cycle. Ten of these cycles would equal only 15% of the least (10 mm or 0.4") ullage that I have ever noted in a 10-year-old-wine.

Although there was little net accumulation of ullage, the size of the ullage bubble did oscillate as predicted. Each cooling increased the ullage by about 3 mm (1 ml). If 3 mm had been lost ten times, then the total ullage would have amounted to 30 mm (10 ml), which would have brought the ullage down to the shoulder. This never happened. Upon warming, 99.5% of the new ullage disappeared. The pressure built up during warming had compressed the ullage bubble. During subsequent cooling the ullage bubble had re-expanded.

The passage of six months between temperature extremes as occurs in annual cycles might have altered the outcome of this experiment by allowing more time for the pressure to expel wine. (Storing bottles upright for six months would also have dried out the corks, with probable disastrous consequences.) I've seen bottles stored continuously on their sides in a passive cellar with a 14°F (8°C) annual temperature range undergo a seasonal expansion and reciprocal contraction of their ullage bubble, while others, subject to a 22°F (12°C) annual swing acquired an additional 3 mm of ullage every year.

These observations suggest that modest annual temperature oscillations produce very little net ullage, but oscillations that are a bit more extreme elicit rampant ullage. Some bottles that experienced the 22°F oscillations did not ullage heavily. This suggests that the threshold for temperature induced ullage varies, perhaps with the quality, length, and fit of the individual cork.

If a modest 0.15 mm annual ullage were to occur as a daily event, as might easily occur in a dining room with a set-back thermostat or a wine shop where the air conditioner is turned off after closing hours, you could get catastrophic ullage in excess of 50 mm (2.5") in one year. One temperature cycle per year is trivial, perhaps even beneficial, but not 365.

Larger daily oscillations, such as those that occur when wine is stored in direct sunlight, bring wine to a premature senility. It's doubtful that such prematurely aged wines pass, even fleetingly, through the ideal mature stage that cellaring is all about. In most aboveground situations, except for air conditioned facilities or enormous wine-filled warehouses with tremendous thermal mass, the temperature rises during the day and falls at night. Storage in direct sunlight or in the vicinity of a variable heat source such as a stove or heating duct can have especially disastrous consequences. Oxygenation (breathing) for an hour before drinking is often desirable, but during the years of storage, oxygenation, though apparently required, must be exceedingly slow.

Temperature influences oxygenation in two ways. First, as described above, temperature oscillations create pressures which, if of sufficient magnitude, move oxygen-laden air. Second, there is what the physicists refer to as the partial pressure. The air outside the bottle contains 20% oxygen. The air inside the bottle contains no oxygen. Oxygen has a tendency to slowly penetrate through or pass beside the cork in response to this oxygen gradient or partial pressure despite constant temperatures. Once inside the bottle, the oxygen reacts chemically with the wine, which keeps the internal oxygen concentration at virtually 0%. High temperatures make all molecules, including oxygen, move more rapidly. Thus, wine stored at a constant high temperature should oxygenate more rapidly than wine stored at a constant low temperature.

For example, a 375 ml bottle of '79 Palmer stored for half a summer in my warm garage was rated as less complex, less tannic, and less interesting than a matched cellared bottle when evaluated, in 1985, by my expert tasting panel.

Why magnums mature more slowly

Given comparable storage conditions, wine in half-bottles matures more rapidly, and wine in magnums more slowly, than wine in standard 750 ml bottles. All three bottle sizes are made with necks of identical diameters and receive similar corks. The only conceivable explanation for the difference in aging speed is that identical amounts of oxygen are delivered for the maturation of drastically differing amounts of wine.

As described above, oxygen can enter wine bottles in two ways; (1) total pressure via temperature oscillation induced expansion and contraction, and (2) partial oxygen pressure in response to the greater concentration of oxygen outside the bottle. The partial pressure of oxygen-driven movement through the cork is governed by the size and condition of the cork, which is unrelated to bottle size. In contrast, air migration induced by total pressure from warming and cooling the bottle is proportional to bottle size. Thus, doubling the bottle size would double the amount of total pressure oxygen, and all bottle sizes would mature at identical rates. Since all authorities agree that large formats age more slowly, the unavoidable conclusion is that partial oxygen pressure, not temperature driven pressure oscillation, is the dominant oxygen mover for properly stored wines. This also supports the notion that wine corks resist the pressures generated by modest temperature oscillations. Perhaps some day half-bottles will be made with slim necks which retard aging to match that of 750 ml bottles. Wine completely sealed in glass might never change. You could open such a bottle by breaking the neck with port tongs. The new plastic corks may provide a more complete seal than cork.

If a cork's resistance to oxygen is related to its length, then it should be possible to manipulate maturation speed by adjusting the length of the cork. With no change in equipment, cellar-worthy wines could be bottled with a range of cork lengths. Those customers intent on near-term enjoyment would select short corks, while those with long-term investment in mind would specify long corks. Collectors desiring to enjoy a case over a period of decades would request a mix of cork lengths and would consume the short corked bottles first.

Extreme pressure

As suggested earlier, there's a limit to a cork's ability to contain pressure. Temperature oscillations below a threshold that appears to be around 14°F (8°C) are no problem, but the pressure built up by larger oscillations appears to move air past or through the cork. This contradicts the truism that gradual temperature changes are O.K., but rapid temperature shifts are not. The magnitude and frequency of the temperature changes are actually the critical factors.

Even more extreme pressures, such as those generated when I intentionally stored a bottle of '79 Cos d'Estournel on its side atop a heating duct, can actually push the cork through the capsule and several centimeters beyond. My tasting panel unanimously preferred the wine from an unheated control bottle.

In another experiment, a single, sunlight-generated excursion from 50 to 102°F (10 to 39°C) did not disturb the cork, but produced 5/8" (16 mm) of ullage in one day, which is equal to the ullage found after two decades of ideal storage. Such extreme temperature changes can occur in unventilated trucks, on loading docks, in car trunks, or even indoors if wine is exposed to direct sunlight.

Heat vs. Oxygen

In addition to introducing oxygen, heat itself probably accelerates maturation, and excessive heat is surely deleterious. The literature on winemaking refers to cooked wine that has gotten too hot during fermentation. To taste the effect of oxygenation without heat one merely has to recall the consequences of recorking and storing a half emptied bottle of wine. The oxygen in the bottle destroys the remainder within a few days. No heat is required. This is why one adds nitrogen or marbles to fill the space, or transfers the remainder into a smaller bottle. The warming of bottled wine without a quick, corresponding release of oxygen is not so easily examined. The wine bottles would have to be kept in oxygen-poor rooms. If lowered cellar oxygen did permit warmer or longer or better storage, it could be accomplished by flooding well-sealed wine cellars with nitrogen, or by consuming the ambient oxygen via combustion. One would simply light a candle or oil lamp before closing the cellar door. When the oxygen in the cellar was used up, the flame would go out. Burning, unfortunately, also produces heat, light, and soot, and the measures required to seal the room from migrating oxygen may be considerable. Nevertheless, due to the immense and possibly easily achieved potential benefit, the notion warrants further study.

Whatever the mechanism, if wine is held below optimal temperatures, say in the low 40's°F (4.5°C), maturation will be delayed. This can be advantageous when preserving wine for resale or for future generations to sample, but if you want your wine to mature, you'd best avoid such low temperatures.

Temperatures below freezing must be avoided at all times – the wine would expand on freezing and the bottles would burst. This disaster is possible in unheated car trunks, carports and even garages, but not in super-insulated wine cellars. Even if the pipes in the rest of the house freeze up, the wine should be safe so long as the uninsulated cellar floor is below the deepest regional frost line. Incidentally, the consequences of freezing the recorked remainder of half-consumed bottles is less disastrous. The air in the bottle seems to cushion the pressures generated when the wine freezes. Some report using freezing to preserve unfinished bottles, microwave thawing being used when thirst returns. I've not personally been thrilled with the gustatory results.

Humidity

Dry air will evaporate wine through the corks. Plastic or wax seals and foil capsules don't seem to completely prevent this evaporative loss. Screw-type closures permit even more evaporation than corks, which is why corks are the closure of choice. Storage of bottles on their sides keeps the corks moist, preventing shrinkage and therefore looseness of the corks, but doesn't eliminate evaporation. Only 100% relative humidity would completely eliminate evaporative loss. Unfortunately, extreme humidity leads to mold, which is the subject of Chapter 8. Very little mold forms in cellars below 80% relative humidity, making that the ideal for home cellars. Many wineries, including Chateau Lafite Rothschild, store corked bottles at very high mold-inducing humidities. They avoid label damage by delaying labeling until just before shipment.

Ullage

It's possible to find 20-year-old wines with only 12 mm (1/2 inch or roughly 4 ml) of ullage. Those wines have surely been stored at high humidity and cool relatively constant temperature. You can also find 20-year-old wines on the shelves of shops without regulated temperature and humidity with wine levels well down into the shoulder. Having tasted such wine, I'd avoid any bottle with more than 12 mm (1/2 inch) of ullage per decade of age.

Even newly released bottles can vary in fill and in the soundness and tightness of their corks, so if buying a single bottle from a bin, pick the one with the best fill. The bottler need leave no more than 1 ml of air in the bottle, which is equivalent to a 3 mm (1/8 inch) air space. The bubble left in at bottling is probably needed to cushion the pressure built up by cork insertion. Another source of uneven levels in new releases can occur if wine is exposed to heat or cold during shipping. Obviously, the bottles at the perimeter of the container will be affected more than the interior ones.

Lighting

Direct sunlight should be avoided, if only because it heats the wine. Whether sunlight itself filtered through the glass bottle has any detrimental effect isn't known. It's entirely possible that sunlight triggers chemical reactions. This should be no problem in dark wine cellars.

Some warn, but without data, against the high frequency wavelengths of fluorescent lighting, suggesting that lower frequency incandescent lights or candles are safer. The tinted glass of wine bottles may offer some protection, and even untinted glass blocks some wavelengths. If there's anything detrimental about fluorescent (or natural) light, then it incriminates most wine shops. Wine on display in shops typically sits all day in open display racks under fluorescent or natural lighting. Rare shops keep only single sample bottles on display, or display only price lists in restaurant wine-list fashion. The shopkeeper then fetches your selection from the dark cellar. Some merchants dispense the "good stuff" for special customers in this manner. To avoid the possible effect of light on wine displayed in wine shops you could purchase by the closed case-full, or ask for a single bottle from a closed case.

If your only choice is wine on display, it's best to select from the bottom of the display rack where the light has been filtered by the overlying bottles. Bottles stored at the bottom of a display rack also tend to be cooler by being closer to the floor. This also applies in home cellars. Some enophiles cellar the 12 bottles from each solid case vertically in a column from floor to ceiling. They drink the upper, warmer, more rapidly maturing bottles first.

The exposure that your wine might get to fluorescent lighting when you briefly visit your otherwise dark wine cellar would seem to be of minimal concern, but you may be storing the wine for a lot longer than the shop did. To be entirely safe, you could store your wine in closed cases or protect your bins with drapes. An alternative is to use incandescent lighting. However, incandescents put out three times as much heat as fluorescents for the light generated. I use a single 40-watt overhead fluorescent. When my fluorescent light was inadvertently left on overnight, the cellar temperature jumped 1°F (.5°C), demonstrating how the heat from even fluorescents can disturb cellar temperature. Keep your wine cellar in total darkness between visits, even if your best laid plan is for a hasty return.

Vibration

Some recommend avoiding vibration such as from compressors or passing trucks. However, there's no evidence attesting to any deleterious effect. In April, 1985 I placed two bottles of '82 Gruaud Larose on their sides in my cellar. Ten months later I subjected one of the bottles to 13 continuous days of violent jiggling in a home-made vibrator. This exceeded the worst imaginable shaking that a bottle of young Bordeaux could receive en route from the Medoc to the United States. The vibrations wore through the label. Five hours after the shaking ceased, my expert blind tasting panel marginally preferred the shaken bottle to its undisturbed companion. So much for the myth that vibration can induce travel sickness in young wines.

Racking and bottling shock at the winery, temperature changes during transportation, and travel sickness in mature wines are separate matters. The anecdotal evidence is that temperature extremes during shipping can do considerable damage, only some of which heals after a few months. During racking at the winery SO_2 is introduced to prevent bacterial contamination. It takes weeks for the wine to recover. Unfiltered wines, which are usually the ones with the best cellaring potential, are said to be more susceptible to temperature shock during travel. The pity is that it costs only a few cents more per bottle to ship from Bordeaux to a US shop or distributor in temperature-controlled containers. Some importers use them, but others may only say that they do. Bottles opened immediately after removal from temperature-controlled containers show beautifully. The Bordeaux shippers should make temperature control mandatory on the sultry Panama Canal route to the West Coast and Gulf route to Texas.

Sediment

Excessive vibration might interfere with the compacting of sediment, but that's only important during the week before serving. Sediment is bitter – it should be kept out of your glass. It's safe to stand a bottle up for a week prior to serving so as to bring sediment from the side down to the bottom. To compact the sediment at one side of the bottom, stand the bottle at 45° from vertical. It's convenient to have a small, portable 45° wine stand for this purpose. Such stands are found in wine accessory catalogs, or you can build one. Draw the cork with the bottle still in your 45° stand, and decant without returning the bottle to the upright. I always keep all the labels in my cellar uppermost so I always know which side of the bottom contains the sediment.

Chapter 5 ✹✹✹✹IN THE ABSENCE OF A SUITABLE CELLAR

It's been estimated that 98% of all U.S. retail wine purchases are consumed within 24 hours. Given the strong consumer response to wines that need cellaring, that figure is difficult to believe. Perhaps 95% is closer to the truth. Many of the 2 to 5% who buy well in advance of anticipated consumption proceed to subject their wines to conditions that are more appropriate for the housing of wine consumers than for the storage of wine.

If you find yourself unable to place wine in a suitable storage facility, it would seem preferable to forego wine storage and (**a**) Buy single bottles of ready-to-drink, professionally matured wine on the way home for dinner, (**b**) drink restaurant-aged wine, or (**c**) switch to whiskey, beer, or mineral water. Each of these options is explored in this chapter. As unacceptable as the notions may seem to avid enophiles, they're the norm in this country.

(a) Buy by the bottle as you need it

Neophyte enophiles often purchase single bottles of older wines from warm shops, relying on the recommendations of newsletters, wine consultants, or vintage charts. Unfortunately, the newsletters and vintage charts assume proper storage.

One shop that I visited near Miami Beach, Florida, specialized in classic vintages of first-growth Bordeaux, but left them to swelter in 100°F (35°C) midsummer heat. Most of their upscale customers only winter in Miami, at which time the store's climate is more reasonable. Despite the academic curiosity, I resisted the experimental purchase of an older wine. I wasn't surprised when the proprietor decided not to offer this book for sale in his shop.

Even year-round air conditioning in the wine shop is no guarantee of a proper storage history. Merchants can acquire wines with a questionable storage history from private cellars or bankrupt shops and offer them, un-sampled, for sale from a 55°F (13°C) environment. Unfortunately, spoiled wine is not improved by chilling, though further deterioration is prevented. At one shop I found the front wine sales room to be noticeably colder than the staff-only main storage area. As a misguided economy measure an occasional shop manager may set the thermostat back daily after closing hours, thus creating a destructive daily temperature oscillation. Liquor chains may use a central warehouse from which they ship to local stores as needed. The storage conditions in the warehouses are usually unknown to the retail customer.

The best shops have temperature-controlled storage that you can inspect. Reputable wine consultants sample questionable wines before offering them for purchase. They sample new lots of wine as they come into the shop to verify their sound condition and to prepare for customers' gustatory inquiries. Increased sales volume from satisfied customers compensates for the wine lost to sampling. If you are so fortunate as to have such a merchant on the route of your daily commute, then you could do quite well to purchase by the bottle on the way home for dinner. Of course, you would still be unprepared for unexpected guests and spur-of-the-moment celebrations.

Most enophiles do not commute daily past an ideal wine shop. A shopping expedition is typically an infrequent and lengthy interstate affair. Even when your wine merchant is down the street, the best offerings can sell out, or become prohibitively expensive as they mature. The best limited production wines sell out to cellar masters as pre-arrival futures and never hit the shelves.

(b) Buying restaurant wine

Wining while dining in a restaurant can be quite elegant, but storage conditions, especially of older wines, can be a problem. If a restaurateur does not permit you to visit his cellar, or disclaims responsibility for the condition of the particular wine that you've selected, then assume the worst. Only the most naive will escort you to a wine rack next to the stove, but some do store their wines there. Unless they're extremely busy, restaurateurs who have gone to the trouble of acquiring exciting wines and of providing good storage for them will proudly escort you to their wine cellar. Conversely, those who display their wines in room temperature racks behind the bar are obviously not courting the fine wine trade. If in doubt about storage, order a recent vintage that you've previously enjoyed. This gives you a basis for comparison, and a stronger argument should the proprietor protest when you return an "off" bottle. Even when storage and selection are ideal, restaurant markups to double or triple retail will strain most budgets, especially so as the palate matures.

Even if you are not familiar with the wines on the restaurant's wine list, and few are, don't even consider bringing your bulky wine library into the restaurant. Whenever possible obtain the wine list in advance and check out the offerings against your wine library or internet service at home. If you have a laptop with wireless internet and subscribe to ERobertParker.com, you can have the wine selection advice of the premiere authority at your fingertips, if you arrive at the restaurant in advance of your party.

Recognizing Spoiled Wine

How, you protest, does one recognize spoiled wine? There are two phases to this task: **(1) Before opening,** and **(2) After opening.**

(1) Before opening.

When the wine steward startles you by thrusting an unopened bottle before you for approval, do you give only a cursory glance at the label and vintage and an approving nod while your dinner party stares? Actually, you can make a flamboyant and elaborate ceremony of the ritual if you are prepared with a script and the proper equipment. You might consider (a) the temperature of the bottle, (b) the condition of the label, (c) the information on the label,

(d) the condition of the cork, (e) the transilluminated wine (f) the amount of sediment, and (g) the ullage.

(a) **Bottle temperature.** Grasp the bottle with both hands. If it is cool to the touch then it has been fetched from a cool environment, probably a cool wine cellar, and it is safe to proceed. If the bottle is warm or only at room temperature, then it has probably been stored improperly and is too warm to serve anyway. Reject it unless it is a very recent vintage.

(b) **The condition of the label.** Proper high humidity can cause mold damage to labels, but not to wine. When evaluating older wines, welcome a bit of label deterioration. So long as you can correctly identify the contents, a moldy label is a good sign. A sunlight-bleached label is another matter, and is best passed up. When wine is aged in a humid winery, labeling may be delayed until the time of shipment, in which case you get a perfectly sound bottle with a suspiciously crisp label. Look for dried wine stains around the capsule of red wines. They indicate that wine has leaked or been pushed out of the bottle during bad storage. Unfortunately, most wine stewards will wipe the bottle off before they present it to you.

(c) **The information on the label.** See if the label conforms to what you ordered: the correct year, the correct property, the correct varietal, the correct quality level. Don't accept Robert Mondavi 1972 Cab when you're paying for Robert Mondavi Reserve 1974 Cab. Older wines often bear secondary labels. These can sometimes tell you where the wine has been. Wines sold at auction sometimes acquire a secondary label naming the auction house, whose reputation you may have heard about.

(d) **Corks.** If a bottle is stored upright in low humidity for a few months the cork will dry out and shrink, loosening its grip in the bottle. Press on the top of the cork through the capsule with your finger. If you can advance the cork, point this out to the steward and request a replacement bottle or alert him of your intention to reject the bottle, once opened, if the contents are less than sublime.

(e) **Color.** Much has been written about the color of red wine in the glass, but I've found nothing on the color evaluation of unopened bottles. I've transilluminated many bottles of red wine, and conclude that for red wine color in the bottle is a useless predictor of color or quality in the glass. The thick colored glass of the bottle and the thick layer of wine you must look through are the problems. When you evaluate the color of wine in a glass you don't actually have to look through glass, and you observe a narrow rim of wine in a tilted glass. The one exception is that cloudy wine will not transilluminate the bright light from the high intensity flashlight that you pluck from your jacket pocket. Cloudiness suggests bacterial contamination.

With vintage ports transillumination is useless as both the wine and the bottle are too dark to see anything. With white dessert wines, however, there's an obvious progression with age from pale straw to dark caramel. Old and heavenly bottles of Sauternes can be quite dark. If the color is too dark for the age, then maturation has been too rapid. Sauternes that have turned black, so called "black beauties," have been mistreated, but are said to still be drinkable. Even properly aged dessert wines may not be to your liking. They trade the luscious fresh fruit and some of the sweetness for an exotic complexity that not everyone appreciates.

(f) **Sediment.** A bit of sediment in a bottom corner is to be expected in older red wines, but a wine that has dropped a bounty of it is probably dead. You note the sediment at the same time that you transilluminate the wine - but be careful lest your examination disturb the sediment.

(g) **Ullage.** Ullage is the final and critically important feature of unopened wine evaluation. Some ullage with age is inevitable, but anything more than 12 mm (1/2 inch) per decade is avoidable. When measuring ullage, take the temperature of the bottle at the moment of examination into consideration. Warming, by expanding the wine, reversibly compresses the ullage bubble. When the bottle is chilled to proper cellar temperature the ullage bubble re-expands. Excessive ullage indicates a loose cork, widely or frequently fluctuating storage temperatures, or low humidity.

To examine ullage production empirically, I selected two identical bottles of Conn Creek 1978 Zinfandel. I carefully measured the ullage in both bottles, and then returned one to its wine cellar bin. I placed the other bottle on its side in full sun on a wooden deck on a hot afternoon in July, 1984, from 2 to 10 p.m. The thermobottle (thermometer-containing wine bottle full of water) that I placed beside it peaked at 102°F (39°C) at 4 p.m., but the cork held. Both wine bottles then rested side-by-side (on their sides) in my cool wine cellar. When the ullage levels were compared five months later in December, the previously heated bottle had gained 14 mm (5/8 inch) of ullage, which is more than one should find after a decade of ideal storage. The ullage in the never-heated bottle was unchanged. No additional differential ullage developed during three subsequent months of storage, which demonstrated that the ullaging process initiated by the heating was complete. The pressure build-up during the one-time 40°F (22°C) heating had forced wine through or around the cork. After the wine cooled, the resulting vacuum had sucked air into the bottle. The two bottles were comparison-tasted blind by a distinguished ten-person panel the following March. All preferred the wine from the never-heated bottle.

Low humidity alone can also produce excessive ullage. When the air is dry, moisture evaporates, despite the capsule, from the outer end of the cork. Replacement wine wicks outward through or around the cork to remoisten the exposed end. Oxygenated air enters to replace the lost volume. The oxygen accelerates and probably impairs the maturation process. I have heard from despondent cellar masters who were shocked to discover low fills after just a few years of low humidity but cool storage.

An absence of ullage is, unfortunately, not a foolproof indicator of wine abuse. Wine subjected to prolonged unvarying moist heat can age rapidly while maintaining a good fill. With upright storage, which keeps the gas bubble next to the cork, daily temperature oscillations will not increase the ullage, but will nevertheless pump gas in and out of the bottle, each intake delivering another toxic dose of oxygen. Thus, wine that is assaulted by temperature oscillations while in an upright position will develop less ullage than identically mistreated bottles that are stored on their sides, thus concealing from view the deteriorated condition of the wine.

While on the subject of upright storage, a few months of upright storage at moderate temperatures such as in an air-conditioned restaurant is not always as disastrous as the preceding discussion suggests. To provide objective evidence on the matter, in 1984 I took a bottle of Chateau Dillon from the tannic 1975 vintage that I had personally cellared from first release. I stored it upright for ten months in my 72°F +/–(22°C) summer-air-conditioned dining room away from direct sunlight. A matched comparison bottle remained in the cellar. The ullage levels, upon returning the dining room stored bottle to cellar temperature, were, as predicted, still identical to one another. My blind tasting panel felt that the dining room stored sample was more advanced. Some preferred the dining room sample, suggesting that the cellared bottle was unready, while others preferred the cellared bottle. The results, had the vintage been less tannic, the wines older, or the temperature excursion longer or more extreme, would probably have been more favorable to the cellared bottle.

To get back to our trip to the restaurant, when the storage is ideal go for the oldies. When the storage is suspect, choose the latest vintage available. Before you give the wine steward the nod to proceed, note that it should be perfectly acceptable to bring a pocket-model Screwpull to a restaurant whose wine stewardship worries you and to insist on opening and decanting an old bottle personally. For that matter, bring your own decanter and stemware if you don't like what the restaurant offers. You're paying for the wine and should be permitted to do what you want with it. Occasionally, an old cork begins to break up during removal, especially when a solid stem corkscrew is presented. Try angling the worm of the corkscrew. As a last resort, push the cork into the bottle and then remove it with a cork retriever. An emergency cork retriever can be made from a wire clothes hanger.

Bend a small hook onto the end of the wire. Don't attempt to pour the wine out with the cork still inside the bottle unless you've got a bent wire holding it below the neck.

While waiting for the approved and decanted wine to arrive at table, examine your empty wine glass. Hold it up to the light to detect dirt and stains, and wipe or return it if not clean. Bring the glass to your nose and give it a long careful sniff test. The most common offender is the awful odor of dishwasher detergent, which gets stronger when it dissolves in the wine. If in doubt, rinse the empty glass out with water from your water glass. I recommend learning to identify the odor of dishwasher detergent-contaminated wine in advance at home. Once experienced it is never forgotten. Unfortunately, contaminated glasses will not readily reveal the detergent odor until wine or water is poured into them.

(2) Evaluating Wine After Opening

Now that the bottle is finally opened, and if red, decanted off the sediment, wine evaluation should be a simple matter of personal pleasure. However, before you take the socially disruptive step of returning a "bad" bottle to a shop or restaurateur, or decide against a purchase for cellaring, you need a bit more than current appeal to go on. If you expect barnyard stink, tannin, or high acidity to indicate a bad bottle, then you'll reject wines that are merely unready and require airing or a few more years of cellaring.

The most readily accepted reason for returning a bottle is because it is "corked". This is a bacterial condition attributed to the growth of an organism that was present in the cork when it was first placed in the bottle. The overwhelming odor is of stale wet cardboard. You should be able to detect the odor from the cork, which is why it is classically presented to you to examine, and especially from the wine itself. Once you have experienced a corked bottle, you'll never doubt the diagnosis again. A substitute bottle from the same case is usually fine.

The color of wine that has suffered poor storage, or is simply past its useful life, is pale and a bit brown. Tired out wines do not proffer much odor (or just a bare whiff when the cork is first remove) and not much taste – perhaps a bland hint of cardboard. Over-aged wine will eventually become awful, but for a long time it just tastes weak and pasteurized. Tired, even dead, but not yet putrefied described the 1920 Federico Paternia Gran Reserva that I discovered in an un-cooled shop in Madrid in 1980.

It doesn't take 60 years for poor storage to destroy wine, though 60 years of even ideal conditions is too much for most wines. One afternoon on a hot dock, or a year in a warm shop, warehouse, restaurant, or dining room can do considerable damage. No self-respecting restaurant should offer decadent wine for sale, and should take it back without a fuss even if the death is merely from old age.

While on the subject of wine service, I always insist on decanting red wines, no matter the age, varietal, or bad advice. If the wine is young and has no sediment then it probably needs a good dose of air before drinking. If it is old it has to be separated from its sediment. Finally, wine tends to stratify in the bottle with heavier elements sinking towards the bottom. Decanting gives the wine a good stirring making it uniform again.

(c) Whiskey, Beer and Mineral Water

After a few disappointing experiences with older wines, many stop drinking all but the latest releases, or switch to less finicky libations. Old wines can provide sublime pleasure, provided they had the potential in the first place, and are treated with proper respect. Unfortunately, when that combination is infrequent the searching behavior extinguishes. The ultimate solution, of course, is to buy only new releases, to cellar them personally to maturity, and to live long enough to enjoy them.

Section 2

✶✶✶✶✶✶✶✶✶✶✶✶✶✶✶✶✶✶✶✶✶✶✶✶✶✶✶✶✶✶✶✶✶

PLANNING

Chapter 6

✶✶✶✶✶✶✶✶✶✶✶✶✶✶✶✶✶✶✶✶✶✶✶

TEMPERATURE CYCLES

Soil Temperatures

Outdoor temperatures rise and fall both daily and annually. The daily temperature cycle of warm days and cool nights penetrates only about a foot (30 cm) into the ground, and therefore has no impact on underground wine cellars. The annual temperature cycle of warm summers and cold winters penetrates much further. Taming the annual temperature cycle is the primary mission of passive wine cellar design.

When averaged over an entire year, the temperature at any given location on the earth is approximately constant, no matter the depth. At the surface, the annual temperature excursions above and below the average are extreme. The annual excursion diminishes as a hypothetical thermometer burrows deeper into the soil. By the time you get down 20 feet (6 meters), the annual temperature cycle becomes inconsequential, plus and minus around 2°F (1°C) in most populated regions.

Figure 6-1 is a representative annual soil temperature profile, this one for Amherst, in western Massachusetts, USA. The curved lines of figure 6-1 describe, at progressively greater soil depths, the average temperature for the coldest and warmest months of the year: January and July. Note that the greatest reductions in the annual temperature spread occur in the first several feet below the surface. This curve can

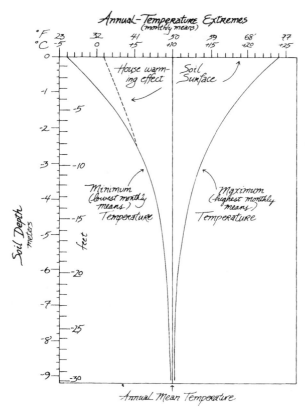

Figure 6-1. The annual soil-temperature profile for Amherst, Massachusetts, USA. Maximum and minimum monthly-mean temperatures are given at progressively greater depths. As depth increases, the temperature becomes more stable.

---

be adjusted to serve your particular location. Should you wish to derive, *de novo,* a soil temperature profile specifically for your location, instructions await you at the end of this chapter.

The goal in designing a passive wine cellar is to approach the constant conditions found at great depth without the expense, technical complexity, and ground water problems of 20 foot (6 meter) depth.

If your deep soil temperature is too high, then no combination of digging and insulating can create a passive wine cellar, so air conditioning is required. In chapter four I concluded that an annual temperature cycle that does not exceed plus or minus 7°F (4°C) from the mean is satisfactory for a passive wine cellar. On figure 6-1 an annual cycle that modest is obtained at a depth of 8 feet (2.2 meters). Unfortunately, most contemporary basement floors are only about five feet (1.5 meters) below grade, which would yield an unacceptably large annual cycle of plus or minus 12°F (7°C). Fortunately, the ameliorating influence of the overlying house and of the freezing and thawing cycle of the soil, which are not represented in figure 6-1, will assist your enterprise.

Soil Temperature Physics

In order to understand how different construction options would influence wine cellar performance, it is necessary to master the rudiments of temperature physics.

Specific Heat is the ability of materials to absorb or release heat as they change temperature. Materials, such as water, which have a high specific heat, absorb a great deal of heat as temperature rises. When these materials cool, they release that heat. Table 6-1 gives the specific heats of a variety of materials found in wine cellars.

TABLE 6-1 SPECIFIC HEATS
(calories per cubic cm per degree C)

Water	1.0
Concrete	.6
Glass	.4
Wood	.16
Air	.00024

Thermal Mass carries specific heat one step further by taking into account the amount of material. Water, no matter the amount, always has the same specific heat, but two gallons have twice as much thermal mass as one gallon. A room with a large thermal mass will remain at a more constant temperature in response to a fixed dose of heat than will a room with a small thermal mass.

Houses heated by passive solar energy depend on thermal mass to store the sun's heat in the daytime for slow release through the night. The greater the thermal mass, the less the temperature oscillates. The amount of thermal mass needed to store one day's solar gain without uncomfortably overheating the occupants of a house is typically supplied by a concrete floor, masonry, water tubes, and furnishings.

Passively cooled wine cellars also rely on thermal mass to modulate temperature cycles. For a wine cellar, the thermal storage must be some 100-times greater than for a passive solar house (since the entire summer's heat must be stored for release during the winter). The concrete floor, walls, and grape juice in a 1,200 bottle wine cellar would store only a few days' solar gain. Even a Bordeaux chais (winery) containing the equivalent of 20,000 cases of wine doesn't have enough thermal mass to safely absorb a summer's heat.

Virtually all the thermal mass required to accommodate a summer's heat is provided by the soil. Compared to the thermal mass provided by the soil, attempting to increase the thermal mass of a wine cellar by using clay tile storage bins or adding extra concrete to the walls is pointless. The thermal mass added is trivial, and the soil displaced by extra concrete is far better at resisting heat penetration.

Adjusting the Soil Temperature Profile

If your part of the world is warmer or cooler than Amherst, Massachusetts, adjust the curves of figure 6-1 laterally to your region's average annual temperature.

Ascertaining your local annual average or deep-soil temperature is not as difficult as you might first imagine. If you can locate a nearby meteorological station they should be able to tell you the average annual air temperature. A more direct and closer-to-your-own-home measure of the average annual soil temperature is the temperature of water as it leaves deep wells of more than 50 feet (15 meters). Ask the people that drill wells, your local water department, or measure your own water temperature if you have a deep well. To measure well-water temperature run the cold water tap full force for several minutes and then measure its temperature as it continues to flow full force.

If the deep soil temperature at your site is above 60°F (16°C), then a passively cooled wine cellar is not possible no matter how far down you dig. The one exception is when an extremely dry climate permits you to utilize evaporative cooling, described in chapter 10. Even 60°F (16°C) is often too warm. The constant deep-soil temperature must be several degrees cooler than the highest acceptable cellar temperature, because some annual temperature cycle is unavoidable.

If your climate is snow free most of the year, then the deep soil temperature will precisely equal the average annual above ground temperature. If the ground carries a snow blanket for part of the winter, then the snow will insulate against soil-to-air heat loss because snow is 90% air pockets, and the annually averaged deep soil temperature will be a few degrees warmer than the annually averaged air temperature. (Summer heat penetration into the soil is of course not slowed by the winter snow blanket.) In Amherst, for example, the average air temperature is 48°F (9°C), but well water is 50°F (10°C).

An additional factor to keep in mind is the predicted global warming attributed to the greenhouse effect. It is predicted that an accumulation of carbon dioxide in the atmosphere due to the burning of fossil fuels and the destruction of forests permits sunlight to enter the atmosphere while blocking radiant heat loss from the earth. By the year 2010 global warming is predicted to reach 4°F (2°C).

In 1996 the World Meteorological Association reported that 1995 had been the hottest since records were first kept in 1861, exceeding the prior 30 year average by 0.72°C. This was quickly surpassed and 2005 was again the hottest ever recorded. Faced with this trend, it would be prudent to design for a wine cellar that will accommodate soil temperatures a few degrees warmer than they are now.

Brace yourself for a thorough discussion of factors that can influence the soil temperature profile. The purpose is twofold. First, it will enable you to adjust the arms of figure 6-1 to more closely approximate your local conditions. This will give you a more accurate prediction of wine cellar performance. Second, an appreciation of the things that influence the soil temperature profile will enable you to select design options with an eye towards diminishing your wine cellar's annual temperature excursions.

Siting

The siting, or placement, of your wine cellar within your basement, is your first major decision.

The deep-ground temperature for your location would determine the average annual wine cellar temperature if your wine cellar were placed below an open field. If your climate provides a deep-soil temperature that is cool enough for a passive wine cellar, then you surely have to heat your house in the winter more than you cool it in the summer, which brings your average annual house temperature above the annual outdoor temperature. Heat from the house will therefore have a net warming effect on the soil beneath your house. Sewer lines carrying warmed waste water from the kitchen and bathroom are routed under parts of the basement and then through the adjacent soil, injecting additional heat into the ground. On the other hand, during the summer your home shades the soil from direct solar heating. If you air condition during the summer, the soil beneath your home will be further protected.

The effects of warming and cooling your house upon soil temperature are greatest beneath the center of the house, and diminish towards the periphery. This occurs because of the insulating value of soil. The greater the distance through soil between your wine cellar and the climate, the greater the insulating effect. This consideration predicts the outcome of locating a wine cellar beneath the center versus the periphery of your house. A central location will most closely reflect the temperature of the overlying house, and will have the smallest annual temperature cycle, but will usually be too warm.

In frigid Alaska or Siberia, wine cellars belong beneath the center of the house to avoid freeze-ups and to protect from the low outdoor temperatures that would retard maturation. In balmy Texas, the soil beneath the center of your air conditioned house will be cooler than the soil at the periphery. You need wine cellar air conditioning in Texas regardless of siting, but beneath the center of the house your air conditioner's efforts will be assisted by insulating soil. In intermediate climes such as the northern half of the United States, passive wine cellars should shun the warm center of the basement. An outside corner gives maximal access to the desirable cooler away-from-the-house soil temperatures.

The formulas used to prepare figure 6-1 do not take into account heating of the ground by the house. To correct for the effect that heating will have on the soil temperature minimum, move the left hand (low temperature) curve of figure 6-1 to the right. At greater depths the correction drops off. As an estimate, at the typical cellar floor depth of 5 feet (1.5 M) below grade, house heat will raise the winter minimum by 4°F (2°C). This correction should be increased if you have a heated and un-insulated basement, and reduced if you have the optimal situation of an unheated well-insulated (including the ceiling) basement that does not house a heat source such as a furnace, dehumidifier, or hot water heater.

The shading effect of the house moves the right hand curve to the left. On the north side of a house (in the northern hemisphere) the

42

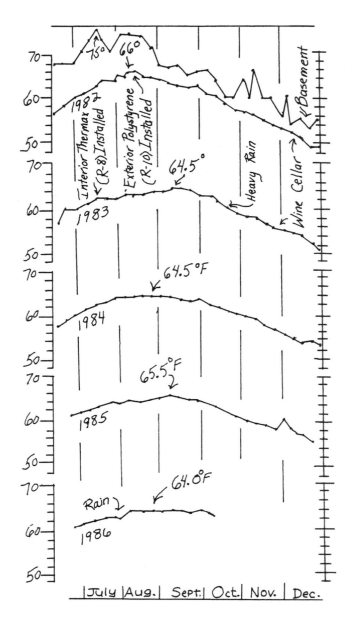

Figure 6-2. Four and a half annual temperature cycles in the author's wine cellar. The floor is 5 feet (1.5 M) below grade.

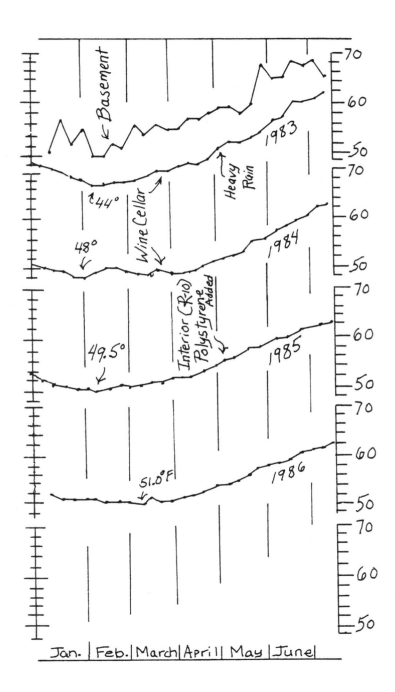

Basement

1983

↑ 44°

Wine Cellar

48°

Heavy Rain

1984

49.5°

Interior (R-10)
Polystyrene
Added

1985

51.0°F

1986

Jan. | Feb. | March | April | May | June

44

shadow cast by the house also cools the soil adjacent to the house. The soil to the east and west of the house will be shaded part of the day, the soil to the south not at all.

The correction of the right hand curve for house shading is therefore greatest for the north side of house, least for the southern exposure. If you use central air conditioning extensively in the summer, then move the right hand curve a bit more to the left to reflect this cooling influence upon the soil. The ideal topography for a wine cellared house is a site with a south-facing slope which permits a deep wine cellar under the northern uphill side of the house combined with easy underground drainage onto the downhill slope.

The annual freezing and thawing of soil (actually of its water content) increases the thermal mass of the soil because water releases heat as it freezes, and absorbs heat as it melts. Figure 6-1 doesn't take freezing and thawing into account. This correction would bring both arms of figure 6-1 closer to the midline, the size of the correction being determined by the depth of the frost and the moisture content of the soil. A $2°F$ ($1°C$) adjustment on each side at the depths that concern us most would be typical.

Shade trees will prevent the summer sunshine from reaching the ground. Ground-cover vegetation such as grass and pachysandra shades the soil while it insulates by trapping air pockets. Vegetation also aids the evaporation of water from the surface, which lowers the temperature of the soil. Low humidity permits more rapid evaporation, making evaporative cooling a potentially more potent factor in dry climates. In dry climates, soil temperatures suitable for a passive wine cellar can, at marginal latitudes, be a fringe benefit of an automatic lawn sprinkler.

If you prefer no vegetation, a thick mulch ground cover will retain moisture longer than bare soil between rainfalls to provide more continuous evaporative cooling, and white concrete or marble chips will reflect sunlight away. The worst surface is black asphalt pavement, which absorbs sunlight. Asphalt is also dry most of the time so there is little evaporative cooling. Bare unshaded soil is nearly as bad.

The conditions immediately adjacent to your wine cellar will have the greatest impact, but heat travels laterally as well as vertically within the soil. Thus, your wine cellar should be as far as possible from your driveway and the street, but close to trees. If there are no trees nearby, plant a few. If you live near a large body of water, especially fresh water that freezes in winter, then the curves of figure 6-1 should be brought a few degrees closer to one another, because bodies of water modulate local temperature extremes.

The temperature and humidity of the living space directly above your wine cellar site are an important consideration. If you only air condition one ground-floor room, such as a bedroom, then try to situate your wine cellar beneath it.

Soil Wetness and Heat Penetration

Figure 6-1 was computed for slightly damp, sandy soil containing 10% moisture, which is not the most favorable condition as far as heat penetration is concerned. Heat penetration through soil depends upon two factors: its insulating value and its specific heat. Soil contains tiny spaces which make up 40% or more of its volume. When these spaces are filled with air, the soil has its greatest insulating value but its lowest specific heat (heat capacity). When the spaces are filled with water, the insulating value is low, but the specific heat is high due to the specific heat of the added water.

The specific heat of soil increases in a linear fashion as water content increases: an increase from 0 to 10% moisture content increasing heat capacity just as much as an increase from 30 to 40% moisture. The changes in insulating value, in contrast, are not linear. Most of the decrease in insulating value occurs between 0 and 10% moisture. **Resistance to heat penetration** is the combination of a soil's ability to absorb heat with its ability to insulate. The greatest resistance to heat penetration is found in soil that is completely dry.

The differences in resistance to heat penetration as moisture content varies are quite large. For example, the **thermal conductivity** (inverse of resistance to heat penetration) of loam (a mix of sand, silt and clay) increases by 150% as the moisture content rises from 0 to 10%, and then falls off 20% from that peak as the moisture content increases to saturation at 50% water. (Loam can hold more water than sand.) The ideal situation alongside a wine cellar is soil with maximum resistance to heat penetration – which means dry soil. When the soil is sandy, the change from half-saturated (20% moisture) to dry decreases the annual temperature cycle by approximately 6°F (3°C), which is equivalent to excavating more than one foot (30 cm) deeper into the ground.

You cannot tell the clouds to stop dropping rain onto your roof and yard, but you can divert rainwater and upgrade drainage. Warm rainwater percolating through the ground also directly transports heat downward, which is another reason for gutters with long runouts and surface drainage. My own wine cellar confirms this notion: with each spring deluge the cellar temperature jumps.

Soil Porosity

A soil's porosity is the percent of its volume that is space, space that is occupied either by water or by air. The porosity of soils increases as the content of organic (usually vegetable) material increases. Sand and clay, with low organic content, have 40% porosity, whereas highly organic peat has 80% porosity. Clay and highly organic soils drain poorly, whereas sand, where the spaces are connected, drains rapidly. When waves wash up onto a sandy seashore they do not roll back to the ocean. The seawater percolates down to sea level through the good draining sand. Around your wine cellar, sandy soil plus good subsurface drainage assures close to the optimal 40% air content nearly all the time.

Ideal conditions alongside a wine cellar are thus a canopy of trees over lush ground vegetation growing in poorly draining organic topsoil with a constant supply of moisture for evaporative cooling. The soil beneath the surface layer should, in contrast, be highly insulating bone-dry sand.

Beneath the wine cellar, high thermal conductivity, like that found in non-porous bedrock or moisture retaining soils, is best. The high conductivity maximizes the rate at which summer heat is conducted out of the cellar floor into the ground.

Bedrock

The least porous material that can be found in the ground is solid rock. It contains virtually no insulating air spaces, and therefore has much less insulating value than soil, which gives it high thermal conductivity. If you discover bedrock during the excavation for a new house-with-wine-cellar, rejoice. If the bedrock adjacent to your house is covered by an insulating blanket of soil, but extends down a respectful distance, then it will serve as an ideal wine cellar floor which will rapidly conduct summer heat down out of your wine cellar. Beware, however, of rock attached to nearby surface outcroppings. They might conduct summer heat into your cellar rather than away from it.

If you discover bedrock, then you can lighten up on the insulation, as the effective insulating (or R- value) of the floor is 50%, or less than what it would be on a soil base. A wine cellar a few blocks from mine is built on bedrock; mine is not. That cellar's annual temperature cycle, with minimal ceiling and wall insulation (roughly R-5), a conventional hollow-core door, and no exterior wall insulation, is nearly identical to what I have had to super-insulate to achieve.

Multi-Day Cycles

We have discussed daily and annual temperature cycles. In between those extremes there are cycles of several days duration such as occur during a hot or cold spell. A three or four-day summer heat wave, followed by more temperate weather, will penetrate several feet into the ground. There will first be a rise in the temperature of the top layer of soil as it absorbs heat more rapidly than it is transferred into the subsoil. After the heat wave is over, the surface soil temperature will gradually fall back as the extra heat is transferred into the subsoil, back into the atmosphere, or is used to evaporate water at the surface.

If the walls or ceiling of a basement are not insulated, then the basement temperature will also cycle in response to heat waves and cold spells. During a typical summer heat wave I observe a rapid rise in the basement air temperature alongside my super-insulated wine cellar, but no detectable effect within. After the heat wave passes, the basement temperature returns almost to its previous level. This pattern repeats many times each year. The temperature within the wine cellar follows a smooth curve, while the readings in the basement, on the other side of the cellar wall, gyrate in response to the weather. Wine cellar temperature stability through multi-day cycles is attributable to the thermal mass of my wine collection acting in concert with super-insulation which slows the influx of heat to a rate at which the concrete floor can transfer it into the subsoil.

Micro-Cycles

There is one final type of summertime wine cellar temperature oscillation. A blast of relatively warm air enters your wine cellar with you through the door, and you then heat the air with your body heat. Electric lighting adds to the heat burden as you tarry to examine a few of your cellar treasures and catalog and bin your latest acquisitions. This extra heat is added to the summer heat that continually enters the cellar through the walls and ceiling. This combination can raise the air temperature in a small wine cellar several degrees in just a few minutes. Minutes after you remove the extra heat sources, the air temperature will return to its previous level as heat enters bottles or leaves through the floor.

Don't be alarmed by these temporary temperature deviations, as the wine within the bottles won't warm anywhere near as quickly as the air. As shown in Table 6-1, air has a tiny thermal mass, which means that a very small amount of heat will noticeably raise the air temperature. Wine has a very high thermal mass, 4,000 times that of an equal volume of air. Even if all of the heat required to raise the air temperature in a wine cellar by ten degrees were transferred to a few hundred wine bottles, the rise in wine temperature would not be detectable with a conventional thermometer.

Thermobottles

If you spend an hour working in a wine cellar, or if you forget to turn off the light or to close the door, then you can raise the wine temperature as heat continues to flow from the warmed air into the bottles. To measure wine temperatures directly, assemble a thermobottle by introducing a thermometer into the center of a water-filled recorked wine bottle. The thermometer can either be entirely enclosed within the bottle, or can protrude via a hole drilled in the cork. Place your thermobottle in the wine cellar in a permanent location where it will be convenient to read. During long projects, such as taking inventory, monitor the thermobottle periodically. When the thermobottle temperature rises detectably, it's time to leave the cellar. A thermobottle is also the most reliable way to monitor wine cellar temperatures because its reading won't change rapidly when you enter the cellar.

A thermobottle can also be useful for monitoring wine temperatures when you transfer bottles from one place to another. For example, should you want to determine how long to leave a bottle of dessert wine in the freezer to rapidly cool it to serving temperature, you could put the thermobottle and the wine into the freezer together and check the temperature periodically. (I get 1°F of cooling with every two minutes in the freezer.) Similarly, if you're serving red wines from a very cold midwinter cellar and want to warm them up a bit upstairs you could move the thermobottle along with the wine.

Deriving a Soil Temperature Profile

The annual soil temperature profile of figure 6-1 was derived via the formulas in Table 6-3 using values given in Table 6-2. Although it isn't really necessary, some of the physicists and engineers amongst you might enjoy deriving a *de novo* soil-temperature profile for your location. A few sample calculations are provided to help you get started.

TABLE 6-2 THERMAL PROPERTIES OF SOILS

Soil Type	Porosity	Wetness	K Thermal Conductivity	C Heat Capacity
Sand	0.4	0.0	.0007	0.3
	0.4	0.2	.0042	0.5
	0.4	0.4	.0052	0.7
Clay	0.4	0.0	.0006	0.3
	0.4	0.2	.0028	0.5
	0.4	0.4	.0038	0.7
Peat	0.8	0.0	.00014	0.35
	0.8	0.4	.0007	0.75
	0.8	0.8	.0012	1.15

TABLE 6-3 DERIVING SOIL TEMPERATURE PROFILES

$$\text{Tmax (at depth Z)} = \text{Ts} + e^{(-Z/d)}\,\text{Dt}$$
$$\text{Tmin (at depth Z)} = \text{Ts} - e^{(-Z/d)}\,\text{Dt}$$

Tmax = the highest monthly mean temperature in degrees C
   (July for the northern hemisphere)
Tmin = the lowest monthly mean temperature (January)
Z = the depth below the soil surface in centimeters
Ts = the mean annual temperature in degrees C
e = 2.718
d = the damping depth = $(2K/CW))^5$
K = thermal conductivity of the soil (cal/cm sec°C, from Table 6-2)
C = the heat capacity of the soil (cal/cm °C)^3, from Table 6-2)
W = 2 x 3.14159/3.15^7 = 2 x 10^{-7} (3.15^7 = seconds in a year)
Dt = the mean ambient temperature deviation, in °C, from the annual mean temperature for the warmest (or coldest) month.

Sample calculations:

When Z = 100 (1 meter), Ts = 10°C, K = .002, C = .4, and Dt = 14, then Tmax = 18.95 and Tmin = 1.05 (°C)

These K and C values are for sand containing 10% water, and were used in preparing Figure 6-1.

If, instead, the soil is bone-dry sand, with K = .0007, and C = 0.3, then Tmax = 17.27, and Tmin = 2.73

If the soil is sand containing 20% water, with K = .0042, and C = .5, then Tmax = 19.91, and Tmin = 0.09

If the soil is saturated sand (40% water), with K = .0052, and C = .7, then Tmax = 19.70, and Tmin = 0.30

Chapter 7

❊❊❊❊❊❊❊❊❊❊❊❊❊❊❊❊❊❊❊❊❊❊❊❊❊❊❊❊❊❊❊❊❊❊❊❊

INSULATION

During the summer, heat flows into a corner wine cellar from (a) the house above through the ceiling, (b) the adjacent basement through the interior walls and door, and (c) the outdoor environment and warmed superficial soils through the exposed and buried parts of the upper foundation walls. This heat exits the wine cellar through the floor and lower foundation walls. The rates at which heat enters and departs, and therefore the temperature inside, are determined by the temperature gradients that push heat through the ceiling, walls, and floor; by the heat resisting insulation; and by the surface areas.

To simplify the explanation of how temperature gradients and insulation determine cellar temperature, let's initially ignore the walls and focus on the ceiling and floor. Since both the ceiling and floor have the same area, surface area can at this stage be ignored. If the ceiling and floor were equally insulated, heat flow would be resisted equally at ceiling and floor, and the temperature of the air in the cellar would equilibrate exactly halfway between the house and soil temperatures. On a typical warm midsummer day these temperatures might be 75°F (24°C) in the house, and 55°F (13°C) in the soil, yielding 65°F (18.5°C) in the cellar. If the ceiling and floor were not identically insulated, the wine cellar temperature would be closer to the temperature beyond the less-insulated surface.

To predict the effect on cellar temperature of varying amounts of wine-cellar ceiling insulation you need the house temperature, the soil temperature, and the R-value (insulation) of the cellar floor. If you air condition your home the house temperature above the cellar will be around 72°F (22°C). If the overhead room isn't air conditioned, use a higher value. The seasonal under-cellar soil-temperature peak was determined in the preceding chapter. For our demonstration site the summer high at four feet below grade is 60°F (15°C).

TABLE 7-1 R—(insulating) VALUES

	per inch	per cm
Aluminum	0.0007	0.0003
Steel	0.003	0.001
Concrete & Stone	0.20	0.08
Brick	0.21	0.08
Water	0.24	0.09
Ice	0.064	0.025
Snow (fresh)	3.00	1.18
Dry Sand	0.44	0.17
Dry organic Soil	0.80	0.31
Hardwoods (oak)	0.82	0.32
Softwoods (pine)	1.32	0.52
Fiberglass batts	3.30	1.30
Cellulose (blown)	3.90	1.54
Extruded Polystyrene	5.00	1.97
Polyisocyanurate	7.2	2.9

The third number needed to determine wine cellar temperature, the R-value of the cellar floor, is the difficult one. The concrete of a cellar floor has a tiny insulating value of only R-0.2 per inch (see Table 7-1). Insulating concrete with inclusions of wood chips etc. insulates only slightly more. Unfortunately, you cannot consider the insulating value of a four-inch concrete cellar floor to be R-0.8 (four inches x 0.2), as you would if moving air or water were on the other side of the concrete sweeping heat away as it arrived. As heat penetrates a concrete floor, it encounters insulating soil. The underlying soil is a part of, indeed is most of, the floor insulation. A dirt cellar-floor is therefore essentially identical, insulation wise, to a concrete floor.

Fiberglass and foam insulation have negligible thermal mass, so it's appropriate to think of them only in terms of resistance to a flow-through of heat. Soil and concrete, however, have thermal mass in addition to their insulating properties. Nevertheless, for our purpose we conceptually separate the soil's insulating and heat-absorbing properties. The cellar floor-plus-soil acts like an insulator beyond which there's a heat absorber such as flowing air or water.

Let's first conservatively hypothesize that the effective insulating value of floor-plus-soil is only R-2.5. That's the concrete plus two inches (5 cm) of soil. Using values of 75°F (24°C) for the house temperature, 55°F (13°C) for the soil temperature, and R-2.5 for the cellar floor, the effects on wine cellar temperature of varied amounts of ceiling insulation can be calculated. As insulation is added to the ceiling, the cellar temperature will fall closer and closer to the underfoot temperature. But at some point additional insulation will no longer significantly lower the cellar temperature. When is that point of diminishing returns reached?

To bring our model closer to reality, we now factor in heat transfer through the interior and exterior cellar walls. The total area of the two interior wine cellar walls of a corner-of-the-basement wine cellar (walls between the wine cellar and the rest of the basement) is typically double that of the ceiling, but the temperature gradient is typically only half that between the wine cellar and the overlying house. Under these approximations, the greater surface area and smaller temperature differential conveniently balance each other out. So, if equally insulated, the interior walls and the ceiling each admit identical amounts of heat. We therefore estimate the total heat transfer through the interior walls plus the ceiling by doubling the amount of heat transfer through the ceiling. With this approximation, equal ceiling and floor insulation place the cellar temperature closer to that of the house. To get back to the midway cellar temperature, the ceiling and interior walls require double the insulation of the floor. During the summer, the exterior (foundation) wine cellar walls admit heat at the top from warm exterior air and warmed surface soils, and lose heat at the bottom to cooler deep soils. It's sufficient for present purposes to say that those two effects cancel each other out.

Using the aforementioned rationale, Figure 7-1 shows the effect of varying the amount of ceiling and interior wall insulation if the R-value of the cellar floor were indeed R-2.5. Going from no insulation (R-1.2 for a single layer of drywall on the wall and an un-insulated ceiling) to a ceiling and walls with 3.5 inches of fiberglass between studs (R-12), lowers our model cellar's temperature by a whopping 10°F (5.5°C). Upgrading to 6 inches of fiberglass (R-21) lowers the cellar temperature only another 2.3°F (1.2°C). Progressing to 9 inches of fiberglass (R-30) in ceiling and interior walls (we'll deal with wall construction later) gains an unimpressive additional 1°F (.5°C). The space between the joists in the ceiling will be filled with fiberglass by this point, so to insulate further you would nail foam boards across the ends of the ceiling joists. The most efficient of these boards are foil-backed polyisocyanurate and go by brand names such as Thermax and High R. Extruded polystyrene boards are less expensive, nearly as effective, and are less likely to give off toxic fumes. A 4-inch (10 cm) layer of Thermax, or 6 inches of extruded polystyrene, would double the

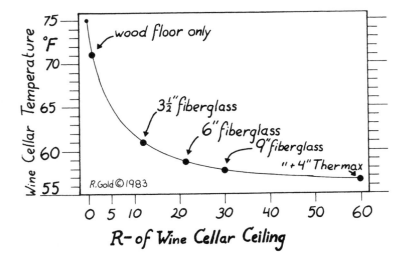

Figure 7-1. Floor at **R-2.5.** Wine cellar temperatures as the R-values of the ceiling and the interior walls increase.

R-value of your 9 inches of fiberglass to yield a super-insulated R-60 ceiling. All of this extra insulation gains you only an additional 1.3°F (0.7°C) of coolness.

A higher estimate for the insulating equivalent of the cellar floor, say R-10 for 12 inches of soil, gives quite another result, as seen in Figure 7-2. Under these conditions, going from no insulation to 3.5 inches of fiberglass (R-12) lowers the cellar temperature only 6°F (3.3°C). Progressing to 6 inches of fiberglass (R-21) adds 3°F (2°C). Going to 9 inches of fiberglass (R-30) adds 1.7°F (1°C), and a further doubling of the insulation with the Thermax or extruded polystyrene to R-60 significantly lowers the cellar temperature an additional 3°F (1.7°C).

To indirectly measure the R-value equivalent of a wine cellar floor, I have examined the overnight effects of adding and then removing ceiling insulation, and have compared the temperature in my super-insulated wine cellar with that of the less well-insulated

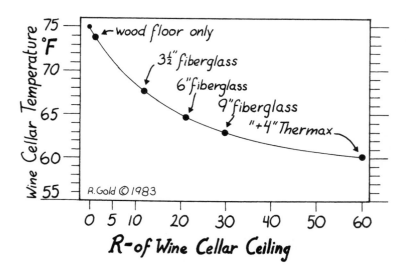

Figure 7-2. Floor at **R-10.** Wine cellar temperatures as the R-values of the ceiling and the interior walls increase.

adjacent basement. My observations indicate that the effective summer R- value of the outside corner of a basement floor is even more than the R-10 (for one foot of soil) estimate used in preparing figure 7-2. This seems reasonable since if your cellar floor is 4 feet below grade, then the outdoor air is separated from the cellar floor by 4 feet (120 cm) of insulating soil which provides R-40 insulation. A wine cellar having a floor with an R- value in this range would profit greatly from super-insulation of its ceiling and walls.

This is indeed what happens in my cellar. As shown in figure 6-2, in midwinter my super-insulated wine cellar with an R-55 ceiling and R-38 foundation walls remains 5°F (3°C) cooler than the rest of my unheated basement, which has an R-20 ceiling and un-insulated foundation walls. In the summer the difference grows to 10°F (5.5°C). Such temperature differentials confirm that the cellar floor does indeed insulate in excess of R-10, necessitating super-insulation in the ceiling and walls.

One summer day I spread a single sheet of plastic loosely over my entire wine cellar floor. 24-hours later the air temperature in the wine cellar had risen 2°F (1.1°C). I removed the plastic and by the next day the temperature elevation was gone. The plastic had trapped a layer of insulating air beneath it, which was sufficient to detectably impede heat transfer into the floor. A sheet of plastic or a pane of glass is rated as R-1. R-1 is therefore not insignificant in comparison to the R- value of the floor, suggesting that the R-40 estimate was too high. The additional lesson learned from this experiment is that unless you want to raise your cellar temperature, place no insulating material like rugs, plastic, wooden flooring, wooden bin floors, or cardboard or wooden boxes directly on the floor, and never place insulation beneath a concrete floor.

The argument for wine cellar super-insulation is similar to the argument for super-insulation of a solar heated house. The fuel saved is not alone enough to justify the added expense. The justification comes when you can forego the expense of a conventional furnace and ducts. Similarly, super-insulating a wine cellar may give you only a few degrees of extra coolness, but if that difference permits you to forego air conditioning, then super-insulating is well worth the effort.

There's an additional reason to super-insulate. All summer heat enters the soil and gradually raises the soil temperature, which in turn raises the cellar temperature. During the winter, the heat stored over the summer escapes back to the cold atmosphere. Wine cellar insulation slows the seasonal heating of the near soil. Every time you double the R-value of the ceiling and walls, you halve the heat transfer into the soil. Lateral heat transfer within the soil will tend to deplete your cool soil bank. Nevertheless, super-insulation can keep the summer temperature of the soil beneath a wine cellar several degrees below that of the surrounding soil at the same depth.

The insulating value of a cellar floor will vary with the type of soil. If the cellar is on solid bedrock, which conducts heat four to five times better than dry soil, the cellar floor will have the equivalent of a very low R-value, necessitating less ceiling and wall insulation. The lower the R-value of the cellar floor, the less insulation you'll need in the ceiling and walls.

You've seen, in figures 7-1 and 7-2, how the first few inches of insulation have the greatest effect on heat transfer. It follows, and is advised in all insulation guides, that you should insulate evenly. Upstairs, in your house, R-60 walls make no sense alongside un-shuttered R-2 double-glazed windows. Similarly, if you have a super-insulated wine cellar ceiling, you need a super-insulated door, a design for which is provided in Chapter 14, and super-insulated walls.

The "insulate evenly" rule assumes equivalent temperature gradients, but this isn't usually the case in a wine cellar. Surfaces facing greater temperature gradients deserve the greatest insulation. Thus, if the ceiling faces a 20°F (11°C) gradient, but the interior walls face only a 10°F (5.5°C) gradient, then the ceiling deserves twice as much insulation as the walls. This is likely to be the case if the rest of the basement has some ceiling and foundation insulation and isn't heated. In this situation an R-60 ceiling is well matched to R-30 interior walls.

A not readily obvious gap in the insulation occurs when you insulate the interior but not the exterior surface of your foundation walls. Compare Figures 7-3 and 7-4. Even if you insulate the interior surface from floor to ceiling, the concrete foundation walls themselves, at only R-0.2 per inch, will conduct heat from the outside air down into the cellar floor. Five vertical feet (150 cm) of concrete wall yield only R-12 insulation.

Insulation of the interior surface is better than no foundation insulation at all. Five feet (150 cm) of concrete at R-12 is a lot better than 8 inches (20 cm) at R-1.6, but is still not enough—the upper part of the foundation walls can face temperature gradients in excess of 50°F (28°C). The exterior surface of the above-grade foundation wall is the most critical region to insulate, and requires the most insulation of all. Because of the extreme temperature gradient, I recommend both exterior and interior insulation against the foundation wall, as shown in Figure 7-6. R-10 to R-20 on the outside, plus an equivalent amount on the inside, is a good combination. If required to prevent condensation, place a polyethylene vapor barrier against the interior of the foundation wall before installing the interior insulation.

In new construction, exterior foundation insulation is easy to install. You merely attach 8-foot-by-2-foot extruded polystyrene boards, running vertically, to the exterior waterproofed surface of the concrete using beads of an appropriate, foam-friendly adhesive, such as Contech PL200. At R-5 per inch, the standard 2 inch (5 cm) thickness is only R-10. Three or 4 inches is more in keeping with the level of insulation elsewhere around a super-insulated wine cellar. It may be possible to special order 3 or 4-inch thick boards, but you may have to apply a double layer of the 2 inch boards. When double-layering, stagger the seams to avoid gaps and to resist moisture penetration. The upper part of the foundation faces the greatest temperature gradients, so you could use a singl e full height vertical 2-inch layer covered with a horizontal layer over only the upper two feet of the foundation.

In a pre-existing house without foundation insulation, you have to dig to install exterior insulation. To dig to the base of the foundation and then refill would require two visits by a back-hoe, which is expensive to rent and will tear up your landscaping. Such an excavation done by hand, even for the perimeter of a modest wine cellar, takes a week of back-breaking labor, and risks life-threatening cave-ins. It isn't essential to go that deep. Ninety percent of the heat that enters un-insulated concrete foundation walls does so through the foot (30 cm) or so that is above grade, and the first foot or two below grade (refer to Figure 6-1). It is usually sufficient to place only one width (2 feet or 60 cm) of polystyrene board horizontally against the foundation. This requires only a 1-foot (30 cm) deep excavation, since most foundation walls extend 1 foot (30 cm) above grade. More than the standard 2-inch thickness is still desirable. Go past the perimeter of the wine cellar when applying exterior insulation, because heat would otherwise travel laterally through the foundation wall. Even this amount of hand-digging will keep you busy for several hours.

Your excavation for exterior insulation will extend at least a foot from the wall. With only moderate extra effort you can excavate for horizontal, within-ground polystyrene insulation extending out 2 feet from the lowest edge of the vertical insulation. Use a gentle pitch for drainage, as shown in figures 7-5 and 7-6. At R-5 per inch, a 4-inch layer of horizontal polystyrene yields R-20 as compared with R-3.2 for the soil that it displaces. If it doesn't bring soil too close into proximity to wooden parts of the house, you can use the displaced soil to raise the surface, thus retaining the R-3.2 as well. Extension of the skirt to 4, 6, or even 8 feet from the wall would provide additional advantage, but would require more digging. To minimize the labor

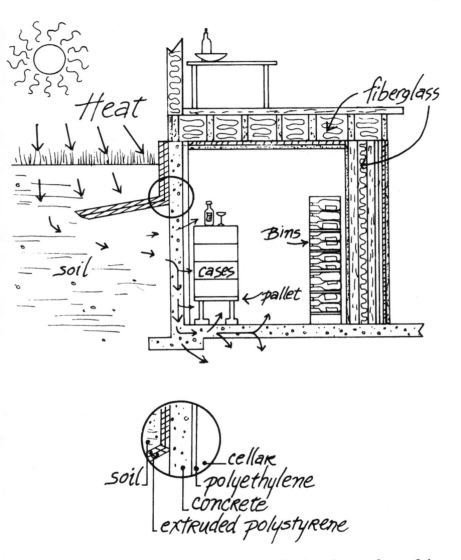

Figure 7-3. When insulation is limited to the interior surface of the foundation wall, summer heat and winter chill will readily flow down the foundation wall into the cellar floor.

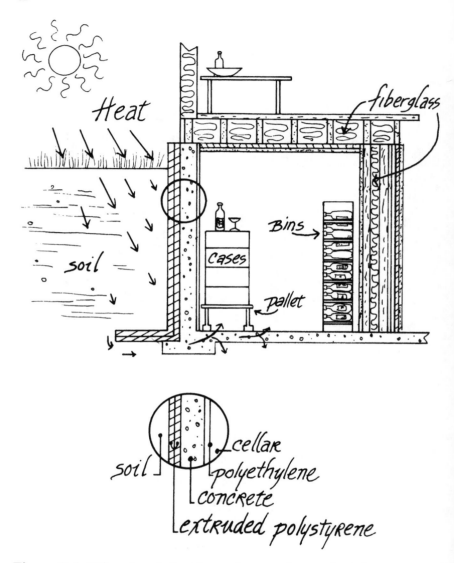

Heat

fiberglass

soil

Bins

Cases

pallet

soil — cellar
polyethylene
concrete
extruded polystyrene

Figure 7-4. When insulation is on the exterior surface, heat penetration to the cellar floor is slowed by the insulating value of the soil.

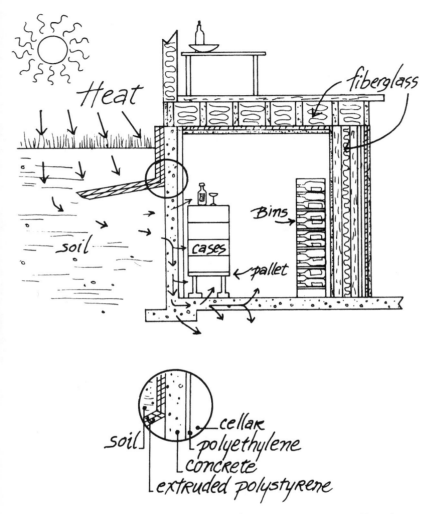

Figure 7-5. For retrofitting un-insulated foundation walls, place two to four inches of extruded polystyrene against the upper exterior surface, plus a horizontal skirt. Apply a UV cover above grade.

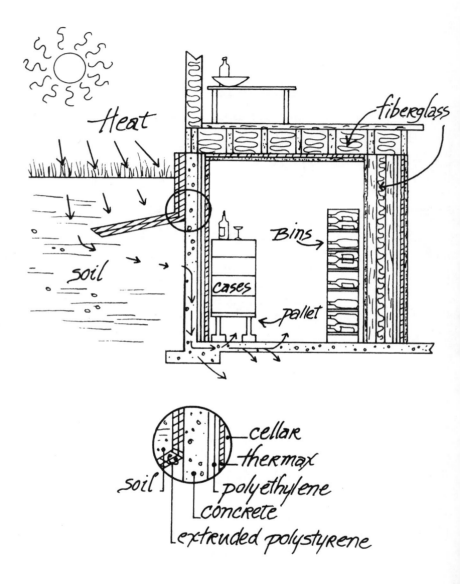

Figure 7-6. The full recommended treatment: Exterior plus interior insulation, with a horizontal in-soil insulating skirt and a polyethylene interior vapor barrier.

required, try to deposit soil being dug at one spot directly onto insulation that's already in place. Any large rocks that you encounter are poor insulators and are best removed. Horizontal insulation is also a good idea in new construction, and should be located at the base of the foundation as in Figure 7-4.

A precise calculation of the effect of within-soil insulation on wine cellar temperature would be a complicated three-dimensional affair. As an estimate, 4 inches of horizontal within-ground insulation is equivalent to sinking the wine cellar an extra 21 inches (53 cm) into the soil. Figures 6-1 shows that this would lower the peak summer temperature 3°F (1.5°C).

The soil beneath any within-ground insulation must be compacted and leveled before the insulation is applied or it will break. A two-by-four aided by a carpenter's level can be used to sweep the surface level. Backfill carefully to avoid piercing or crushing the insulation. Only extruded polystyrene is recommended for contact with soil. Less compact, expanded or molded bead-polystyrene, polyurethane, and foil-faced polyisocyanurate (e.g. Thermax), all pick up moisture with soil contact, which degrades them to 85% to 65% or less of their original R-value.

Stronger 3 or 4-inch thick polystyrene boards are especially welcome when installing horizontal insulation. A new type of extruded polystyrene is advertised as being especially resistant to compression. This would be a good idea for horizontal insulation where a riding lawn mower or construction truck might roll over the buried insulation. Since the interiors of wine cellars are rather damp places, extruded polystyrene, despite its slightly lower initial R-value as compared to Thermax, also has appeal for use on the interior cellar walls.

Above-surface polystyrene deteriorates in a few years due to weathering and ultraviolet light. Its garish pink or blue color is also aesthetically objectionable. Fortunately, products with a bonded and impact resistant UV shield are now available. A material that coats like stucco is also available, but I have no experience with it.

Having gone to the trouble of insulating the exterior surface of the foundation, don't neglect the more accessible, but easily overlooked, top of the foundation wall. This surface is an extension of the spaces between the ceiling joists and is easily reached from inside the basement. Insulation should extend out above the top of the foundation wall all the way to the exterior siding.

One final source of heat exists via the concrete floor and walls shared by the wine cellar with the adjacent basement. Heat will enter the concrete floor adjacent to the wine cellar and travel laterally into the cooler concrete of the wine cellar floor. To combat this heat invasion you can insulate the upper surface of the concrete floor alongside the wine cellar and, by the same logic, the inner surface of foundation walls adjacent to the wine cellar. The easiest way to do this is with foam insulation laid on the floor and propped against the wall. To store things on top of the insulation, use boards to distribute pressure.

Most readers will not be devoting their entire basements to wine storage, but a few words of advice are in order for those exceptions such as restaurants, wine shops, and people with tiny basements or who run home wineries, or invest heavily for resale. If the entire basement is to be used for wine storage, then build a super-insulated room around the furnace, heating ducts, water heater, and hot water pipes, and also wrap the water heater heavily. Insulate the furnace room floor but not the furnace room ceiling. Any foam insulation near a furnace must be protected from fire by 5/8" drywall. Super-insulate the rest of the basement ceiling and the foundation walls.

Chapter 8 * HUMIDITY

As we have seen, ideal cellar temperature cannot easily be achieved. Neither can ideal humidity. Excessive humidity inflicts the torment of mold and inadequate humidity brings the heartbreak of ullage. If you live in the desert where it's always dry, you can skip the first part of this chapter on high humidity and mold, but don't overlook the second part on low humidity and ullage, and also check out evaporative cooling in Chapter 10. For everyone else, this entire chapter is required reading.

High Humidity and Mold

Moisture enters unfinished basements, often surreptitiously as water vapor gas, without visible sign through concrete or cement block foundation walls. Some moisture also enters through the floor. This moisture escapes through the basement ceiling. If your new wine cellar ceiling and interior walls prevent the escape of this moisture, then excessive humidity in the 90 to 100% range can result.

Excessively high relative humidity inevitably leads to mold. The carbohydrates in your wine cellar: cork stoppers, paper labels, paper surface of the drywall, and wooden shelves can all become mold food. The microscopic creatures secrete enzymes which digest cellulose into glucose, which they then metabolize. They also release allergenic spores into the air. Epidemics of the most common mold produce a white but smelly Christmas-in-May. Black molds are even more depressing. Once mold has staked claim to a cellar, it is extremely difficult to eradicate. Preventive measures which avert the extreme humidity that encourages mold growth can ensure that your acquaintance with this organism remains vicarious.

Why cellars tend to be damp

There are two measures of humidity: absolute and relative. **Absolute humidity** is simply the amount of water vapor in the air, and is usually expressed as grams per cubic meter (g/m^3). **Relative humidity** is the amount of water vapor in the air expressed as a percent of the maximum amount of water vapor that air is capable of holding at that temperature. For example, when air is at 22°C (72°F) it can hold no more than 19.4 g/m^3 of water vapor.

For a better idea of how much water this is, imagine a 5' x 7' x 12' wine cellar which contains about 10 m^3 of air. At 22°C this cellar can hold up to 194 g of water vapor. One g = one ml. As liquid water, 194 ml would fill 1/4 of a 750 ml wine bottle. If the air in the cellar only contained 3/4 of the 100% maximum, or 14.6 g/m^3 of water vapor, then the relative humidity would be 75%.

Figure 8-1 shows how the moisture capacity of air dramatically increases as temperature rises. The warmer the air, the more moisture it can hold. For example, air at the typical household temperature of 72°F (22°C) can hold up to 19.4 g/m^3, whereas air in a 59°F (15°C) wine cellar can hold only 12.8 g/m^3. The points on figure 8-1 representing these two temperatures are circled.

If the room above the wine cellar and the wine cellar itself were both at 100% relative humidity (that is, if they actually contained 19.4 and 12.8 g/m^3 of water vapor respectively) then water vapor, if not stopped by a vapor barrier, would travel from the region of higher (19.4) absolute humidity down to the region of lower (12.8) absolute humidity. Since the wine-cellar air was already fully saturated, these water vapor acquisitions would have no option but to leave the vapor state and deposit as liquid water upon the coolest surface available. This is how dew forms. The water vapor content of the wine cellar air would remain unchanged at 12.8 g/m^3, so water vapor would continue to migrate from upstairs.

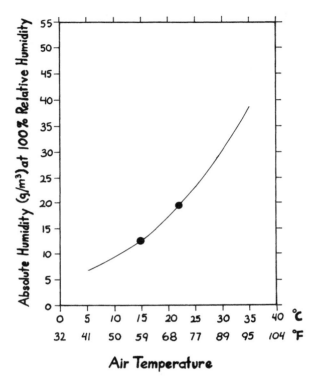

Figure 8-1. As air temperature rises, its water vapor capacity increases.

In practice the air in the room above the wine cellar is almost never at 100% relative humidity. Nevertheless, the overhead house can, and indeed often does, contain more moisture than cool wine-cellar air can retain.

Humidity is impossible to gauge accurately without instruments. You need a hygrometer, which is the technical name for a device that measures relative humidity. Don't wait until a mold epidemic reveals that the relative humidity is too high. A simple $10 hygrometer is available at your hardware store, and fancier versions can be had from wine-accessory firms and scientific supply houses.

Inexpensive hygrometers are often inaccurate at high humidities, which is where you'll be working. If in doubt, calibrate against a dry-and-wet bulb hygrometer. Dry-and-wet bulb hygrometers and the similar sling psychrometer are a nuisance to use routinely as they require a water supply, fanning, and reference charts. To monitor small changes in humidity you have to interpolate the values in the charts. These devices are, however, excellent for calibrating. Most hygrometers available today have a dial and pointer, and are easy to dismantle and adjust. After calibration, place your hygrometer permanently in a convenient eye-level niche. Readings will vary with location even within a small cellar.

A simplified model

Ignore for the moment moisture entering or departing your wine cellar via the walls, door, or floor, and consider only the interaction between the wine cellar and the house above. Assume also that the temperature and humidity in the room above the wine cellar remain constant. Figure 8-2 uses upstairs temperature and humidity plus cellar temperature to predict the relative humidity in the cellar.

To use figure 8-2, measure the temperature and humidity in the room above the proposed wine cellar. Find these values on the axes of the figure. For example, one cool day in May the temperature is 69.5°F (21°C) and there's 50% relative humidity upstairs. That places you at position "X" on figure 8-2. The curved line that passes through "X" represents a 50°F (10°C) wine cellar at 100% relative humidity.

You predicted the annual soil temperature extremes at the level of your wine cellar floor in Chapter 6. Early in the spring the temperature at the cellar floor will still be close to its winter low. If the cellar floor temperature is 50°F (10°C) on our glorious spring day, then the air down there will rise to 100% relative humidity.

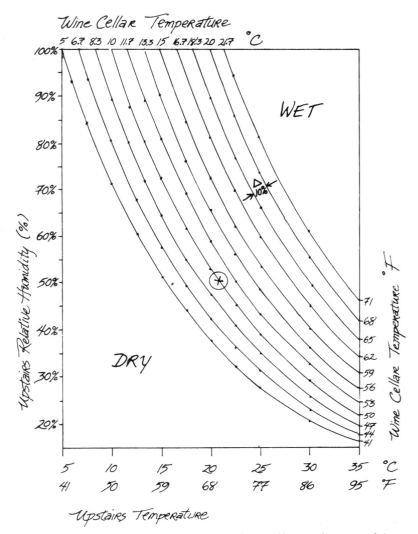

Figure 8-2. Each curve represents a wine cellar at the stated (top and right side) temperature and 100% relative humidity. Equilibrium is assumed with the upstairs conditions of temperature (bottom) and relative humidity (left side). Adjacent curves represent approximately 10% shifts in wine cellar relative humidity.

When the upstairs temperature and humidity place you at a point on figure 8-2 that's cooler than the actual cellar temperature, the relative humidity in the cellar will be lower than 100%. The spacing between curves was selected so that each curved line represents approximately a 10% shift in relative humidity. For example, if figure 8-2 yields 50°F (10°C) when your actual wine cellar temperature is 53°F (11.7°C), which is the curve just to the right of position "X", then the equilibrium cellar-humidity is 90%. For a 56°F (13.3°C) cellar, (the next curve over), the cellar humidity would be 80%.

When figure 8-2 yields a cellar temperature that is warmer than the actual cellar temperature, for example 50°F (10°C) when the actual cellar temperature is only 47°F (8.3°C), then the cool cellar air is unable to retain all of the water vapor that would be delivered, and condensation of water on the coolest surfaces would result.

The upstairs temperature and humidity will only occasionally bring the predicted wine cellar humidity to 100%. A polyethylene vapor barrier above the wine cellar can slow water vapor so effectively that it would take many hours of adverse conditions before the wine cellar reached 100% relative humidity. The upstairs temperature and absolute humidity usually fall at night, which offsets the influence of occasionally less favorable daytime conditions.

The greatest risk of mold occurs in the spring and early summer when wine cellar temperatures are still near their coolest, meaning low water-vapor capacity, but the upstairs indoor absolute humidity has already risen from its winter low. Later in the summer the cellar will be a bit warmer, giving it greater moisture capacity, and a humidity lowering air conditioner is more likely to be in operation upstairs.

In winter, moisture from upstairs is rarely a problem, as the absolute and relative humidity of the heated household air will both be quite low, approaching equilibrium with the low absolute humidity of cold outdoor air. So long as the interior surfaces of your windows are colder than the coldest spot in your wine cellar, there can be no winter humidity problem in your wine cellar. However, if your house has vapor barriers and thermal window shutters and you zealously humidify your home for health reasons, you could conceivably create midwinter moisture problems in your wine cellar.

Recommendations: The walls

It's now time to expand our discussion to include the cellar walls. The interior wine cellar walls, those that face the rest of the basement, require a vapor barrier. This is because the basement, lacking a perimeter vapor barrier, and being warmer, will at times have a higher absolute humidity than the wine cellar. The continuous polyethylene layer should go on the warmer basement (not wine cellar) side of the wall, just under the drywall. Alternately, if you are using fiberglass batts, make sure they're faced, and put the facing, which is a vapor barrier, furthest from the wine cellar. Finally, if you've placed foil-faced foam or extruded polystyrene insulation on the outside, that will serve as your vapor barrier.

The exterior wine cellar walls that face soil also require a vapor barrier. Imagine a completed wine cellar, with vapor barriers in the ceiling and interior walls, but unmodified exterior walls. The humidity at the wine cellar floor increases to 100%, and the lower part of the exterior walls becomes damp. If figure 8-2 indicates that the air spaces around the wine cellar don't contain enough absolute humidity to account for the high wine cellar humidity, then the moisture must be entering through the foundation. The basic problem is more water vapor resistance on the ceiling and interior walls than on the exterior walls. Moisture is entering the wine cellar from the soil more rapidly than it can escape into the rest of the house. The solution is not to eliminate or degrade the ceiling's vapor barrier–that's needed to protect against warm humid dog days–but to upgrade the vapor barrier on the foundation walls.

During new home construction, prevent water seepage by waterproofing the exterior surface of the foundation wall around your prospective wine cellar. The standard treatment is one layer of brushed-on black asphalt designed for exterior damp proofing. It must be applied to a dry wall. After the asphalt has dried, apply your exterior polystyrene insulation using an appropriate adhesive such as Contech PL200. (Wet asphalt doesn't hold foam boards in place.) Consider waterproofing the exterior surface of the concrete foundation with modified asphalt, rubberized asphalt sheets, or sprayed-on bentonite clay instead of the standard unmodified asphalt. Don't forget the peripheral drainage system to carry ground water away from the foundation – this is part of proper home construction and is especially critical near a wine cellar.

I recommend placing drainage board against the exterior surface of the foundation insulation before back filling. The porous drainage board provides a low-resistance channel that carries rainwater downwards to peripheral drains or to the soil beneath the cellar floor. The drainage board also protects your foam insulation from nesting rodents.

The surface soil level should grade away from the house to promote runoff. Settling after backfilling can create rainwater-retaining depressions which should be filled. Figure 8-3 depicts the total recommended treatment for new construction at a wet site, less the exterior insulation.

If you're building a wine cellar in a preexisting basement, soil moisture can usually be stopped from the inside. The simplest and probably best interior vapor barrier is created by hanging six-millimeter or thicker polyethylene directly against the interior surface of the foundation. A staple gun is the only tool you'll need to attach the polyethylene to the ceiling or sill and to wall studs at the edges. The poly doesn't have to adhere to the foundation walls. A narrow air gap can be left between the poly and the wall.

How, you ask, can a vapor barrier that doesn't cling to the foundation possibly work? Moisture passes through concrete via tiny pores.

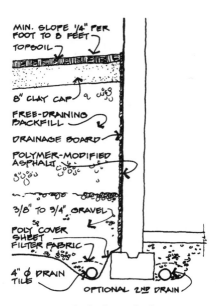

MIN. SLOPE 1/4" PER
FOOT TO 6 FEET
TOPSOIL
8" CLAY CAP
FREE-DRAINING
BACKFILL
DRAINAGE BOARD
POLYMER-MODIFIED
ASPHALT
3/8" TO 3/4" GRAVEL
POLY COVER
SHEET
FILTER FABRIC
4" ⌀ DRAIN
TILE
OPTIONAL 2ND DRAIN

Figure 8-3. The recommended foundation treatment to exclude moisture. (Progressive Builder, Sept., 1985, page PB 17.) In addition, exterior insulation is recommended beneath the drainage board.

When the moisture reaches the inner surface, surface tension holds it inside the pores unless it can evaporate into the air space or is under enough pressure to break free of the concrete pores and run down the wall as liquid water. The polyethylene vapor barrier isolates a thin layer of air that quickly reaches 100% relative humidity. The moisture in the pores of the wall will thereafter stay in place, as additional water molecules cannot evaporate into 100% humid air.

If the air layer trapped by the poly were warmer than the air in the wine cellar, droplets of water would condense on the cooler poly and run down to collect on the floor. This is prevented by a layer of insulation interior to the poly vapor barrier, which keeps the surface of the poly at wall temperature. If you have the temerity to defy my vapor barrier advice, at least limit your initial wine storage bins to the interior walls. This precaution will leave the foundation wall accessible when an unseasonable indoor white Christmas reveals that you erred.

The messier, more expensive, and less-effective waterproofing treatments that you apply with brush or trowel aren't needed unless you have cracks that rainwater flows through. These treatments come in two forms: water-base waterproofing paints, and spirit-base treatments. The water-base paints contain portland cement. The spirit-based stuff soaks into the wall to fill the pores, after which the solvent evaporates. The toxic solvent fumes can become quite concentrated in the close confines of a wine cellar. They might, among other ill effects, damage the olfactory epithelium in your nose, after which you'll have no further need for a wine cellar. For cracks and gaps, including the crack between the wall and the floor, use waterproofing concrete-patching compounds. Don't apply conventional paint to concrete; it prevents the penetration of any subsequent waterproofing material.

When a cellar master is outwitted by mold, nature's whitewash is invariably concentrated on the bottles and shelves closest to the floor. If you raise and lower your hygrometer during the summer, allowing an hour for the device to fully respond at each site, you'll discover that the relative humidity is lower at the ceiling than at the floor. This occurs because the ceiling is a few degrees warmer than the floor. The absolute humidity will be uniform at all levels, but at the floor it constitutes a greater percentage of capacity.

If the relative humidity at the floor is 100%, then at the ceiling it will be around 90%. Additional water added to the 90% upper region will distribute equally throughout the wine cellar, which means that the relative humidity at the floor will attempt to exceed 100%. Excess moisture will come out of the air as water droplets, or dew, deposited on the coolest surfaces available such as the lower walls, floor, and the lowest wine bottles. The moisture enters the cellar via the dry upper surfaces and is only deposited on the wet lower surfaces. The initial – and incorrect – impulse is to waterproof the wet lower surfaces. Since mold doesn't grow rapidly below 80% relative humidity, wine can even be stored during the summer in a basement through which a stream passes, if the vertical temperature gradient is steep and the wine is kept near the ceiling. A mild wine cellar mold problem can often be cured simply by raising the lowest wine storage one foot (30 cm) off the floor. Another tack is to temporarily increase the cellar temperature a few degrees, thereby increasing its moisture capacity. Do this by increasing the R-value of the accessible floor with a layer of polyethylene or foam board.

Recommendations: The Door

During the heating season the basement adjacent to your wine cellar will have a relatively low water content. Come spring, however, the absolute humidity of the adjacent warmer basement will increase, often to a level greater than the still cool wine cellar could tolerate. Figure 8-2 can be used to track this relationship. When the basement is moist, wine cellar door openings should be brief and infrequent. Needless to say, the door, being part of the interior wall, requires a vapor barrier.

Recommendations: The Floor

The floor is not usually a source of wine cellar moisture because any water that gets beneath it should percolate down into the soil. You could waterproof a new basement floor by placing a layer of polyethylene on the ground before the concrete is poured - but this will leave undesirable permanent insulating air pockets. Another notion is to spread a thick layer of small washed stones on top of the concrete floor. The stones trap insulating air next to the floor. This creates temperature and humidity gradients. In summer, the relative humidity at the bottom of the stone bed may reach 100%, but at the top of the bed, where the air is warmer, the relative humidity is lower. Stones on the floor are not very practical as a seasonal remedy since removing them annually would be a chore. If your wine cellar is too wet I'd try polyethylene on the floor, placing boards over it in the traffic areas. Poly or stones work because they raise cellar temperature, so only do enough to solve seasonal excessive moisture problem.

Recommendations: The Ceiling

Without a continuous layer of polyethylene, the vapor barrier facing the overlying house would have gaps between insulating foam boards and through the floor joists - but that vapor barrier **should** be less effective than the one facing the soil. This arrangement will prevent the build-up of upward traveling moisture in the wine cellar. The wine cellar also needs protection from the downwards migration of high absolute humidity that will infrequently occur in the house. The case for a good but imperfect ceiling vapor barrier is compelling.

The ceiling vapor barrier goes uppermost, against the overhead floor. If you combine unfaced fiberglass between floor joists with Thermax or polystyrene boards across the face of the joists, you will have the boards, the better vapor resistor, on the wrong side. Faced fiberglass insulation or polyethylene strips should go in first, with the vapor barrier uppermost against the overhead floor boards. Wrapping the floor joists with polyethylene creates a vapor barrier that is too effective, and is inappropriately located in relation to the floor joists, inviting condensation and rot on the lower surface of the floor joists.

Moisture from Within

Mold-inducing humidity can arise from within a wine cellar itself. One reader wrote that he found mold shortly after installing 1,000 clay wine-storage tiles that had been stored under the stars. Rain had soaked into the tiles. A long session of human breathing while taking inventory can also release a fair amount of water, as will burning candles, and broken wine bottles.

Electric Dehumidification

If despite your precautions, or perhaps because you took none, your humidity soars, you may be tempted to install an electric dehumidifier. This can benefit both your wine and items stored elsewhere in the basement. Put your electric dehumidifier outside the wine cellar, because the phase change from vapor to liquid releases lots of heat, as do the compressor motor and fan. A dehumidifier located in the basement outside your wine cellar will pull water vapor out through your interior cellar walls – provided they're not equipped with a super-efficient vapor barrier.

Dehumidifier coils tend to ice up in cool places. If this happens, plug the dehumidifier into a timer that prevents it from operating for about 5 minutes out of every 15. The down time allows accumulated ice to melt. Water from the dehumidifier should be drained via a hose. Raise the unit off of the floor to provide enough gravity for the drainage. If you persist in the folly of placing an electric dehumidifier inside a wine cellar, initially set the controls for the humidity level that just barely turns it on, and monitor the temperature consequences.

Ice Dehumidifier

An enterprising reader reports that he can lower the humidity in his wine cellar by suspending a gallon milk jug full of ice over a drip bucket. During the mold season he rotates two jugs daily between his cellar and his freezer. Moisture from the air condenses on the cold surface and drips into the bucket. Let me know if you try this one and whether it really helps. I doubt it.

The Dry-Well

A dry-well is an air-filled hole in the floor that can magically eliminate mold by lowering humidity. Throughout the spring and summer the ground warms from the surface down, creating a vertical temperature gradient. During this warming process the bottom of a dry-well, being at greater depth than the cellar floor, will be cooler than the cellar floor. Whenever the absolute humidity exceeds the dew-point at the bottom of the dry-well, water vapor will condense to liquid water there, and will seep into the ground.

When conditions are favorable, water vapor leaves wine cellars through the ceiling, the internal walls, and the dry-well. When conditions are not so favorable, as during an extended period of high absolute humidity upstairs, the flow through the ceiling and internal walls can reverse, leaving the dry-well to save the labels.

The dry-well depth required to obtain satisfactory humidity control depends upon the steepness of the soil's vertical temperature gradient, which is a function of the extremity of the climate. The more extreme the seasons, the steeper the temperature gradient will be. Dry-wells are most effective at inland sites where the seasons are severe and there is a steep temperature gradient. Sites tempered by large bodies of water, such as San Francisco, have a much smaller vertical temperature gradient. A dry-well would have questionable utility in San Francisco.

A guestimate of what to expect at your location can be derived from the temperature and humidity gradients within your wine cellar or wine cellar site. For example, suppose that during the spring the ceiling of your 6-foot (180 cm) high wine cellar has a 10% lower relative humidity and is some 2°C (4°F) warmer than the floor. By extrapolation, a 3-foot (90 cm) deep dry-well would go to work whenever the wine cellar floor was above 95% relative humidity. As a rule of thumb, excavate to a depth equal to the height to which mold extends above the cellar floor.

The preceding design considerations are only estimates. The practical approach is to dig until you get the degree of humidity reduction that you require. Take temperature and humidity readings at the floor before you begin. Dig until the soil at the bottom of your hole is measurably colder than the cellar floor. Wait overnight and see how much you've lowered the humidity. Doubling the depth should roughly double the effect. To verify that you've not been deceived by coincident changes in the weather, seal the dry-well overnight and see if the floor level humidity rises. Don't go to the trouble of digging a dry well when a simple polyethylene vapor barrier on the inner surface of external walls would adequately control humidity. If you've got a really wet situation, however, a dry-well could be your solution. All this assumes that your dry-well does not reach the water table. Also, the water table is not constant. Heavy rain can raise it and drought can lower it.

How wide should a dry-well be? An adequately wide dry-well is of course one which excess water vapor migrates as rapidly as it accumulates at the cellar floor. The rate of water vapor accumulation at the cellar floor depends on the local climate, vapor barriers, and cellar size. The rate of water vapor migration from the floor into the dry-well will depend on the diameter of the dry well (wider is faster), and the absolute humidity differential. An absolute humidity differential between the cellar floor and the bottom of a dry well will only occur when the dew-point at the bottom of the dry-well is exceeded. It follows that the humidity lowering action of a dry-well only occurs when the humidity is very high. The one working wine-cellar dry-well that I have visited was quite effective, I was told, despite being only about 2 feet (60 cm) in diameter and in a very large 12-by-14-foot, poorly vapor-barriered wine cellar. However, I didn't have the opportunity to personally evaluate the effectiveness by covering it for a day.

In rocky soil, dry-well walls may need no support, but in softer soils, especially near the foundation, or when great depth is desired, retaining walls are required. For cylindrical retaining walls you can obtain well tiles from a building supply company. Well tiles are concrete rings that you stack in place. Don't seal the bottom of your dry well with concrete, because the water that collects there has to be allowed to drain into the soil. If heavy spring rains raise the water table beneath your cellar, the flow could reverse, your dry-well becoming a "wet" well. That's no problem if the water stays below floor level, but if your basement is subject to seasonal flooding you will need a sump pump. The bottom of your formerly dry dry-well is a ready-made site for that sump pump. Conversely, any hole that you dig for a sump pump automatically becomes a dry-well, so locate it within your wine cellar, and make it deep.

Dry-wells are frequently placed underground out-of-doors in order to provide rapid drainage of rainwater from storm gutters into the soil. When placed underground they are filled with rocks to keep the overlying soil from collapsing into the well. When placing a dry-well in a wine cellar, your contractor may reflexively begin filling it with rocks. Stop him. Rocks would slow the migration of water vapor.

The top of a dry-well must be left open to permit the migration of water vapor. To protect inebriated dessert-wine searchers from stepping into it, use a grating or stack an additional tile above the level of the floor. Since the action of a dry-well depends upon its bottom being colder than the cellar, it becomes inoperative during the winter. Fortunately, high cellar humidity is not a problem when the outdoor air is colder than the wine cellar.

Having a thick concrete cellar floor and controlled humidity, I personally have not been able to field test the dry-well notion. I'm eager to hear from anyone who has.

Low Humidity and Ullage

Despite your success at overcoming excessive spring and summer humidity, your attentiveness to matters of moisture must not go into winter hibernation. Beware! Your cellar's relative humidity may sneak down past 60%. Under such low humidity intra-bottle moisture will evaporate away via the corks. The lost wine will be replaced by oxygen-rich air, which in sufficient excess will destroy your wine.

If the 75% relative humidity threshold is breached, turn on your unpatentable towel-and-basin wine cellar humidifier (Figure 8-4). This inelegant apparatus consists of a water-filled plastic wash basin perched on high with a towel wick draped over the side. Humidification is adjusted by raising or lowering the towel overhang. The lower the towel, the more the humidification.

Water will evaporate off the towel, and some water will drip onto the floor from whence it evaporates. If additional evaporative surface is needed, try a stack of cement blocks, perhaps perching the basin atop the blocks. Within four days, a towel-and-basin humidifier increased my cellar's humidity from 60 to 75%. One basin of water lasted several weeks. When you evaporate water in order to raise humidity, you also reap the secondary benefit of evaporative cooling.

For as little as $100 you can get an ultrasonic electric humidifier. They come with built in humidistats and can efficiently raise and maintain humidity. They will not warm your cellar like a steam vaporizer would, because the water is not heated. Ultrasonic humidifiers shake up an ultra-fine mist. At the cavernous Opus One winery cellar in California they have installed the equivalent of an ultrasonic humidifier. They call it a misting system and regulate the humidity at 87%. The down side of ultrasonic humidification in a home cellar is that if the humidistat sticks in the "on" mode when you're away for a few days extensive label damage can result. Just because it's less efficient, the towel-and-basin approach is safer. Whatever you do about humidity, it will change gradually, so wait a couple of days after each treatment.

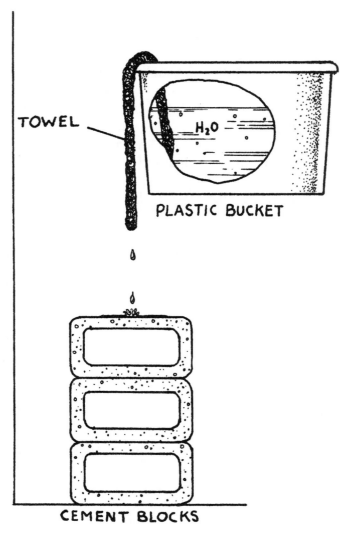

Figure 8-4. An unpatentable towel-and-basin passive humidifier.

Chapter 9 * REFRIGERATION

Climatic cooperation has always been needed in order to produce great wines. Before the age of refrigeration wine makers were at the mercy of the weather even after the harvest was completed. Potentially great vintages could be spoiled when promising fermentations overheated during unseasonably hot autumn weather. Modern refrigeration at the winery now permits the realization of the grapes' full potential.

The same is true for bottled wine. Before refrigeration, bottled wine not stored in deep, cool, humid cellars deteriorated rapidly. The other chapters of this book focus on the construction of traditional passive (no refrigeration) wine cellars with the assistance of modern materials. I recommend this approach to all who are blessed with appropriate climates and basements. Passive wine cellars can succeed as far south as Washington, D.C. or San Francisco.

If your climate is too warm, or you have no basement, refrigeration is the way to go. Refrigeration equipment is durable, electrical supplies are generally reliable, and the thermal mass of your wine will protect against brief outages. Nevertheless, lengthy power outages or mechanical failures as trivial as a tripped circuit breaker while you're touring in Burgundy, are still possible.

There are six routes by which private oenophiles can achieve refrigerated wine storage. The options are:

(a) Rented storage space,
(b) Window type air conditioners,
(c) Ducting from central air conditioning,
(d) Specialized refrigeration equipment in your cellar or spare room,
(e) Self-contained, pre-built refrigerated chambers, and
(f) Old refrigerators.

(a) Rental Storage

Refrigerated or underground rentable wine lockers are common in England. Though still sparse in the United States, they can be found in major metropolitan areas including New York City, Chicago, and Los Angeles. Your wine merchant should be able to direct you.

A storage facility should be inspected, preferably in August, before being rented. I'd discretely leave a minimum-maximum thermometer (which holds an indication of the highest and lowest temperatures reached) in my locker. Rental lockers may not have controlled humidity, which means that the humidity may be lower than ideal.

A typical charge is $1 (US) per case, per month, which works out to $1 per bottle per year, assuming a full locker. Insurance against theft and climate control failure may be extra, if available. By the time the wine is ready to drink, the accumulated storage charge can exceed the original cost of the wine. The cost of rental storage space compares unfavorably with the one-time 5 to $10 per bottle purchase price of a self-contained, refrigerated home locker (option (e)), or the $1 or less per bottle materials-cost for a passive or air conditioned home cellar. To be fair, if you live in a high rent inner city apartment you should factor in the rent that you are giving your landlord for the storage space.

At some lockers there's a fixed monthly charge for a private chamber. You get a key and have unlimited access during business hours, just as with a bank vault. At others your labeled cases are stored in a common facility. The proprietor fetches a specified case, sometimes for a handling fee, upon 24-hours notice. The latter arrangement doesn't lend itself to the withdrawal of a single bottle for an evening's pleasure. The greatest inconvenience is the trip to the storage facility.

Rental storage is your savior when your wine needs temporary protection while you're between houses. For the longer haul, however, even the priciest self-contained refrigerated home locker is more economical and more convenient. Private arrangements, should you have a friend with a good cellar, and consortium cellars are attractive notions that often lead to strained relationships when the cellar master suddenly needs the storage space or you come to fetch a bottle without sufficient notice or at an indelicate moment.

The store from which you buy your wine may provide free storage of your purchases for a few months, especially if you shop by telephone and are tardy in retrieving your wine. Some shops, however, have less-than-ideal storage conditions. They also may not be able to guarantee you're paid for wine against the unlikely occurrence of fire or theft. If the shop should be sold or enter bankruptcy while storing your wine, both also unlikely, you might have to join a line of creditors.

(b) Window-Type Air Conditioners

The cost of electricity to cool a well-insulated, independently air-conditioned wine storage space should be around $100 per year; and the initial investment in a small window-type air conditioner is modest when compared with specialized refrigeration equipment. If a suitable opening to the outside, such as a basement window, is available, then definitely install your air conditioner so as to export the heat outside.

Lacking an appropriate aperture, it's easy to install an air conditioner in the interior wall between wine cellar and basement. In the first case your air conditioner will occasionally strain against an outdoor heat wave, but in the latter case the basement surrounding your wine cellar will be heated through the summer, making its task progressively more difficult. If the equipment or power fails, it's best to have a cool basement alongside your wine cellar.

In most window-type air conditioners the fan stays on regardless of the temperature. The thermostat only cycles the compressor on and off as needed. When people occupy a window-type air conditioned room they turn the thing on and off as needed. This is not as likely in a wine cellar where the unheard fan may run on for weeks when not needed, or the air conditioner may be left off by oversight when cooling is required. Some window air conditioners offer the option of having the fan and compressor cycle on and off together. It's called an "energy saver" switch. Look for it. If not available, then consider getting a separate air conditioning thermostat that can turn the entire air conditioner, including the fan, on and off in response to the temperature.

When air conditioners designed to cool for human comfort-levels are asked to operate at wine-comfort temperatures in humid locations, the condensate freezes onto the coils instead of dripping off as water. This ice build up interferes with, and finally completely blocks, air flow through the air conditioner, leaving the room hot and the compressor and fan straining.

There are two satisfactory fixes for this problem. The first uses a timer that requires the air conditioner to rest 5 minutes out of every 10, or 15 out of every 30. The air conditioner plugs into the timer. Ice that forms during the on minutes melts and runs off during the down time.

The alternate fix uses the blast of cooled air from the air conditioner to turn itself off, providing down time for ice build-up to melt and run off. Bypass the air conditioner's built-in thermostat, which monitors the temperature of the warm air coming into the air conditioner, by turning it to the coldest or constant-on setting. Control the air conditioner's electrical supply with a second, separately mounted air conditioning thermostat. Direct a stream of cold air from the air conditioner directly at the auxiliary thermostat. When the cellar warms, the air conditioner will operate, but only for a few minutes at a time. As a stream of cold air is generated it will chill the thermostat, and the air conditioner and fan will shut down until the thermostat warms up again. If the on-cycles are too long no matter where you mount the thermostat, you may have to break some air-diffuser vanes to generate a more concentrated cold air stream. If the cycling is too rapid, protect the thermostat with an air deflector.

Conventional air conditioners dehumidify as water vapor condenses on the cooling coils. The 50% humidity that results is nice for people, but not for wine. You can automatically recycle the condensate by placing a drip pan beneath the exterior coils and channeling the condensate water to a towel and basin humidifier inside the wine cellar. A less elegant but simpler option is to transfer the drip-bucket water to the towel-humidifier by hand every few days.

Sizing Your Compressor

Air conditioners are rated in BTUs per hour. BTU stands for British Thermal Unit and is a measure of heat. One BTU is the amount of heat required to raise the temperature of one pound of water one degree F. The metric equivalent, a calorie, raises one gram of water one degree C. One BTU equals 252 calories.

Your air conditioner's compressor must be large enough to remove BTUs as rapidly as they enter your cellar during the hottest day of the year. Given the dimensions of your cellar, its insulation (R-factor), the desired cellar temperature, and the temperatures it faces, you can compute the BTU rating needed.

First, convert the total R-factor of each surface (ceiling, interior walls, exterior walls, and floor) to the conductance, which is the reciprocal of the R-factor. For example, a 2-inch thick layer of extruded polystyrene has an R-factor of 10 (5 per inch) and a conductance of 1/10 or 0.1. If the upstairs air were 1°F warmer than the cellar, and the ceiling had a conductance of 1, then, by definition, each square foot of ceiling would admit 1 BTU per hour.

For a realistic example, take an upstairs wine storage room that you want at 55°F with living spaces above and on two sides that never exceed 80°F, exterior walls on the remaining two sides, and R-10 in the ceiling and interior walls and R-20 in the exterior walls. A ceiling that measures 5-by-12 feet (60 ft^2) would admit (80–55) x 0.1 x 60 = 150 BTUs per hour. Add to this 7-by-17 feet of interior wall for

$(80 - 55)$ x 0.1 x 119 = 297 BTUs per hour. Add also 7-by-17 feet of exterior R-20 wall that faces at most 105°F for $(105 - 55)$ x 0.05 x 119 = 297 BTUs per hour. Finally, add in a 5-by-12-foot R-10 floor that faces, at most, a 70°F crawl space for $(70 - 55)$ x 0.1 x 60 = 90 BTUs per hour. Totaling the four BTU values gives a conductance load of 834 BTUs per hour.

To this conductance load you must add something for air diffusion. A tight wine cellar might diffuse one total air change every two hours. A 5-x-12-x-7-foot cellar contains 420 ft^3 of air less 20 ft^3 for the volume of the contents. 400 ft^3/2 hours = 200 ft^3/hour. Diffusion brings 70°F basement air into the cellar. The heat capacity of air is 0.018 BTU per ft^3 per degree F. 200 x $(70 - 55)$ x 0.018 = 54 BTUs per hour. Nothing need be added for the heat generated by occupants or lights, as you won't be in the cellar often or long enough for these to be important. Your total cooling load is 834 + 54 = 888 BTUs per hour. When sizing for a basement wine cellar you have to estimate R-factors for the floor and the below grade walls, but the result will be in the ball park of the example. Air conditioners designed to produce 70°F bedrooms will be less efficient than their advertised ratings at 55°F, especially if you cycle them on and off to prevent icing. The smallest standard window type air conditioners are rated at 4,000 to 5,000 BTUs per hour, which, if my example is representative, should be more than adequate for insulated wine storage spaces.

(c) Borrowing from Central Air

Warm climate readers who can afford serious wine can afford, and usually have, centrally air conditioned homes. In that situation, a thermostatically regulated damper on a central air duct to the wine cellar seems an attractive concept. The damper is opened by an air-conditioning thermostat in the wine cellar. The thermostat is also wired to turn on the compressor when only the wine calls for cooling, typically in the fall. This is called "zoned cooling." If you borrow from central air without benefit of thermostatic regulation you'll get unacceptable temperature oscillations.

Ducts come in two types: un-insulated rigid sheet metal and insulated flexible plastic. The flexible is much easier to install, though short segments of sheet metal ducting are needed for dampers and connections. In most cases a four or five-inch diameter duct is adequate. To avoid cold spots, distribute the cooled air via a perforated pipe, diffuser, or holey section of duct. To get the air to move you must provide a return or exhaust duct of equal diameter, and herein lies the problem.

If members of your family are subject to mold allergies, then recycling air from the wine cellar back to the central air and hence to the entire house is not recommended, even with the fanciest filter. The only alternative is to direct the return to the outdoors with one or more flap closures on the line. The flap closures designed for stove hoods or clothes dryer exhausts should work nicely, as would a second electronically controlled damper. The cost of air conditioning will go up a bit, but some air exchange is always desirable anyway. Replacement air will be drawn in from the outdoors via the routes by which air feeds the furnace flame during the heating season.

The greatest danger when zoning from central air comes on the switch-over to the heating season. If you forget to disconnect the wine cellar duct, furnace heat will cook your wine. The electronic damper in the wine cellar line must therefore be wired so that it can only open when the air conditioning circuit is on. Dampers don't completely block air flow, so seal the line each winter.

If the preceding two paragraphs have not dissuaded you, then the final task of this section is to size the wine cellar duct. Calculate the cellar's BTU per hour requirements as described above in section (b). The duct size that will deliver that many BTUs per hour is determined using the temperature of the air delivered by your air conditioner (which you measure with a thermometer inserted via a small hole), the rate of air flow per cross-sectional inch of duct, and the heat capacity of air, which is 0.018 BTU per foot^3 per degree F.

To get back to our section (b) example, you need 888 BTU per hour. Suppose that your central air delivers air at 45°F, and you want a 55°F cellar. The temperature differential is 55 − 45 = 10°F. Cut a one square inch hole at the point where your wine cellar duct will come off the main duct. With a stopwatch and large plastic bag determine the rate of air flow. Let's suppose that a 1- cubic-foot bag fills in 15 seconds. This equals 240 feet^3 per hour. 240 x 0.018 x 10 = 43.2 BTU per hour per inch^2. To deliver 888 BTU per hour requires a duct with a cross section of 888/43.2 or approximately 21 inches^2. Ducts are sized by diameter. To get cross sectional area from diameter, the formula is radius (diameter/2) squared times pi (22/7). A conversion table follows.

Duct diameter in inches	Cross section in square inches
2	3
3	7
4	13
5	20
6	28
7	38
8	50

The exampled wine cellar therefore needs a 5 or 6-inch diameter duct.

(d) Specialized Refrigeration Equipment

For under $1,000 US you can purchase a designed-for-wine-cellaring refrigeration-humidification unit for your self-built cellar. Some of these have the usual drip pan astride the hot compressor with the special added feature of venting the heat-evaporated condensate back into the cooled space. They are, of course, engineered so that they don't ice up at low operating temperatures.

Several wine accessory catalogs feature these units. Use the instructions in section (b) to determine the correct size. Some have the very-desirable split-system design common to whole-home air conditioners with the compressor and heat dissipation coils outdoors.

There is also commercial refrigeration equipment that cools your grocer's meat locker and milk cooler. The hot compressor and heat-dissipation coils go out of doors as in a whole-house central air conditioning system so your basement doesn't heat up. Special consideration is required to achieve the relatively high humidity that wine requires. I've heard from several readers who have been delighted with the results using this, albeit more expensive, approach.

(e) Self-contained Refrigerated Vaults and Refrigerators

With this option you go to your local Home Depot or equivalent, purchase the largest wine fridge that will fit into your minivan, drive home and stock up. For larger wine fridges from wine specialty catalogs, wait for the delivery van, plug in, and stock up. Some models require screwdriver assembly of prefab panels, a good idea if you'd have trouble getting a pre-assembled unit through doorways. If, due to a busy schedule or lack of carpentry acumen, your alternative would be to hire a custom contractor, then this option could be less expensive than a passive cellar. If you're likely to be moving from time to time, they're a lot more portable than a basement wine cellar. They still take up a lot of space.

For the convenience you'll pay $5 to $20 per stored bottle, plus electricity. The smaller units, which hold as few as 40 bottles, cost the most per bottle space. If you're serious enough about wine to be reading this book and to buy refrigerated storage, then you're likely to keep buying wine, more than you may currently realize, so get the largest unit that you have space for, or be prepared to buy several of the smaller ones. Individual bottle racking costs more and uses space less efficiently but is more convenient than grouped stacking on two or three shelves. Double depth, some requiring nesting-necks, is common in the larger sizes, and adds inconvenience vis-a-vis the behind bottles. Furniture-quality exteriors are dearer than plain paneling, but if they blend into the decor they may make the endeavor more palatable to spouses. Discounts and disparaging comments about the competition are often available, as the purveyors of these big-ticket items are in lively competition.

If you buy by the case, then each vertical column of ten bottles (five high by two deep) can contain the same wine so you won't have to dig for a buried bottle. A mix of half-case and individual-bottle purchases is more typical. Put the half-case lots in the rear in one-bottle vertical columns, the single bottles in the front, with those most ready to drink on top. To keep track of your shifting inventory draw a map in erasable pencil.

Three-temperature versions are available at extra cost and contain colder and warmer compartments that are supposed to adjust white and red wines to their respective serving temperatures. These are primarily for restaurants. The special chambers use space that you will need for long-term storage. Also pass up the glass door feature as the glass is not a good insulator. A key lock would be a more useful option. Beware firms that advertise a lowball price, take payment, and fail to deliver. Pay by credit card. This ensures a refund if the unit never arrives.

The mechanical components should be at least as reliable as your home refrigerator's, as they work on the same principle, but without the complexity of a freezing section, and will suffer far fewer door openings. Most refrigerator service people should be able to fix one. Unless noted in the catalog, these units have no heaters, so don't locate one on an unheated porch or in a detached unheated garage.

The compressors also have their high temperature limits, so no un-insulated attics please. A 1,200 bottle pre-fab cellar might fit into a large, unneeded bedroom, but check with an architect first about the weight-bearing capacity of any above-cellar location for the larger sizes.

Proper regulation of humidity should not be presumed. The literature on some models claims that by re-evaporating condensate, humidity is kept at 70%. However, if the air around the chamber is too dry, as it might be in Arizona or in mid-winter, there may not be enough condensate to re-evaporate. For example, air with a moisture content of 33% relative humidity in a 68°F (20°C) room translates to only 50% humidity inside a 55°F (13°C) chamber. If you humidify your home to at least 50% relative humidity in winter, there's probably no danger.

The humidity inside any wine storage chamber should be monitored. Those who have checked on my behalf have been surprised by low, mid-winter readings. It's easy to add moisture. The lowest or highest level of two-deep storage chambers is usually only one deep because the compressor is in the back. Turn those bottles neck out and put wet sponges between the necks. Trial and error with a hygrometer will indicate how many sponges to use and how frequently to wet them.

If you can, inspect an operating unit, noting the noise level in a quiet room when the compressor kicks on. Check the general construction, thickness and type of insulation, soundness of the shelving, and the door fit. A tight door should not allow a piece of caught paper to slide out easily. If the distributor has already placed one in your part of the world, he should be able to direct you to asatisfied local customer who you can call and visit. For the small units from Home Depot and the like I recommend plugging it in at the store and browsing for an hour. I didn't and can't get the thermostat to go above 50 F.

(f) An Old Refrigerator

An orphaned refrigerator that still has good door seals might serve as a poor man's wine vault. Even at its lowest setting, it may be too cold for wine storage, but you can take care of that. Use rigid insulation to divide the box into two compartments; one containing the thermostat and ice chamber, the other containing the wine. The insulation will keep the wine chamber warmer than a refrigerator usually gets. Adjust the size of holes in the insulation to get the desired effect. For better regulation, mount an air conditioning thermostat inside the refrigerator and wire it to turn the refrigerator on and off. To augment humidity, add wet sponges as needed. In a basement that gets down to 55°F in the dead of winter, defrost a nonfrost-free refrigerator annually by shutting it off and opening the door. The biggest drawback of refrigerator storage is the meager capacity.

The refrigerator route makes no monetary sense compared to the alternatives if you have to buy a new refrigerator for it. Can a refrigerator that has been retired as not up to the job of cooling milk ever be trusted with the task of guarding Mouton? I've never tried to use a refrigerator, retired or otherwise, for wine, and have yet to communicate with anyone who has. If you've taken this trip please let me know how you set it up and how it went.

Chapter 10 * COOLING WITH EVAPORATION, WATER, AND AIR

Evaporative Cooling

If you've ever paid a summer visit to an old, aboveground winery where they age in small wooden casks, then you've experienced evaporative cooling in action. Despite intense summer heat outside and lack of insulation in the winery's wooden walls, the closely spaced casks are moist and cool without benefit of mechanical cooling. Moisture from the wine seeps out via pores in the wood and evaporates into the winery air, eventually escaping through the winery walls. These evaporative losses of up to 20% concentrate the wine as they cool the winery. The taste of oak is added as well. The smaller the cooperage, the greater the surface of cask to volume of contents ratio, and therefore the greater these effects. Topping up with wine keeps the barrels full.

A wine-filled winery has considerable thermal mass, which tames daily temperature oscillations. This amount of thermal mass cannot, however, account for the winery's cool condition through the summer. When porous wooden casks are replaced with stainless steel, the thermal mass is not changed, yet the wine maker discovers that his old winery has acquired an appetite for insulation and mechanical cooling. You don't have to evaporate wine to achieve evaporative cooling in your home cellar: water does the job quite nicely. The evaporation of water absorbs prodigious quantities of heat. Comparisons between the heat absorbed by evaporation and that absorbed without the phase-change illustrate this point.

Evaporation absorbs sixty times as much heat as is absorbed bringing the same amount of water (or wine) through the upward run of an 18°F (10°C) annual passive wine cellar oscillation. Put another way, the evaporation of one drop of water every three seconds absorbs as much heat every day as is absorbed when 1,200 bottles of wine gain 18°F (10°C), a process typically spread over half a year. Conversely, condensation from water vapor (as happens when using a dehumidifier or a dry-well) releases all of the previously absorbed heat. It is therefore essential that the water vapor generated during evaporative cooling leave the wine cellar to permit continued evaporation, and do so without condensing back to liquid water.

The basic requirements for evaporative cooling are:

(1) A continuous, slow release of water onto
(2) a large evaporative surface.
(3) Insulation to retard the entry of heat, but
(4) no vapor barrier, and
(5) dissipation of the water vapor to the outdoors.

The most economical approach for a water supply would be to set up several towel-and-basin humidifiers. A more precise approach involves a plumbed, slow-drip water supply. A drip regulator designed for desert irrigation should serve admirably. You can obtain one at a garden supply store or catalog. A third tack is to use a humidistat-regulated ultrasonic humidifier which will throw a fine mist of water into the air whenever the humidity is low enough to receive it.

Every form of building material has some resistance to the passage of water vapor, but there are enormous differences. For insulation with high water-vapor permeability, you can do no better than unfaced fiberglass batts. Foam boards of all types should be avoided because they block water vapor – as does polyethylene, and – to a lesser extent - paint, varnish, and plywood or paneling. Wood is moderately permeable to moisture. For a sheathing surface that is highly water vapor permeable but resists air infiltration the desert cellar master is blessed with several modern types of building wrap. The original was TYVEX, now out in an improved version. The major competitor is called TYPAR HouseWrap. They come in a roll that you attach with staples or large headed "roofing" nails. TYVEX blocks more air infiltration, TYPAR is more tear resistant. TYVEX has a coating on the printed side that resists ultraviolet radiation and sheds rain drops, but will nevertheless be degraded within a few months if left exposed to sunlight. TYPAR is not degraded by sunlight.

House-wraps are normally used on the outside of houses, just beneath the exterior sheathing of wood or perforated vinyl siding. For wine cellar cooling, however, you could use TYPAR and nothing else on both sides of the unfaced-fiberglass-filled wall through which you want moisture to pass. Only after the cooling effect is clearly demonstrated would I experiment with external sheathing such as wooden shingles or wooden siding or vinyl siding. To keep the moisture going, air must be allowed to circulate freely between the pieces of siding, the gaps being kept open with spacers. Vinyl siding comes with pre-formed holes for breathing. Augment those holes liberally with a drill. On interior walls I see no structural reason for covering the TYPAR or TYVEX. However, if too much moisture gets out - if your temperature goals are met but the humidity gets too low despite your humidification – then unpainted, 3/8-inch (the thinnest standard size) drywall on the interior surface should slow the rate of moisture penetration and protect your house wrap. Paint would further slow moisture penetration, water based paints less than oils.

Evaporative cooling should work admirably in a continuously dry desert climate where water vapor will readily exit to the environment. Adding moisture to keep the cellar humidity at 80% will help in any climate. Residing in cool, moist New England, I've no personal experience with evaporative wine cellar cooling in a desert setting. I'll be watching my email for reports from desert-dwelling readers.

Cooling with Well Water

If you have your own deep well, then the water comes into your home at deep soil temperature. In case you've fantasized using this water to cool your wine cellar, here are my musings on the matter.

If you were to run your home's incoming water pipe through the wine cellar air, even in a baseboard hot-water radiator, it would not pick up much heat, as the air surrounding the pipe or radiator is too good an insulator. When filled with hot water, baseboard radiators heat houses, but the radiator is over 100°F (55°C) hotter than the room it has to heat. Your cooling water, in contrast, would only be about 9°F (5°C) cooler than the cellar.

If you use well water to cool the soil beneath your wine cellar you could get more efficient pipe-to-soil heat transfer. The thermal mass of the soil will also smooth out temperature fluctuations. To accomplish this heat transfer you would route your water supply through pipes or a tank in intimate thermal contact with the floor of the wine cellar. In new construction you could run loops of copper pipe around the perimeter of the wine cellar prior to pouring the concrete floor. The pipe would become encased in the new floor. Connect to the water inlet with two tees, retaining a bypass line with a shut-off lever, and install shut-off levers at both ends of the wine cellar loop so that, in case of a leak, you can isolate the loop. To avoid burying relatively vulnerable solder joints in concrete, use a continuous coil of copper tubing. For a dirt floored wine cellar, burying a coil in the floor should work nearly as well, but to protect the copper pipe, screen rocks out of the dirt that you use to back fill.

While household water is running, the amount of heat absorbed will be determined by the surface contact area, which suggests a long run of thin pipe. On the other hand, when the water stops running, the cold water contained within the wine cellar loop will have plenty of time to absorb heat. Since household water-use is generally a sporadic affair, with long gaps between hand washings, showers, and toilet flushings, perhaps the amount of water in the wine cellar at one time is more important than the contact area. This means large diameter pipes. The logical extension of large pipes is to run your household water through an un-insulated 30 gallon water tank standing upright in a corner of the wine cellar or lying on its side half-buried in the floor. The least expensive way to obtain an un-insulated water tank may be to remove the insulation from a standard hot water tank. Condensation leading to rust on the cool, exposed steel can be avoided with a coat or two of black paint suitable for metal. Don't use silver, which is heat reflecting.

I've never tried water cooling, being served by a town water supply, but I know of one major winery that has. Opus One in Napa, California circulates 45°F water through miles of pipes in the floor and ceiling of their shallow cellar that keep the winery at a constant 55°F. (They were unable to have a deep cellar due to a high water table.) If your deep soil temperature is cool enough to provide the cool water you would need, then your climate is surely cold enough for a standard passive cellar. However, if your water table is too high for a deep cellar, then Opus One's approach is worth considering.

Cooling with Air

Another free source of cooling which some misguided oenophiles have actually attempted to harness is cool night air blown through the wine cellar with a fan. For this approach you need two flap-valved ducts, an intake and an outgo. A standard bathroom exhaust fan is adequate. A heating thermostat (turned on by cold) is mounted out doors, and an air conditioning thermostat (turned on by heat) is mounted inside the wine cellar. The two thermostats are wired in series so that both conditions – outside cool and inside warm - must be met to turn the fan on. The system will cool, with an undesirable daily temperature rise, and unpredictable humidity, until the inevitable series of hot nights. Air cooling is NOT RECOMMENDED. It's been described only to dissuade you from trying it should the concept appear spontaneously in a dream.

Section 3

\|\|*\|*\|*\|*\|*\|*\|*\|*\|*\|*\|*\|*

WINE CELLAR CONSTRUCTION

Chapter 11

\|\|*\|*\|*\|*\|*\|*\|*\|*\|*\|*\|*\|*

CAPACITY AND DIMENSIONS

To derive dimensions prior to cellar construction, the consummate oenophile must estimate the greatest number of bottles that she will ever want to store at one time. To obtain this figure she projects her future wine consumption, and the anticipated average cellaring time. Part of the appeal of a home wine cellar is the availability of an appropriate mature wine for both anticipated and unanticipated occasions. No one expects you to make your daily wine selections ten years in advance. But you can predict your averaged behavior.

Let us suppose a love of classic red Cabernet Sauvignon-and Merlot-based Bordeaux and their California counterparts which, for the years that matter - the vin de garde years – are best after an average of 15 years of cellaring. Suppose further that you anticipate the consumption of two and a-half bottles per week. Two and a-half bottles times 52 weeks per year times 15 years brings you to 1,950 bottles or 162 cases in simultaneous storage.

Before we proceed to actual dimensions ...

WARNING: Please fix into permanent memory the concept that you are generating a prediction that you must never consider yourself under any obligation to fulfill. An occasional enophile, after investing his psyche in cellar construction, goes on a buying rampage. He behaves as though he considers empty cellar space to be an abhorrent vacuum in desperate need of immediate obliteration. There will be great vintages in your future. Save cellar space for them.

A case of wine occupies one ft^2 (0.1 M^2) of wall space, so your 162 cases need 162 ft^2 (16.2 M^2) of wall. Dividing by 5 feet (1.5 M) of usable storage height, the area nearest the floor being susceptible to high humidity and mold, yields 32.4 linear feet (9.7 M) of storage wall.

The most efficient way to arrange bins is to have a long narrow cellar with storage on both sides. Each storage rack will be one foot (.3 M) deep, that being the length of a bottle on its side. Storage racks arranged along both walls plus a 3-foot (1 M) wide aisle yields an interior width of 5 feet (1.5 M). Two-foot wide (0.6 M) aisles are possible, but make it difficult to maneuver. If you'll be storing wooden Bordeaux crates along one of the long walls, then allow for their 20" (.5 M) length, which brings you up to a 5' 8" (1.7 M) cellar width.

One of the short-end walls will be usurped by the door. The opposite short wall could be used for 3' of storage across the width of the aisle, but that would block 2' of long-wall storage (the end 1' on each side). I suggest instead that you place your bins only on the two long walls. Save the middle of the back wall for newly arrived stacked cases and boxes that can be moved if you need to access the furthest long-wall bins. Dividing the 32.4 (9.7 M) linear feet that you need by two walls gives you a 16.2 ft (4.8 M) long wine cellar. If basement space is not at a premium, err on the side of a larger cellar, as extra space is easier to deal with than extra wine. Besides, a larger size should be a bit cooler by diluting the impact of lateral heat transfer into the soil beneath the wine cellar.

If the available space suggests a wider design, consider double-depth bins that are 2-feet (.6 M) deep. With that arrangement, access to the rear bottles is a bother, but you can usually use the rear slots for duplicates of the forward bottles.

For a more detailed prediction of your future vinous requirements, see Chapter 19, "Planning Ahead," which goes into much greater depth concerning the anticipation of future consumption.

Chapter 12 * CRAWL SPACE EXCAVATION & NEW CONSTRUCTION

Houses lacking basements sit over crawl spaces or on concrete slabs. If you have a crawl space, then you may be able to excavate a passive wine cellar. If your home is on a concrete slab, forget it–your only routes to passive wine cellaring are a cellared addition or moving to a different house.

(a) Crawl space Wine Cellaring

A crawl space, for the uninitiated, is a two to 4-foot high (.6 to 1.2 M) dirt-floored space beneath a house. Because of the restricted headroom, crawl spaces can only be navigated on all fours. The dirt floor of a crawlspace is usually level with the surrounding terrain.

If your house is built over a crawlspace, you may be tempted to store wine there. Unfortunately, in most climates crawl spaces, lacking access to the more stable deep soil temperature, have an excessive annual temperature oscillation. They are also terribly inconvenient. A typical crawlspace is entered through a trap door in a closet floor or a tiny outside ground-level window. After a while even the most devoted connoisseur begins to resent wrestling with hanging coats, banging his head, and doing the three-point crawl (one hand being committed to the wine). It gets especially bad when, with a dining room full of distinguished guests and a belly full of dinner and wine, you impulsively decide to fetch the Graham's. Consider also the embarrassment when visitors request a wine cellar tour. Crawlspace wine storage is at best a stop-gap solution. Do not despair. If the water table is suitably low year-round (and lack of a basement suggests otherwise), you can excavate.

For access more convenient than your closet floor, the very first step is to cut a generous trap door in the floor of the room above your prospective wine cellar. If the floor joists are the typical 16 inches

(40 cm) on center, you will have to remove a portion of one floor joist, thus making room for a 30" (75 cm) wide trap door. To compensate for the missing section of joist you double, if possible, the entire lengths of the adjacent joists and cross brace against the cut end of the joist from which you have removed the section. An alternative to joist doubling is to support the cut joist ends with metal cellar posts set onto concrete footings or onto buried solid cement blocks.

An insulated trap door is a smaller version of the door described in Chapter 14. To match existing wooden floor boards, preserve in labeled sequence and reuse the original floor boards. If you recess the trap door handle there will be no tell-tale bump in the floor. For additional security you could install a recessed key lock, but the best security is obtained through tight lips combined with a throw rug that hides the trap door. Avoid locating your trap door in the center of the dining room. Such placement inevitably leads to, "Pardon me. I need to move the dining room table and roll up the rug to fetch another '70 Giscours."

A fixed wooden or aluminum ladder provides adequate access. Use hooks or screws rather than nails to anchor the ladder – you may have to remove the ladder intermittently during construction. Flat ladder-rungs are more comfortable than the round variety.

Since footings usually extend 4 feet (1.2 M) below grade, and crawl space ceilings rise at least 2 feet (.6 M) above grade, you should be able to dig a 6 foot (1.8 M) high wine cellar without undermining the foundation. Occasionally a deeper excavation is needed. Undermining of the foundation could have disastrous consequences, so if you must go deeper, a retaining wall is required to stabilize the soil beneath the original foundation footings. Though a daunting task, only the modest length of foundation flanking your wine cellar is affected. Set up form boards and use bags of ready-mix concrete for your retaining wall. Hire or at least consult with a concrete contractor before messing with your footings.

Figure 12-1. "Pardon me. I need to move the dining room table and roll up the rug to fetch another '70 Giscours."

In soft soil a pointed short-handled shovel and work gloves are your primary tools. If possible, rent a conveyor belt to whisk the dirt out of your crawlspace. This avoids the need for a bucket brigade. Crawlspaces normally come with venting in the form of a small window. This opening could serve admirably for conveyor belt soil removal. With a windowless cement block foundation it is relatively easy to remove a few blocks with a sledge hammer. These can be replaced later with a basement window or new blocks. With a poured concrete foundation, hole punching is out of the question, but you might be able to angle a conveyor belt up and out through your strategically placed new trap door.

A bucket brigade via your trap door is the last resort. You need a few sturdy pails, a rope with hook, and a pulley hoist. A counter weight is a helpful feature. An assistant upstairs to dump the pails into a waiting wheelbarrow will save you several million trips up the ladder.

If your soil is hard or rocky, then hand digging may be impossible. Having no head room to swing a pick ax, you would be reduced to a hammer-and-chisel operation. Rent instead an electric (no fumes) jack hammer for the weekend, and arrange for assistance. If the soil is dry or dusty, wet it down with a garden hose and wear a dust mask.

Don't remove any unattached boulders that you discover in your crawlspace. Bury all but their surface. Being less heat resistant than soil, boulders will conduct summer heat into the cooler deep soil. If you encounter solid rock (see "Bedrock" in Chapter 6), rejoice. Your temperature regulation is virtually assured, and you'll have a reduced need for insulation. Excavate to expose as much rock as possible, but be sure to include all exposed rock within the confines of your wine cellar insulation.

Once your excavation is complete, resist the urge to pour a concrete floor. It's unnecessary. If tracking dirt is a concern, line your cellar aisle with concrete patio blocks.

108

(b) Slab Foundations

When a builder tackles a wet site or a skimpy budget, or desires thermal mass to absorb solar gain, he often pours a slab concrete floor at ground level, leaving neither a basement nor a crawl space for your wine. This type of floor is not reinforced to bridge underlying spaces. You would have to remove the concrete floor from the entire wine cellar location with a jack hammer. The way to deal with a slab floor is to leave it alone and build a cellared addition onto your home.

(c) Building an Addition or a New House

When you hire a contractor to build an addition or a new home, you can specify exactly what you want. Even with new construction, trap door and ladder access in an otherwise basement-free home is a commendable approach. It's economical, easy to hide from thieves, and provides wine storage space that would otherwise be wasted on a stairwell. An addition on the north end of your home is ideal. A wooden floored dining room or extra bedroom would go nicely atop a trap door accessed wine cellar.

With new construction you can specify a deeper than standard cellar – I'd go for 8 feet (2.4 M) below grade – at moderately greater cost. The deeper cellar reduces the annual temperature oscillation while providing more height for wine storage. When building an entire new house you could limit the deeper foundations and basement to the wine cellar location, but some of the savings would be lost to the added complexity. If you make the entire basement deeper you'll have nice head room for the ping pong table. With ranch-style houses a good compromise is to have an extra-deep basement under the northern half of the house complemented by an insulated slab floor on the south to store solar heat from south facing windows. An extra-deep half-basement should add around $3,000 of construction costs versus a standard basement.

The advantages of new versus existing basement construction are that the cellar space is dug out by machine when the foundation is excavated, and exterior insulation, drainage, and waterproofing to your specifications can be applied before backfilling.

(d) Selecting a Pre-built New Home

When selecting among available completed houses, everyone has particular requirements and priorities. The proper number of bedrooms, the neighborhood, schools, and commuting distance are typical considerations. In Europe many older homes come with family wine cellars, but if you want a wine cellar in North America, you usually have to build it. When evaluating a pre-built house as a prospective repository for your wine cellar fantasy, there are very specific requirements. Whether or not you should share this consideration with your spouse or significant other is a delicate and weighty political question that goes beyond the scope of this book.

Look for a deep basement with plenty of head room, with a tree shaded north, north-east, or north-west corner not already usurped by a furnace or crisscrossed by heating ducts and hot water pipes. Heat sources anywhere in the basement such as heated rooms, furnaces, and water heaters are undesirable but usually unavoidable. The lack of a basement furnace or ductwork favors expensive-to-operate baseboard electric heat. Houses on a south facing slope will have the deepest north basements, which is ideal. Relatively new houses may have the benefit of exterior foundation insulation installed during construction. Old houses may have the benefit of an excavatable dirt floor or dirt-floored root cellar.

Chapter 13 *WALLS AND CEILINGS

Exterior Walls – New Construction

You can insulate your new concrete foundation walls at the same time they are poured by having your concrete contractor use the Nudura System (Nudura.com) which uses insulating forms made with expanded polystyrene which are left in place after the wall is poured. They have an R-22 insulating value.

Electrical Wiring

Your first task when placing a wine cellar in an already built house is to install an electrical outlet. As electrical jobs go, this one is trivial, and in some areas, it's legal to do it yourself – but if you are electrically naive, take no chances - hire a professional. If installing a wine cellar air conditioner is even a remote possibility, then serve your outlet with a 12-gauge or heavier 3-wire 110-V electrical line from a 20-ampere circuit breaker that is dedicated only to the wine cellar. You certainly don't want to risk having your air conditioner shut off by a short or an overload elsewhere in the house on a shared circuit. The one exception would be a frequently used, single-shared item that will, by being off, signal that your wine cellar air conditioner circuit is down. That item might be an illuminated doorbell button. If no air conditioning is contemplated, you can tap into any convenient electrical box. You need one grounded (3-prong) double-receptacle wall outlet near the place where the air conditioner would go. If that place can be high on the short-end wall, it's less likely to get blocked by wine storage bins or be attacked by moisture. To avoid an insulation gap at the outlet, dangle it by its cord until you finish insulating the intended location.

Now you have convenient and safe power for your work lights, electrical tools, and work radio. It's not at all pleasant to trip over extension cords while manipulating awkward expanses of drywall.

Later on you can run wires from your outlet for permanent lighting. Once you're wired, turn on the radio or CD player and bid temporary farewell to your family and TV.

Footings for Interior Walls

If your house is an antique with a dirt floor, you'll need a footing for the new interior walls. You could pour a four-inch thick by ten-inch wide concrete footing using old lumber for forms and a few bags of ready-mix concrete. Since the wall will not be load-bearing, you can more simply fill a shallow trench with a row of solid pre-cast concrete blocks. Carefully level the upper surface with the aid of a spirit level. A thin layer of sand beneath the blocks will facilitate the leveling operation. Backfill and tamp around the blocks to prevent movement. An alternative possibility is to use a nominal 4 x 6 (actually 3.5" x 5.5") pressure-treated landscaping timber as your sill and place it directly on leveled sand. If you already have a poured concrete floor, you can build your non-load-bearing walls right on it without an additional underlying footing.

Stud Walls

Now that you're on solid footing, mark out the wall and door locations on the floor and against the foundation wall. Be sure to allow enough room so that the finished wine cellar, after all the layers are installed, will still be as wide as you wanted it to be. A basic wood-frame wall is made from nominal 2" x 4" x 8' lumber (actual dimensions 1.5" x 3.5" x 8'). In load bearing walls the studs (verticals) are spaced 16 inches (40 cm) apart on center. Since your walls will not be bearing any load, you can place the studs further apart, on 24 inch (60 cm) centers. Fiberglass insulation comes in batts precut to friction fit precisely into the resulting 14.5 or 22.5-inch wide spaces.

For the interior wall with no door, place a horizontal 2 x 4 on the floor. This is called the sill, and should be one continuous piece. If any part of your wall ever rots, it will be the sill, but unless you have an unusually wet situation or are going directly onto soil, I don't recommend pressure-treated (moisture resistant) lumber. Pressure-treated lumber has been impregnated with arsenicals. Its use in closed spaces is controversial. If you do use pressure-treated wood, do so only for the sill. An adhesive such as Contech PL 200 is applied with a caulking gun to the concrete floor beneath the sill. Apply the adhesive at the beginning of a long work session so that it will still be pliable when you install the studs that will press it against the floor.

A second continuous horizontal board, the header, is then nailed up against the existing overhead floor joists. The header must be precisely over the sill. Use a plumb-line (string and weight) or a spirit-level held against a vertical board to fix the location. If the new wall runs parallel to the overhead floor joists, then the easiest construction is to line your wall up precisely with an overhead joist and nail your header directly to it. Otherwise, you have to bridge the gap between adjacent floor joists. Do this either with 2 x 4 cross braces or 1/2-inch plywood. If building the wall will block access to the space between two ceiling joists, then vapor barrier and insulate there before closing it in.

Measure, cut, and place and nail vertical studs one by one, starting at the foundation wall, to fit snugly between sill and header. An electric utility saw, tape measure, battery-operated drill, pencil, and two saw horses are needed for the cutting process. The stud that abuts a vertical concrete foundation wall should be attached with adhesives and be braced from the adjacent stud overnight while the adhesive dries. Toe-nail the studs (nail at an angle) into the sill and header using 8-penny (2.5 inch) or 10-penny (3 inch) common nails. Mark the locations for the studs in advance with your pencil, as studs try to slide during toe nailing. An alternate and less physical technique is to use screws instead of nails. For this you will need a battery-operated drill as screw gun. You may have to pre-drill the holes. To accommodate full 4-foot widths of untrimmed drywall, the distance from the concrete wall to the center of the third stud should be exactly 4 feet, and the distance to the center of the fifth stud exactly 8 feet. When the vertical studs are in, with the floor adhesive still pliable, secure the sill if you're working over a concrete floor by pounding in several 1 5/8 or 1 3/4 inch concrete nails (use 3 1/4 inch concrete nails if you've used double sills). Don't do this to concrete blocks as they might crack.

An alternative technique is to assemble the entire stud wall (sill, header, and studs) horizontally on the floor, nailing or screwing straight through sill and header into the ends of each stud with two, 10-penny (3 inch) nails or comparable screws. A brief moment of drama and apprehension follows as you attempt to raise the entire heavy completed wall into place. The tension of this moment will only be rivaled when, towards the end of your project, you first open your fully installed, super-insulated door, praying to Bacchus that it will not grind to a halt on the floor. If the wall can be successfully raised, you then use a level to make the wall perfectly vertical. Bridge the inevitable small gaps left between the header and the overhead joists with shim shingles as you nail upward with 10-penny common nails or screws and down with concrete nails that penetrate 1/8 to 1/4 inch into the floor.

There are four difficulties with wall raising. First, you need to be strong enough to lift and maneuver the weight of the wall. If in doubt, get help. Second, you need clearance for the assembled wall past pipes, ducts, and pillars. Third, you cannot remove and trim individual studs that prove to have been cut too long without lowering and disassembling the wall. Fourth, the geometry of wall-raising requires extra headroom. You need clearance for the diagonal of the wall, which is slightly greater than the finished height. If the wall is going parallel to ceiling joists, then you should be able to raise it between joists and slide it into place. If the wall is going perpendicular to the overhead joists, then consider a double sill: the lower sill waiting on the floor to receive the assembled wall.

The second interior stud wall, the one with the door, is built in the same manner as the first, except for the door gap. No sill goes beneath the door opening, but a header is added at the top of the door opening. It's best nevertheless to frame with a continuous sill that bridges the door opening. Only after the wall is finished and secured (don't glue or nail within the doorway opening) do you cut out the sill within the doorway. Further door details await you in the next chapter.

The foundation walls on two sides of your wine cellar don't require a stud wall, though you could build them that way if driven to do so. These walls are best insulated (later) with floor-to-ceiling, free-standing extruded polystyrene panels.

Once the stud walls are in place, run any electrical wires that will be covered by the insulation and drywall, such as wires for a ceiling light, light switch, or interior wall outlet. If you already have your outlet on an exterior wall, and are willing to forego a wall mounted light switch, then just continue with the wall construction. When all the ceilings and walls are in, you can hang a light with a pull cord switch and plug it into your existing outlet.

Should this brief description of wall construction leave you at all confused, fully illustrated, do-it-yourself guides to stud wall construction are available at your lumber yard or bookstore.

Air Conditioner Hole

If you need an air conditioner it should be mounted well above the floor, permitting gravity disposal of condensate and minimizing the condensation on and corrosion of motor parts during the seasons when the unit rests. If in doubt about your site, it's good insurance to frame an opening 18 inches (45 cm) high and 26 or more inches (65 cm) wide near the top of an interior stud wall in anticipation of a possible air conditioner. Framing means nailing in secure upper and lower horizontal 2 x 4s bridging adjacent studs. These must be able to bear the weight of an air conditioner, so a central vertical jack (extra stud below the lower frame) is advisable.

Window air conditioner electrical plugs come with short leashes, so the air conditioner hole and your outlet should be close to one another. Many small air conditioners blow cooled air to their left (your right as you face the unit), so select a spot towards your left. Fill the opening with insulation and cover by screwing in an independent piece of plywood or drywall. Mark the perimeter of the opening on both sides of the wall so you can relocate the opening, and make the bins at that location independently removable. If your climate and construction are proper, you'll never need air conditioning, but it's reassuring to have a backup plan that you can implement quickly on short notice.

Lighting

Fluorescent lights should be used because they give off only 1/5 as much heat as incandescents. Eventually you or someone dear to you will leave your wine cellar light on overnight. It finally happened at my house too. The 20-watt fluorescent bumped my cellar's temperature 1.5°F (0.8°C) overnight. I don't recommend time delay switches that automatically shut off in a few minutes. After many years of faithful service these switches eventually fail, and when they do they stay on. Besides, it would be dangerous for your heart if the lights snapped out when you were inspecting your magnum of 1961 Latour.

With its extra heat production, a 100-watt incandescent bulb could noticeably nudge the summer cellar temperature whenever it took you more than a few minutes to select a wine. A 2-foot (60 cm) long 20-watt, single-bulb fluorescent fixture gives just as much light, casts fewer shadows, and gives fair warning when it's ready to fail. A ceiling mount interferes least with storage space, but put it to one side if head room is tight. The simplest light switch is a pull cord with the end of the string attached above the door so you can find it easily when entering. If you do install a wall switch, place it on the inside of the room so a passing child cannot turn the light on without your key. For the ultimate security, install a red light upstairs that goes on in symphony with your wine cellar light.

Some authorities recommend protecting wine from light, especially the short waves of daylight or fluorescent, but deem the longer wavelength incandescents to be safe. I've seen no data on this issue. The safest route is to go fluorescent but drape the wine bins closest to the bulb.

Insulation

Fiberglass batts come precut to friction-fit between studs spaced either 16 or 24 inches on center. Fiberglass batts have an R-value of 3.2 to 3.5 per inch. The standard thicknesses are 3.5 (R-11), 6 (R-19), and 9 inches (R-29). Marginally higher R-values are claimed for fire-resistant cellulose (treated shredded newspaper), but special blowers are needed to apply cellulose. When moisture gets into the walls the paper might settle or rot, so cellulose insulation is not for basements.

Even higher R-values can be had with rigid foam boards. The R-values range from 4 to over 7 per inch. All foam boards are not alike. The closed-cell extruded polystyrene version that is also suitable for underground exterior applications is your best and strongest choice at R-5 per inch. They usually come colored pink or blue in 2' x 8' x 2" interlocking boards. I've seen ads for an extra strong variety. Other foam boards, usually white, of similar dimensions and lower cost, come in at R-4 and are more fragile and less moisture resistant. The Cadillac of insulating boards is foil-backed polyisocyanurate, under brand names including Hi R, Thermax, and Ultra R. The manufacturers claim an amazing R-7.2 per inch, and more if an air space faces the foil face. It comes in 4' x 8' boards of varying thicknesses from 1/2" to 2". Polyiso-cyanurates swell in moist locations, probably losing some insulating value in the process, and emit noxious fumes if not covered with drywall. Foam boards are too rigid to press between studs. After a great deal of tedious trimming to get them in they still leave edge gaps. Foam boards are, therefore, placed on the face of a stud wall, not within it.

Double Walls Vs Single Walls

Should you want more insulation than a simple 2 x 4 stud wall can provide, and you probably will, you can:

(a) build two adjacent stud walls, filling the spaces within and between them with fiberglass batts, or

(b) build a single fiberglass-filled wall and add foam boards on one side.

(a) The double wall all-fiberglass approach is the least expensive, but requires a bit more space. You build with nominal 2 x 4s or 2 x 3s spaced 24 inches apart on center. The industry standard is the nominal 2 x 4, but so far as structural strength is concerned, nominal 2 x 3s (which measure 1.5" x 2.5") are satisfactory for double non-bearing walls. The savings in lumber cost would be minimal, but the smaller dimension leaves a bit of extra space for insulation, as fiberglass insulates better than wood.

Two independent stud walls are built 0 to 9 inches or more apart from one another. The space between the walls is filled first, with unfaced fiberglass batts laid sideways, one atop the other. The two walls are then filled with vertically oriented unfaced fiberglass batts. Unfaced fiberglass batts will friction fit and hold within the stud walls. For example, two 2 x 4 stud walls placed 6 inches apart yield a total insulating value of R-43. A 9-inch, between-walls space yields R-53.

To minimize the area where there is only the central insulation, offset the vertical studs so they are not directly opposite one another. To achieve this offset, begin measuring the 24-inch (60 cm) stud wall intervals at one end for the inner wall, and at the opposite end for the outer wall. It's worth the extra confusion in laying out the stud spacing.

(b) For a slimmer profile and a bit less work (but slightly greater expense) build a single 2 x 4 stud wall, fill it with 3.5 inches of fiberglass, and then pile on extruded polystyrene boards. The polystyrene is a good vapor barrier, so it belongs on the basement (outer) side of the stud wall only. In order to fasten drywall onto the 4" of foam that you would require for an R-33 wall, you'll need 5.5" drywall screws. Finally, building the stud wall with nominal 2 x 6 lumber adds 2 inches of fiberglass.

Installing Fiberglass

When it's time to insulate with fiberglass, wear a paper dust-mask and change clothes and shower after you're done. Cut fiberglass batts to length with a sharp utility knife. If you cut on a concrete floor you'll need a fresh blade for every stroke, so place a board on the floor at your insulation-cutting station. If, as recommended, you use unfaced fiberglass, just press it into place between studs. With faced batts, staple onto the face of the studs. The vapor barrier facing must go on the non-wine-cellar side of interior walls only. In the ceiling the facing goes up – so no stapling.

If you've used unfaced fiberglass and no foam, then attach a continuous 6-millimeter polyethylene vapor barrier on the non-wine-cellar side of the interior stud walls, extending up between the overhead floor joists, and overlapping the edges of the ceiling vapor barrier.

Vapor Barriers

The inadvisability of totally encasing your wine cellar in plastic can be illustrated by the theoretical consequences of breaking a single bottle of wine. With nowhere to go, the moisture would theoretically raise the humidity to 100%. If the soil beneath your cellar is not saturated by a high water table, some moisture will go down through your concrete floor into the ground, but it's probably also a good idea to allow some water vapor exchange with the overlying house. Any vapor barrier that you apply to the ceiling must go uppermost, against the subfloor. For an uninterrupted barrier you would wrap each floor joist, but don't do it. Use faced fiberglass batts for the first layer of ceiling insulation, with the facing uppermost. Vapor barrier gaps will remain through the floor joists and around the edges and ends of the batts.

The narrow region above the foundation walls needs a vapor barrier too. This small space faces the outdoors, so the vapor barrier must be on the living side. Fill these recesses between the ceiling joists above the foundation wall with unfaced fiberglass batts, and then extend the polyethylene or extruded polystyrene board vapor barrier on the inner surface of the foundation wall upwards (see the next paragraph). A staple gun (not a stationery stapler) is best for attaching polyethylene because it leaves one hand free to manipulate whatever you're stapling, and because hammer blows while using nails can easily damage plastic. (A recent report on the aging of polyethylene questions the durability of standard grades.) Get the thickest and best grade available, and treat it gently. Sunlight and heat both degrade it. By the time you read this a superior vapor-barrier material may be available.

The interior surface of the foundation wall needs a vapor barrier. If you're going to cover the concrete walls with a double layer of interlocking extruded polystyrene board insulation, then a preceding sheet of polyethylene directly on the foundation wall would be redundant. Extend the foam boards up between the overhead floor joists and tape or caulk the seams and the edges to make a tight vapor barrier. The bins that will cover the wall will protect the foam boards and keep them from popping out of place.

The Ceiling

Since the overhead house will usually be warmer then the adjacent basement, the ceiling deserves more insulation than the interior walls. In the ceiling you'll be limited primarily by the available headroom. Completely fill the space between the floor joists with fiberglass batts, beginning with faced (paper

120

vapor barrier) batts, the paper facing upwards. For 12-inch floor joists you may need to use two layers of fiberglass, the second layer unfaced. If spacing between the floor joists is irregular or non-standard, run the fiberglass across the short way, cutting sections to the appropriate length. Pack it snugly. If the floor joists are cross-braced with x-shaped wire or wood, then cut short pieces of fiberglass to fit all spaces. Add 2 inches of extruded polystyrene or polyisocyanurate boards across the face of the floor joists. To give your nails or screws better grip on the boards, use the thin aluminum washers designed for such applications. At around R-40, fiberglass plus 2 inches of foam will usually suffice. If you have the head room and want to insulate further, then you should consider placing the equivalent of an overhead horizontal stud wall at the desired new ceiling height.

Drywall (Sheetrock)

You'll be applying most of the drywall at full width (4 feet), but will have to trim at least the height. The technique for making straight cuts in drywall is best learned by observation. For those who have never seen it done, mark the line to be cut with a pencil and straight edge or chalk line (which is easier) and then, using a sharp utility knife, cut through the paper on one side with a single firm stroke. Next, rap the opposite, uncut side just below the cut with one fist, while holding the drywall above the cut with the other hand. The plaster center will crack beneath the score, and the drywall will fold. Finally, cut the paper hinge, reaching around with your utility knife. Practice on scrap.

Drywall nails are sufficient, but if you have a screw gun or battery-powered drill, use drywall screws. (Battery powered drills rotate slowly enough for screwing. Electric drills are too fast.) Select a nail or screw length that bites into at least 1/2 inch of wood for walls, 3/4 inch for ceilings. The heads of screws or nails should be driven (recessed) 1/8 to 1/16 inch into the drywall, but not far enough to tear the paper facing. You'll be covering the metal heads with joint compound to prevent rust. Even better, use exterior grade screws to avoid rusting.

Ceiling drywall is traumatic to install, especially if you're working alone, as you have to hold it firmly in place while you nail or screw it up at several spots. If it slips after being attached at only one end, it cracks. This operation doesn't quite match the drama of wall raising or door hanging, but it comes close. Get help at this stage. The helper need have no expertise, just enough arm strength to maneuver and hold the heavy sheetrock overhead while you fasten. A temporary wooden support is also useful. The support is simply a floor-to-ceiling length 2x4 with a short board nailed across the upper end to distribute pressure. You lean the support out of the way (but within reach) while you and your assistant maneuver the drywall into position. Hold your end up with one hand and fetch the support with the other. Once the support is in place, both hands will be free to nail or screw while your assistant continues to support the opposite end. A few screws at strategic locations will secure it temporarily, but then fasten to every stud or ceiling joist at approximately 6-inch (15 cm) intervals. Install the ceiling drywall before the wall drywall so you'll have more room to maneuver, and can leave modest edge-gaps which will be covered by the easier-to-adjust vertical drywall.

Drywall comes in several thicknesses. For walls, 1/2 inch or even 5/8 inch is desirable for strength. It also slows heat penetration in the event of a fire. The 5/8 is extremely heavy. The weight of fullsheets make them difficult to maneuver, especially for those whose regular job is sedentary. For ceilings, 3/8 drywall is often used because its lighter weight eases construction, and because ceilings are not usually subject to rough treatment. I'd compromise at 1/2 inch (1.3 cm) throughout, making planning less complicated. Drywall comes in two basic types: the standard grey type and the green water-resistant type. Water-resistant drywall is usually used only in bathrooms, but I advise it for your wine cellar too.

The final step is to seal the drywall joints against air leaks with joint-tape, and to cover the heads of the screws and nails against rust. You'll need one five-gallon pail of joint compound, and a broad putty knife. You will need two coats of this stuff. The basic technique for joints is to apply sticky mesh joint-tape followed by a thin layer of joint compound applied with a broad putty knife. After it dries, usually overnight, add a second layer sufficient to bury the tape. The resulting wall can be left rough without sanding. (The rough finish seems appropriate for a wine cellar.) Cover the nail or screw heads with joint compound too.

Painting

Paint your drywall or it will mildew. Oil-based primer or paint will emit noxious fumes for days while drying in your unventilated cellar. Lest the entire project be nullified by damage to your olfactory epithelium, stick to latex (water based) primer and top coat. Mildew-resistant latex paints designed for damp locations such as bathrooms are available and are recommended. They are applied as two coats of the same paint, the first coat serving as the primer.

Building Wrap

As an alternative to the aggravation of drywall and two coats of paint, there's a modern class of material that should be adequate for a wine cellar. Building wraps are paper thin and come in rolls of various widths, but are oh so much stronger than paper. They are designed for the wrapping of the exterior of houses prior to the installation of the outer skin such as vinyl or cedar siding. Some are degraded by the ultraviolet portion of sunlight, but that's of no concern in a cellar. They also can be punctured or torn if abused. The major brands are TYVEX, which is white, and TYPAR, which is gray. TYPAR is the more tear resistant of the two. You roll it out and staple it onto the ends of wooden studs. The building wraps are highly resistant to the passage of air, but allow water vapor to pass easily, making them ideal for wine cellar interiors. To apply them to a ceiling covered with foam you must first nail or screw 3/8" thick wood strips called furring strips at one foot intervals through to the ceiling rafters. You then staple the building wrap to the furring. The furring also secures the foam.

Now that the rough work is completed, are you ready for the more exacting craftsmanship required for the construction and installation of a super-insulated door?

Chapter 14 *THE DOOR

The need for even insulation, as explained in Chapter 7, also applies to the door. My recommendation is that you custom-build a super-insulated door. But first, let's dispose of several alternatives which I do not recommend.

Not-Recommended Doors

An easy way to avoid having to build and hang a door is to buy what is appropriately called a pre-hung door. For example, a pre-hung, insulated, exterior-type metal door costs around $350. It comes in a frame with all the trim and it's a snap to install. Unfortunately, it offers only R-10 insulation.

You could do better for cheaper by installing a standard, interior-grade, pre-hung hollow core door with two-inch slabs of polystyrene glued onto both sides. With this system you won't be able to open the door completely, and your relatively fragile insulation board will be exposed to damage, and the gaps around the edges of the glued-on insulation will be significant. Nevertheless, if you're careful, this is a good quick fix.

To double the R-value of a standard pre-hung door, you can install two of them, one opening out, the other in. The R-values are additive, and the air space between them adds an R- or two.

You could also arrange your two doors around an airlock entry. This is a space between two doors that is large enough for your body. You close the outer door behind you before you open the inner door. By never having both doors open at the same time, you avoid drafts of hot air. An airlock entry only makes sense for a frequently used entry. For a personal wine cellar, which is entered in-frequently, the air lock feature offers virtually no advantage and wastes a lot of space.

Finally, there are those massive doors that are made for meat coolers. The press-latches on these expensive and pretentious items are designed to be operated no-hands hundreds of times a day by heavily laden meat cutters. The fancy hardware might impress an occasional guest, but you don't need it.

The Recommended Door

A far less elaborate and much superior R-36 or better door is easy to custom build. Use two or three layers of 2-inch thick polyisocyanurate or extruded polystyrene as a core. One version of this door design is shown in Figure 14-1. If your insulating board comes 4-feet wide, cut it in half lengthwise and double it for your 4" x 2' x 8' core. Cut the insulation with a standard wood hand saw. Trim the 8' length to 3" shorter than the final door height. For 4" of foam use the 2 x 6 and 1 x 6 construction shown. For 6" of foam use 2 x 8's and 1 x 8's. You can rip them down for a precise fit around the foam, but don't forget to allow for the notched in diagonal brace made from a 1 x 6. Alternately, you could cut out a 3/4" deep groove in the foam for the diagonal brace. You screw the 1-by's into the ends of the 2-by's using 2" flat head screws. As an alternative, do the entire door in 1 by's, but pre-drill the screw holes or the wood will split. A can of spray foam-insulation can be used to seal the edges against air leaks.

For door stiffness cut full-door facings from two 4' x 8' sheets of thin (1/4") plywood. The remainder of the plywood sheets can be used for the door jambs. The jamb is the wall surface within the doorway. Use wood cement, most easily applied with a caulking gun, to fasten the plywood. Use small finishing nails and clamps to hold the plywood door facings firmly in place overnight while the cement dries. While the door is still lying on its side, apply a water base urethane finish to the interior surface to prevent mold.

Arrange the door opening, direction of swing, and hinge placement so the door opens out at a full 180 degrees to lie flush against

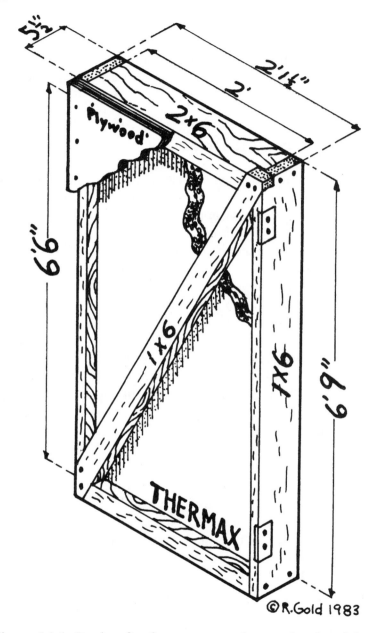

Figure 14-1. Design for the recommend super-insulated door.

the wall, or you'll be squeezing through an opening diminished by the thickness of the door. When framing the wall, a header (two for a double wall) should be placed above the door opening at a height that allows room for the height of the door plus one inch. The inch is needed for a 3/8" threshold at the floor, a 1/4" thick head jamb, and space for clearance.

The door jambs extend the full thickness of the doorway. If you have 12" thick walls, then cut your 12" wide jambs from the 1/4" plywood. The space between the vertical studs flanking the door should provide, for the 6" thick x 25.5" wide door depicted, 1.5" more than the door width, or 27". The extra space is for two 1/4" thick plywood jambs, clearance, and the 3/4" swing-out of the door. As the door opens, its trailing edge will describe an arc whose radius will equal the diagonal of the door as measured from the hinge. With a thin door, the diagonal is barely more than the width, but for a 6" thick, 25.5 inch wide door the diagonal is 3/4" greater than the width. For an 8" thick 25.5" door the diagonal is 1.2" greater than the width. The ideal way to accommodate the swing-out is to build both the doorway and the door 3/4" (or 1.2") wider on the handle end of the hinged side. That way the diagonal measured from the hinge equals the width of the face. (This detail was unfortunately not contemplated before figure 14-1 was drawn.)

Hanging a door is always tricky, especially for a thick door in a thick wall. If you have no experience hanging doors, then this is the moment to enlist a carpentry-competent friend. If the walls and doorway are vertically plumb as measured with a level, if the floor is level, or at least not off by more than the thickness of the threshold, and the door is square and hung straight, then it shouldn't scrape the floor when you open it.

Use three 4" hinges installed with 1.5" flat head screws. Attach the door half of all three hinges first. The hinges should be reset into the door using hammer and chisel to form the reset slot. Drill pilot holes for the screws. This would be a good time to cut the plywood jambs and loosely place them, but don't attach them yet. It's also the best time to install the handles (see below) as they'll make it easier to maneuver the door. Prop the door into place, using shims to raise it off the floor, and mark the precise spot for the wall side of the top and bottom hinges only. Move the door out of the way. Separate the two halves of the top and bottom hinges only by removing the pins, and install the wall side of these two hinges directly onto the studs. No reset is needed here as cutouts in the 1/4" door jamb will provide the recess. Put the door back and, if you did it right, the hinge pins will drop right in, perhaps with a bit of lubrication and a few hammer taps. Cross your fingers before you test the door swing. With the door open, secure the third hinge to the wall. Now use finish nails to install the plywood door jambs, after first making sure that they don't need to be trimmed or padded to get a good door fit, and after making cut outs for the hinges.

A thick door won't take a standard doorknob, and if it could it would be a heat leak. Metal strap handles serve nicely. The exterior door handle can safely be attached at the edge of the door, the screws going into the door frame. To save your fingers from being pinched, keep the interior handle away from the edge of the door, which leaves nothing solid to attach it to - until you attach it to your diagonal brace or to a strip of wood affixed across the width of the door. Weather stripping then goes on the top and both sides of the door. The bottom gets a wood or aluminum threshold. An adjustable threshold is best. When all is done, the opening of the door will be accompanied by air resistance and an audible whoosh of air which attests to your air-tight construction.

The final touch is to paint the exterior face of the door with two coats of mildew resistant paint to match the color of adjacent walls, thus making the wine cellar less obvious to intruders. Strategically placed wall hangings and pictures can also be used to hide the door. The branded end panels from Bordeaux crates make great decorations, but are more safely placed on the interior surface of the door. Oh yes, don't forget to add a padlock.

Chapter 15 * BINS AND SHELVES

Compared to the complexities of the preceding chapters, bin and shelf construction are a breeze. Storage by the case in the original crates and boxes is, initially, even easier.

Storage in the original crates & boxes

Even if you don't currently buy wine by the case, you probably will once you have a wine cellar, so anticipate a few stacks of crates and boxes. Most Bordeaux come in wooden crates with the name of the chateau and the vintage conveniently branded on the end. Bordeaux crates make very efficient use of space, and keep out potentially harmful light. Note the date of acquisition and cost in pencil directly on the crate or on a staple-attached file card, or attach the store receipt. Stack the crates with branded ends exposed. Nothing could be simpler – until you want a bottle from the bottom of the stack.

One reader reported finding luxuriant mold on the interior wooden surfaces and labels upon opening crates that had been closed for several years. I suspect that his crates had been stored directly on the floor in very high humidity. If you keep the cases one foot off the floor and the relative humidity no higher than 80%, it's safe to use Bordeaux cases as supplied. Even the cardboard boxes that most American wines are shipped in can be used so long as the bottles are on their sides.

Moving crates to access the bottom of a stack is minor compared with the frustrating nails that secure the tops. If you've found an ideal tool for removing tops in such a way that they can easily be re-secured, let me know. In my hands, the tops splinter under screw driver and hammer attack, and when I try to reseal a case, the nails are usually bent or go sideways. If you discard the tops you lose some of the strength of the case, making tall stacks dangerous. An inexpensive hinged top would be a useful innovation.

Pallets

In high humidity situations, which you have gone to some lengths to create, placing wooden cases or cardboard boxes directly on the floor invites mold. It also impedes heat transfer through the floor. You must therefore raise your case storage a foot (30 cm) off the floor, onto pallets. Four sturdy 12.5" (30 cm) high pallets can be made from construction lumber using one 8' long nominal 2x10 and two 8' long nominal 2x4s as depicted in Figure 15-1. Nails that are 2.5" long suffice, but longer nails, even 4" long 20-penny (20d) common nails, would prevent lateral sway. Pre-drill before nailing to prevent splitting.

Bordeaux crates are made of thin wood, assembled with a few short nails or staples. I've seen them stacked ten high in wine shops, but I wouldn't risk it, especially if their strengths have been compromised

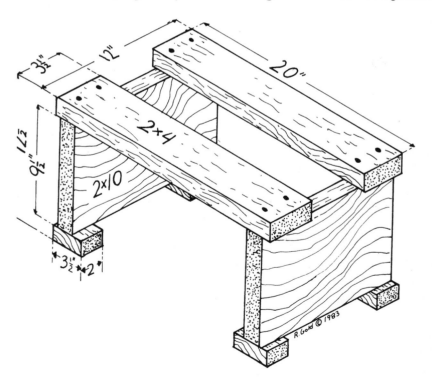

by removing the tops. A stack of four or five crates is probably safe. To go higher, I'd build a sturdy (2 x 4 construction) shelf half-way up the wall. For a convenient 40" (100 cm) high work space, place a piece of plywood atop two side-by-side stacks of Bordeaux crates stacked four high atop wooden pallets.

Once wines approach maturity, stacked wooden crates become intolerable to access. They also become inefficient spacewise as the contents are consumed. I eventually threw out all but one of my pallets which I saved for new arrivals, and converted my cellar from crate storage to bins. I was delighted with the improved access. In retrospect it would have been easier to start out with bins.

Bin design

A six-foot (180 cm) high and 12-foot (360 cm) long wall of bins can hold 968 bottles weighing 2,850 pounds (1,250 kilos), which will easily cost you $20,000. Sturdy storage racks are clearly a wise investment. The racks must rest directly on the floor. Never hang shelves from the walls. For strength the best materials are steel, aluminum, and wood. Steel and aluminum, being excellent thermal conductors, will conduct summer heat into the floor, making the bottles slightly cooler than the air surrounding them. When spring humidity rises, condensation followed by mold will select these cooler surfaces to the detriment of your labels and corks. Wood is a better insulator than steel, but can itself be attacked by mold. Plastics are excellent insulators and are mold resistant, but aren't rigid enough. Most everyone builds wooden bins, ideally with redwood or cedar which resist mold. Pine is much cheaper and more readily available, but needs two coats of urethane to resist mold.

You can purchase ready-made or ready-to-assemble shelves and bins in an assortment of materials and shapes from wine accessory catalogs. The typical cost is under $3 per bottle space. If you choose prefab bins you can skip the rest of this chapter, but I'd suggest spending a day building bins for $200 in materials and using the $2,800 balance for a case of '2005 Cos.

You've surely noticed stylish diamond-shaped bins in shops, restaurants, and interior design magazines. Aficionados of diamond-shaped bins suggest that they have more than a cosmetic advantage over bookshelf-like bins with vertical sides. They might argue as follows: Consider loading a case of Bordeaux size bottles into a 12-inch (30 cm) wide by 9-inch (22.5 cm) high bookshelf bin as at the top of Figure 15-2. The first row of four bottles goes in easily, albeit with a proclivity to roll until the row is full. For the second and third rows you have to hold one, two, and then three bottles in place until you get the fourth in. When you remove a bottle from a filled row, the three remainders roll over and crash into the valleys of the row below. If you decide to replace the bottle you've just removed, you have to first reposition and hold three bottles in place. The moving and rolling disturbs sediment and invites breakage. With diamond bins, the only possible way to stack is in staggered rows, each bottle resting securely in a valley. You can safely remove any single bottle from a diamond bin, even from the bottom row.

Diamond bins are, unfortunately, difficult to construct and leave odd spaces where they meet the walls, ceiling, and floor. Diamond bins usually have sides of equal length, so you get a capacity of 4 (2 x 2), 9 (3 x 3), 16 (4 x 4), or 25 (5 x 5) bottles. None of these sizes are convenient when dealing with 12 bottle cases. Unequal sided diamond bins such as a 4 x 3 (12 bottle) size are more complex to design and assemble, but would be more useful.

Rejoice! You can obtain all of the advantages of diamond bins, except the aesthetic, with bookcase bins by selecting dimensions that accommodate staggered rows of bottles.

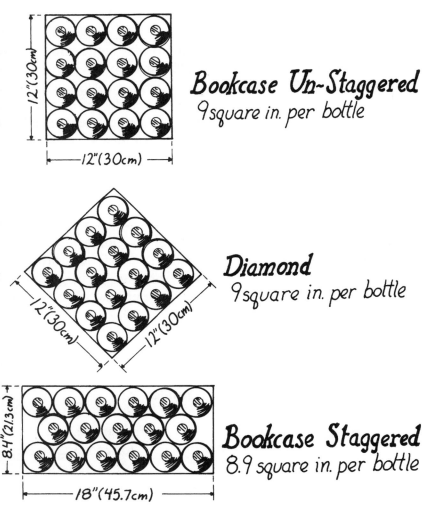

Bookcase Un~Staggered
9 square in. per bottle

Diamond
9 square in. per bottle

Bookcase Staggered
8.9 square in. per bottle

Figure 15-2. Three bin styles. **Top**; an unstaggered row bookcase type bin. Easy to build but inconvenient to use. **Middle**; an attractive, user friendly, but difficult to construct diamond shaped bin. **Bottom**; a staggered row bookcase type bin. Easy to build, easy to use.

Bottle dimensions

The standard 750 ml (roughly 1/5 gallon) wine bottle comes in two basic diameters – 3.0" (7.6 cm) and 3.2" (8.1 cm). The former is the more common, serving Bordeaux, Italy, Germany, Australia, Spain, and most United States wines. The larger 3.2" bottles are traditional in the Burgundy, Rhone, and Loire regions of France, occasionally in Italy, and, in California, for Pinot Noir and Chardonnay.

Bin height

Working initially with the more common 3-inch bottle, the first row will of course require 3inches of height. Due to the stagger, each subsequent row only requires an additional 2.7 inches (6.9 cm) of height. Three-row bins thus require an interior height of 8.4 inches (21.4 cm). Table 15-1 gives the diameters and increments for all of the major bottle sizes.

TABLE 15-1 WINE BOTTLE DIAMETERS
in inches and (centimeters)

	Bottle Diameters		Incremental Height for 2nd, 3rd, etc. staggered rows	
Bottle Size	Bordeaux style	Burgundy style	Bordeaux style	Burgundy style
375 ml	2.4 (6.1)	2.6 (6.6)	2.1 (5.3)	2.3 (5.8)
750 ml	3.0 (7.6)	3.2 (8.1)	2.7 (6.9)	2.9 (7.4)
1.5 L	3.8 (9.6)	4.2 (10.7)	3.2 (8.1)	3.6 (9.7)

TABLE 15-2 BIN DIMENSIONS

Bin Designation	Interior dimensions in inches and (centimeters)	
	Height	Width
Universal	9.0 (22.9)	13.5 (34.3)
Bordeaux – 11 bottle	8.4 (21.3)	12.0 (30.5)
Bordeaux – 12 W (3 high, 4 wide)	8.4 (21.3)	13.5 (34.3)
Bordeaux – 12 H (4 high, 3 wide)	11.1 (28.2)	10.5 (26.7)
Burgundy – 11 bottle	9.0 (22.9)	12.8 (32.5)
Burgundy 12 W (3 high, 4 wide)	9.0 (22.9)	14.4 (36.6)
Burgundy – 12 H (4 high, 3 wide)	11.9 (30.2)	11.2 (28.5)

Bin width

Still working with 3" bottles, the bottom row requires 3" width increments, but the second row is displaced 1/2 bottle to one side. If the second row is to contain as many bottles as the first, then it requires an extra 1.5" (3.8 cm) in width. If the staggered rows are to contain unequal numbers of bottles, likely 4-bottle rows alternating with 3-bottle rows, then the bin width would be an even multiple of 3".

The universal bin

For the greatest versatility and ease of planning, with just a small spatial sacrifice, a universal size of 9" (23 cm) high x 13.5" (34.3 cm) wide would accommodate eleven Burgundy shape (3.2") bottles, twelve Bordeaux shape (3") bottles, or any six magnums. Consider doing all your bins in the universal size save a few odd ones to fill out the wall space. If you favor 18 wine tastings, then a few large tasting bins are desirable as well. Table 15-2 summarizes the shape and capacity of seven of the more plausible bin shapes.

Bin depth

Wooden bins are typically built with nominal 1" (2.5 cm) thick boards, which are actually only 3/4" thick. If the width of the boards is nominally 8" (actually 7.5" or 19 cm), then they will adequately support the fat part of the bottles while lying on their sides, necks facing out. Wider, nominal 10" (actually 9.5" or 24 cm) boards give a broader, more stable structure, with no loss of aisle space, only slight extra cost, and no extra labor.

If your cellar is wide enough, then 18" (45 cm) deep shelves will give you the option of double depth stacking. The rear bottles go neck out, the front bottles neck in, necks overlapping. Plan for staggered rows of unequal width (e.g. 4, 3, 4 rear nesting with 3, 4, 3 front). This arrangement saves a few inches in depth, but if you tilt the shelves (see below), the forward bottles will be tilted incorrectly. If you have the room, full double depth with all necks out requires 22" to 24" (55 to 60 cm) deep bins.

Bin construction

A strong and simple construction technique uses continuous floor-to-ceiling nominal 1" x 10" risers held in place only by horizontal shelves (see figure 15-3). Each shelf rests on shelf clips, available at most hardware stores. The shelf clip has a 1/4" diameter 3/8" long pin that inserts into 1/4" holes drilled into the risers. Two clips can go into a single hole from either side of the board. They're made by Knape & Vogt Mfg. Co., Grand Rapids, MI 49505. Ask for # 346. They come 100 to a box at $30 per box. You need four clips per bin.

This design only works if you go snugly from wall to wall. The risers should go all the way to the ceiling. The shelves are cut from the same stock as the risers. For single depth bins use #2 pine. Select the lumber personally. Sight along the edge of each board to check for warp. Reject warped, split, or severely knotted boards. To be on the safe side, assemble a test column and try filling it with a variety of bottle sizes before cutting all the shelves. Your unglued unscrewed wall of bins will readily disassemble should you move to another house. For double depth bins you won't find 24" wide pine boards. Either rip 4' wide sheets of plywood in half, or use pairs of 12" risers and shelves. For strength, the grain of pine shelves must run from side to side, not front to back.

Urethane all the wood on all surfaces. The first coat soaks in and blocks the pores, the second seals the surface. Once mold gets started, it can continue to flourish even under urethane. Glossy urethane is more impervious to moisture than flat or semi-gloss. Spirit based urethanes are traditional, but eco-friendly urethanes are now available which allow water clean-up and don't emit noxious fumes for weeks after being applied. Marine spar-varnish, designed for boats, is the most moisture resistant, but gives off toxic fumes. Whatever you select, apply it out-of-doors or, in winter, in a well ventilated garage. Do all the boards on one side, by which time they'll be dry enough to turn onto sleepers for the second side. You usually have to wait overnight before applying the second coat. Wait a few days after that before bringing them into the cellar. While waiting, keep the boards away from rain. It might be convenient to seal the shelf boards before cutting them into individual shelves. For cutting your boards a skill saw is required. Drill the shelf clip holes after sealing the boards. If you drill first, urethane will get into the holes and the shelf clips won't fit.

Before drilling all the boards, drill for and assemble one bin and test fill it with real bottles. Then drill all the shelf clip holes before assembling the wall. A modest rearward tilt (the rear of each shelf being one inch [2.5 cm] lower than the front) provides safety. In earth-quake-prone zones use a steeper tilt. The wall behind the bins, assuming you've used a firm material such as drywall, keeps the tilted

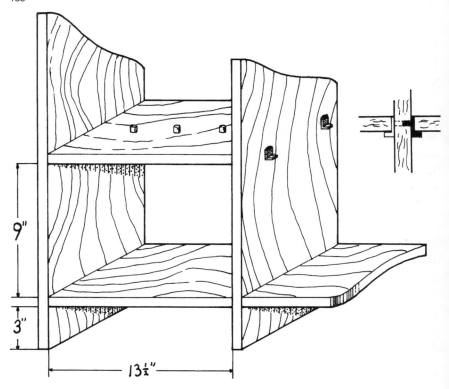

Figure 15-3. Bin construction with shelf clips. The universal bin size is shown.

bottles from slipping out the back. If you've used only building wrap on the wall, or if the bins are not against a wall, then a 1/4" plywood backing is required. The tilt encourages sediment to collect at the bottom of the bottle – which is where you'll want it during decanting. Tapered German-style bottles require a steeper tilt to keep them secure.

You'll probably want to keep your cellar treasures in individual bottle storage. For individual bottle storage leave only 3.5" (9 cm) between shelves for 750 ml bottles; 4.5" (11.4 cm) for magnums.

The best height for the lowest shelf clip hole is 3.5" off the floor at the rear, 4.5" at the front. That will allow good air circulation to the floor beneath the bins, while affording you a slot under the lowest shelf in which to temporarily place a few bottles when rearranging your stock.

When assembling a wall of bins, work your way across from one wall to the other, inserting one mid-level shelf between each pair of verticals. Draft a family member to hold the risers in place until the shelf between the last pair of risers is inserted. That last shelf should be cut to length at the last minute, ensuring a snug fit. As you fill in the rest of the shelves, minor (1/16") width adjustments can be made by selectively notching the edges of shelves where they contact the 1/16" thick shelf clips. To prevent bottles that rest directly on shelves from rolling, get pre-made 1/4" dowels and insert them into holes drilled half-way into the shelves. This is usually only needed for individual bottle shelves.

Ceramic tile bins

Some misguided authorities advocate the use of stacks of round ceramic drainage tiles as individual bottle bins. They cite as advantages the thermal capacity of the tiles and the individual bottle storage. Tiles are wasteful of space, expensive, heavy, and difficult to cut. One oenophile reports nearly destroying his foot when a tile dropped, his eyes when chips flew off the electric saw, his arm when the saw slipped, and his lungs from the dust. The thermal capacity of tiles is negligible compared to that of the wine itself. Large rectangular tiles will stack more efficiently, each holding a dozen or more bottles – but you might have trouble locating an efficient shape. Beware the moisture retained in tiles that have been stored under the stars. One reader reports a mold epidemic after 2,000 previously snow-covered tiles were assembled into a bin wall in her vapor-barriered cellar. A modern version of the ceramic tile theme uses plastic sewer pipe. They're lighter and easier to cut than tiles, but they still waste space.

Milk carton bins

Steel milk cases on their sides offer a reasonable alternative to wooden bins. The biggest problem is to obtain some 50 cases at a reasonable cost. Stealing them from the dairy is definitely illegal. Perhaps you can locate a dairy that is converting from heavy steel to light plastic milk cases as a delivery truck fuel-efficiency measure. The plastic milk cases that dairies have largely turning to are not as rigid as steel ones, so can only be used for the upper one or two rows.

You could, for example, have three rows of steel cases at the bottom followed by two rows of plastic cases. To prevent rust, steel cases should be spray-painted outdoors before assembly into a wall of bins. Brush painting takes forever. Secure adjacent cases to one another using stainless steel hose clamps. Place wooden or plastic insulating blocks under the lowest row of steel cases, the front block being an inch or so higher to produce a modest tilt.

Each milk case has interior dimensions of 12" (30 cm) square. It will hold sixteen 3" bottles in unstaggered rows, fourteen if staggered, twelve 3.2" bottles, or six magnums.

Section 4 * ACQUIRING

Chapter 16 * THE WINE MARKET

Nearly every wine lover can recall an event which served as the launching pad of enophilia. Mine transpired in the Loire Valley of France where I fell in love with the incredibly fresh, fruity, and perfumed local white wine. At the conclusion of our vacation we landed in Boston laden with two assorted cases of Loire Valley wine. That was when you could take liquids into the cabin of the air plane.

To expand my holdings after arriving home, I investigated the displays at my local wine shop. Those early experiences were exceedingly frustrating. No amount of transillumination or label perusal revealed the wine's taste and aroma, to say nothing of aging potential. The few guide-to-wine books that I found at my local bookseller (This was even before Hugh Johnson's Pocket Encyclopedia) gave general descriptions of regions and styles, and rated the vintages, but failed to provide the crucial specific property-by-vintage evaluations needed for informed purchasing.

Your friendly wine merchant

My local wine merchant conducted private tours of his offerings for me. He described the virtues of a dozen or more wines, pointing fondly to each as we traversed the aisles. Unfortunately, I was unable to retain the descriptions offered during these excursions. I was also unable to keep track of the shelf locations of the recommended wines so as to check them against the information in my guide books.

After a few of these frustrating trips, I changed my tactics. I took a shopping cart on the guided tour. As we proceeded down the aisles, I popped a bottle of every one of the recommended wines into my cart. After the delighted merchant left my side to greet a new arrival, I examined the bottles in my shopping cart in a more leisurely manner, checking each property against the wine library in my briefcase, and returned the questionable wares to the shelves.

If you're a new enophile, then you may initially have difficulty locating anyone other than your wine merchant with whom to share your enthusiasm. Experienced wine merchants present ongoing, personalized, private wine appreciation courses for their customers. They learn from your morning-after reports what types of wine you like and the comfort level of your wallet. The tuition is covered by the profit on purchased wine. A job well done leads to and warrants incredible customer loyalty.

Buying recent releases

At this writing the 2005 Bordeaux are getting rave reviews as the vintage of the century. To take advantage of the opening prices and availability, decisions should be made quickly. The most highly rated wines, especially those from the smaller properties, may only hit the shelves for a few days. By the time you read this it will probably be too late for the initial offering of the 2005's, but there will be other vintages of the century.

Actually, the selection that you see on the racks at your wine merchant has already been quadruplicately gleaned. First, some items have been sold as pre-release futures. With pre-release futures the wine merchant circulates and even advertises a formal pre-release price list. The merchant collects his money before the wine leaves the winery – sometimes even before bottling. With futures you get assured availability (if the merchant does not go out of business and properly honors your futures purchase) at the relatively low pre-release price, and the wine merchant gets a sure sale and the opportunity to use your money for upwards of two years. The drawbacks for you are that you only have newsletter tasting notes (see below) or the wine merchant's recommendation to go on, you are obliged to buy by the case or half case, and you can't easily cancel your order.

The second gleaning occurs more informally. Parker (see below) gives a wine from an obscure property a 99-point rating. Someone in another state who gets his copy of the *Wine Advocate* in the mail a day before you do telephones your wine merchant even before the merchant himself receives the wine or gets his *Advocate*, and snags by credit card the shop's entire allocation.

The third gleaning occurs when unsold great wine reaches the shop and the merchant holds his one-case allocation in his temperature-controlled storage room. It never appears on the customer accessible web site inventory or on the store's shelves. He fetches a bottle or two at a time for special customers. You are not one of his special customers.

The fourth gleaning occurs via store tastings. (Pre-release or just-released wines are poured at a store tasting.) Before heading for home, the tasters snatch up by the case-full the shop's entire allocation of the show stoppers, leaving the happy merchant with a pile of credit card slips and checks.

Unaware of this quadruple gleaning, the neo-enophile cruises the aisles in search of liquid treasure. Don't get me wrong. Some great wines at reasonable prices may be on the shelves. But how do you discriminate? Most wine region guidebooks will tell you in varying detail which chateaux or vineyards have the best reputations, but will offer no property-by-property comparison on the particular vintages before you. Nevertheless, after consultation with the wine merchant and in consideration of reputation, you purchase a 12-bottle mixed case (for the 5% mixed case discount) of tasting samples.

Arriving home with your $400 experiment, you're faced with a dilemma. At up to $65 a bottle you're reluctant to open them all at once for comparative tasting, so as a compromise you open one every few days to evaluate and consume with your significant other over dinner. Some of the wines with the best potential are going to be unpleasantly tannic and not at all ready to enjoy. A two-ounce tasting sample is all you need to guess at future development. Consuming the rest of the bottle could be painful.

Being new to the process, you may not be sure what visual, aromatic, and gustatory qualities predict cellaring potential as opposed to current appeal. Each wine will be evaluated against a different food background and in a different time frame. After a few weeks the rolling tasting is completed and you return to your wine merchant to discuss your findings and purchase a case of your favorite, only to discover that it is sold out, and that 12 new and tempting wines have arrived on the container from Bordeaux.

If you're thorough about it, most of your evenings and all of your wine drinking will be consumed by the evaluative process, and you'll still only get to try a tiny sample of the wines on the market. Selecting wine is only supposed to be the overture, not the whole performance. Worse, your mixed case purchases can easily get ahead of your sampling, leaving you with scores of single bottles of never-tasted potentially great wine.

Store tastings

Many wine shops and people in the trade conduct wine tastings open to the public. Get on the mailing lists of as many wine shops in your commute-comfortable zone as possible. Most hold regular Saturday afternoon affairs. Many offer wine "classes" held on a series of weekday evening, or single-evening events. Most fine wine shops also offer formal dinners with wine held at restaurants. The Saturday affairs are typically free, the "classes" kept down to $40 per person, per session. You'll get to sample six to a dozen wines currently available at retail. The education of your palate and stocking of your cellar may be your goal, but the merchant who organizes the event has slightly different plans. He requires a good turnout followed by brisk sales. He's learned to keep the cost down to generate turnout, and usually serves ready-to-drink wines that are in ample supply. Wines in short supply, or of higher price, or that demand cellaring, will not generally be shown at introductory store tastings. They don't need a boost.

The better shops have gotten into a pattern of having one or two huge walk around tasting events a year. Dozens of distributors and importers pour wines that they donate. The admission charge is usually modest to none. If you can get the list ahead of time consult your web service (see below) to plan for the event since it is usually impossible to meaningfully taste more than 50 or so of the several hundred wines offered at such events. A discount is usually offered for wines ordered at or within a week of the event. The best wines may only be poured in the first hour before they run out, so arrive early and head for the good stuff first.

When wines with cellaring potential find their way into introductory tastings, they often are misinterpreted by the neophyte clientele. For example, the great, monstrously proportioned '81 Ch. Beaucastel was greeted with groans of derision at a tasting that I attended in 1984.

Advanced and private tastings

Introductory tastings are appreciated by beginners, but soon you'll be thirsting for something more sophisticated. Your localine merchant will keep you posted on his own events, but may be less forthcoming about the competition. You have to ask wholesalers and other customers who you meet in wine shops or at store tastings about private tasting groups and shops with more advanced events. Many large cities have wine appreciation societies that offer regular tasting series. Watch the internet listings such as the Wine Bulletin Board on ERobertParker.com, and localwineevents.com. Tasting events with a national draw are often advertised in the *Wine Spectator* magazine that you can pick up at most wine merchants. If you are willing to travel to Europe consult *Decanter* for listings. *The Wine Spectator* (winespectator.com) holds an annual 3-day Wine Experience, usually alternating between New York City and San Francisco, that is well worth attending. The Society of Wine Educators (Societyof-wineeducators.org) holds an annual two-week-long meeting in the summer that is open to the public and features a considerable amount of tasting. There is an annual Long Island, NY bash in August (LIwines.com). The Nantucket Wine Festival is held in May (Nantucketwinefestival.com). The Boston Wine Festival stretches for four months in the spring (Bostonwinefestival.net). The best tasting events are the free ones open by invitation only to the trade. This is where your local wine merchant can be leaned on if you are a really special customer. You would have to come as his assistant or as a volunteer pourer. If you fancy organizing a private wine tasting clique, then begin collecting names and phone numbers at store tastings, in wine shop aisles, or at national events. Full instructions are given in Chapter 22.

Buying older wines

Most fine red wines are released for sale to the public three to four years after the harvest. Some is held back by established wineries or in distribution channels, and a few retailers buy in such quantity that they maintain stock, but by and large the better wines disappear from retail shops years before reaching maturity.

When you do find wines with some age, their storage history is unknown. While chilled fine-wine rooms and warehouses are no guarantee of a favorable storage history, they do indicate that the wine is not currently being abused, and suggest that the proprietor is sensitive to proper wine storage. A wine shop that overheats in summer, on the other hand, should be shunned year round.

Most wineries, distributors, and retail outlets have inadequate capital and inadequate storage capacity to enable them to age significant supplies of the classic vintages. Such are the economics of the wine industry. Try to purchase sanely priced and properly cellared 1990 Bordeaux and you'll lament not having cellared these treasures when they were less expensive and more widely available.

Nevertheless, most fine wine merchants display at least a modest selection of older more mature wines, often segregated into a locked and hopefully temperature-controlled compartment. Initially you may avoid this section of the shop in favor of less-expensive recent releases. Unfortunately, limited human life expectancies don't afford the middle-aged connoisseur the luxury of a 20-year wait. The anticipation of palate deterioration after age 60 further restricts one's time frame. Your sales resistance will falter when you discover that you have a cellar full of great wines, but nothing ready to drink. You'll then purchase those older vintages for at least double what they would have cost when you began cellaring.

Right now (2006), twenty-one years after release, the 1982 Mouton Rothschild, acclaimed in *The Wine Advocate* as the best of a legendary vintage, is virtually unavailable at retail. If you do find it, expect to pay $500 a bottle. This is more than ten times the price at first release. Yet, when this wine finally matures, properly stored bottles will be obtainable only at a price that makes $500 seem reasonable.

When you buy older wines, buy only one bottle and, if you're assured that more is available from the same source, open it soon – even if not yet at perfection, it's probably already pretty good. If it's rotten, ask for a refund. If it's merely tolerable, you're only out the cost of one bottle. If it's great, grab a case.

Going to the source

Most enophiles still stock their cellars through traditional retail outlets, but the ultimate connoisseur also goes to the source for rare treasures, a few bottles of which have never left the winery that produced them. Wines have three levels of "sold out". The first level is reached when the distribution channels dry up and the winery decides that there's so little left that they can sell it all from the winery without having to share with the middlemen. Many top wineries sell all of their wine, or at least all of their special reserve, directly to adoring fans. This means that, so far as your local wine merchant is concerned, the wine is always sold out. Some wineries do it the easy (for them) way. You have to appear at the winery when they're open, on the release day if you want to be sure to get some, pay the retail cash-and-carry price, and lug the cases home. Joe Heitz sold most of his acclaimed '85 Martha's Vineyard that way. This system may be practical if you live in San Francisco, but for New Yorkers it's not.

To tap the national market, many boutique wineries have developed a wine-by-UPS trade. Once a year the folks on the mailing list get an order form indicating their allocation. The order form is usually accompanied by the winemaker's tasting notes. In some cases the allocation is just a few bottles. To maintain your place on the list you must purchase your allocation every year – great years as well as not so great. If you pass, there's a waiting list of thirsty enophiles who covet your allocation. A few months after they get your money, the UPS truck arrives. Delivery is timed for the spring when the weather is not too severe. Beaux Freres, Stoney Hill, and Williams & Selyem are but a few of the U.S. wineries with a direct sales program. Wines from the hottest properties like Screaming Eagle have a lively secondary market where the lucky holders of $500-a-bottle allocations sell their three-bottle tickets for double the winery price without ever having to take possession of the wine.

In France you can also get wine at the property. The smaller the chateau and the less famous it is, the better your odds. At Lafite only the latest vintage is for sale, and at the same price that you would pay back home – without the bother of transporting it. Several other Bordeaux properties will sell you the latest vintage as well. Again, these same wines are available at home for roughly the same price.

The second level of "sold out" is when the stock at the winery actually gets low. At that stage the wine disappears from behind the winery counter and the distributor's list, and what's left enters the winery's library (actually a wine cellar). Sometimes a large cache of a wine from a great vintage is held back for a second release at maturity at a much higher price. Wines in the library, or between releases, can sometimes be procured for special events, especially those with a publicity angle. Ask your wine merchant to sponsor an appointment.

Even an un-sponsored visit to the winery when the owner or manager happens to be in a good mood can do the trick. Call or write ahead for an appointment. Even a call from your motel on the morning of the proposed visit will often get you in. Don't even dream about free bottles. Carry and offer cash and don't haggle. By exchanging bottles for cash the wine maker can avoid bookkeeping, shipping, middlemen, and, god forbid, income tax. The folks who serve as tour guides and tasting room clerks to the hordes at the larger Napa wineries are never authorized to release anything but the latest vintage of the big volume wines. To get into the library stock you must talk your way up to the authorized party in the main office. That person will not be at the winery on weekends.

To have even a shot at the impossible-to-get wine you must know exactly what you want and have a rough idea of its retail value. If you don't specifically plead on bended knee for the 1974 Mayacamas, it will not be offered. Once the wine is offered and you have unflinchingly agreed to the asking price, there's nothing to lose by offering to save him the bother of opening the case and wrapping your bottle. Offer to take the whole case. You won't regret it.

The third stage of "sold out" is when there really is not a single bottle left at the winery. You are then out in the secondary market of auction houses, charity auctions, private trades, a few special wine shops, and the internet.

Internet Sales

ERobertParker.com has a section on their Wine Bulletin Board called the Commerce Corner devoted to sales and trades and tastings and wine country trips. There are many other sites that offer to sell you wine as well. Lots of wine is offered on EBay.com. Try wine.com, The Chicago Wine Company (tcwc.com), winebid.com, wineweb.com, winesearcher.com, winezap.com, wineaccess.com, and winecommune.com. Most major wine shops list their entire inventory (except for the 100 point items that are in reserve storage for allocation to special customers) and futures offerings on customer accessible web sites. You can pay by credit card and pick up the wine months later at your convenience, or have it shipped.

Chapter 17

❉❉❉❉❉❉❉❉❉❉❉❉❉❉❉❉❉❉❉❉❉❉❉

NEWSLETTERS & POCKET GUIDES

There are many who are eager to sell their tasting notes to you in the form of books, pocket guides, newsletters, and web sites.

Hugh Johnson's Pocket Wine Book

The first edition appeared in 1977 as *Hugh Johnson's Pocket Wine Encyclopedia*, and has been updated annually, the current (2007) $15 edition being the 30th. Prior to 1977 there were no annually updated guides to wine. Wine books, some with excellent wine reviews, came out from time to time, and became obsolete within a few years of publication. Nevertheless, the stubborn publishers waited as long as 10 years before updating, long after the last drop of blood had been extracted from the earlier edition.

Johnson's Pocketbook, although grown to 288 pages, is still narrow enough to fit into your pocket, and it has a sturdy hard cover. It provides thumbnail evaluations of 5,000 properties from 22 countries around the world. The ratings are based upon information gathered from a variety of consultants. Johnson has not personally tasted all the wines. There are good vintage charts and descriptions of vintage characteristics for all regions. Johnson uses a five-point rating scale (0 to 4 stars) but the rating is only for the property as a whole. Occasionally there are a different number of stars for the reserve wine, but again the stars do not differentiate vintages. Recommended vintages for the property are listed in boldface (ready), blue type (really ready) or light type (not ready) with no further differentiation, except for France and Portugal where an apostrophe indicates an especially good year (e.g. 90'). This two or three-point rating scale is not optimal, and there are never vintage specific tasting notes. In comparison, most newsletters use a 50-point rating scale. The apostrophe given to the 75' La Mission identifies it along with many others of the vintage as highly recommended, but fails to distinguish it as a monumental wine. Perhaps the 31st edition will add a second apostrophe, expanding the scale to four points. Vintages that are not listed are not recommended, or perhaps they were not tasted, leaving the reader in some doubt. Johnson rates over 300 Bordeaux properties, which is excellent, but the worded tasting notes are for the property as a whole, not for individual vintages. The alphabetical ratings of 250 obscure German wines are especially helpful. Elsewhere, Johnson's encyclopedia slips. For California wines he rarely gives separate ratings for the reserve and special selection wines that collectors' prize. Mondavi Cab is just that. There are no vintage ratings for the reserve Cab, and no apostrophes. There are several useful pages of wine and food pairings and extensive vintage charts on the inside covers.

This is the bible for beginners. When the annual edition comes out, the ratings of new vintages are already months behind the first barrel tasting reports in the newsletters, and the opening futures prices are history. For futures and new release purchases this delay is intolerable. For wine selection in restaurants the delay is unimportant, portability being uppermost. Serious collectors quickly graduate to the newsletters which provide more up-to-date and detailed information. Parker's Palm Pilot version, which I have not examined, is a high-tech alternative.

Using the Pocket Wine Book (or Parker Palm) in Restaurants

With the Pocket you can glean any restaurant wine list. Your dinner companions would however be most impressed if you ordered confidently without benefit of a reference book. Worse, the sommelier will disappear for hours if you spend more than 15 seconds with the carte de vins. First, remember that you only have to zero in on one or two wines, not critique or even peruse the entire list. Focus on the region that the wine list seems to specialize in. The one wine from Argentina may stand out by its uniqueness, but it probably won't be a stand out wine. If you want to discretely consult your Pocketbook or Parker Palm, stop by in the afternoon and examine the wine list in the lobby. The occasional restaurant will put its wine list on a web page, or will send it to you on request as an email attachment, or by traditional mail, and some will allow you to take their wine list home. Another good ploy is to examine the wine list while waiting to be seated. Some vain individuals conduct their Pocket or Palm searches in the restaurant's bathroom.

The Wine Advocate

This was the trend setter and is still regarded as the best of the newsletters. It will set you back 65-dollars annually (Domestic) for six issues. Up to 72 pages and over 1,000 wines are reviewed in every issue. The net cost is only 1 cent per review. French wines from Bordeaux, Burgundy, and the Rhone are comprehensively, even exhaustively, reviewed. The major Bordeaux vintages are reviewed in cask before the futures sales, after bottling, and every few years thereafter. Burgundies are also reviewed in great detail. Serious wines from California (Cabernets), Italy (Barolos), and Germany are covered as well. Humbler breeds such as Chenin Blanc and White Zin are virtually ignored. When a Port vintage is declared, Parker reviews it. Vinous excellence from any corner of the world quickly finds its way into the pages of *The Wine Advocate*.

A table of contents on the front page is arranged in the order in which the articles appear, with pagination. The issues are devoid of graphics, save corkscrew logo. They're neatly stapled and conveniently 3-hole punched. The typesetting is sharp and clear, on high quality paper, with the properties listed alphabetically, property names in bold type at the left margin, and price and rating cores conveniently located on the right margin, a nice feature if you only want to read about the 90+ wines. Retail prices are listed, as are the telephone numbers and email addresses of U.S. wineries and importers of the others.

The wine descriptions are excellent, lucid, and accurate when compared with my personal tasting, and are accompanied by predicted cellaring potential. The most pleasant feature of this newsletter is the use of lively sentences as opposed to strings of adjectives. Vintage charts are frequently included in the issues. Articles are often accompanied by summary tables listing the wines by ratings and in quality categories so you can quickly find the wines of the vintage and the sleeper wines and then go to those tasting notes selectively. All the Bordeaux wines are listed alphabetically in one long list so you don't have to know which commune Batailley is in to quickly find its' tasting notes.

The internet version, ERobertParker.com, is a recent addition at $99 a year. It accesses all of the wine reviews from the paper version going back several years. You can call up the review of any wine and vintage very quickly. There are also several additional features including less-formal reviews from dinner engagements and such. A Wine Bulletin Board feature is free and accessible without a subscription.

All of the Bordeaux reviews are by Robert M. Parker, Jr., who has been dubbed "The planet's most powerful critic." Besides being a prodigious tasting feat, this promises, and delivers, consistency over successive vintages versus a publication such as the *Wine Spectator* where the reviewers can vary from year to year. Parker has recently added several co-authors, but each of them tends to concentrate on their own geographic areas, so there still is within-region consistency, but not between-region consistency. The writing style exudes genuine excitement for the best wines, which in turn sets off explosions at the telephones and web sites of the nation's wine shops.

The reader's dilemma is whether to get the mailed paper version, the web version, or both. If you are in the stocking up phase of your life span, then a few days difference can be crucial to getting the single-case allocation that is sitting at your local wine shop before the other subscribers get there and before the staff at the shop gets around to examining their copy and adjusting prices and allocations. The paper *Advocate* is mailed first class usually on a Monday afternoon and two days before the issue is put on to the website around 4 AM Eastern time (1 AM in California) with a notice on the front page that it is up and an email reminder to you if you request it. If you live in Maryland then the paper version will get to you first. If you live in Oregon then the web update should arrive first. If you subscribe to the paper version you probably go to the post office daily anyway, so you will be alerted by the package that it has arrived, but only the fanatics will check the web site Wednesday mornings when a new issue is due, so be sure to ask for the email notice. It would be a great bother to print out the issue to take to the wine shop, and a juggle to bounce between *The Advocate's* website and the wine shop's online inventory. Therefore, for in person or on line purchasing the paper version is best. Since the access on the web site to individual reviews going back many years is instant, you need the web version to most easily review the status of older wines, restaurant wine lists, and the wines featured in a wine shop mailing. The final judgment is that you probably need both versions.

The impact of the reviews on the market place is the drawback of The Advocate. It's so influential that the 90-point wines go quickly. What better lead-in could there be for the other excellent but less-widely circulated newsletters?

International Wine Cellar

Stephen Tanzer started out in 1985 with a market survey of the New York City wine shops, with occasional tasting notes. It was aptly called the *New York Wine Cellar*. Over the years the focus has evolved to that of a traditional newsletter, and new name. Six issues per year for $70 print, $80 web (Internationalwinecellar.com), or $120 combined. Roughly 500 wine reviews per issue. The coverage is excellent. The subscription list of *The International Wine Cellar* is, fortunately, shorter than that of *The Wine Advocate*. All the major wine regions such as Bordeaux, Portugal, Rhone, Oregon, etc. are covered.

The Cellar is highly recommended and the web version is just as easy to navigate as the Parker site.

However, there are a few really annoying features. The paper issues are not three-hole punched, and the reviews are in paragraph style so that the 100-point rating scores, which are not in bold type, are buried within the paragraphs instead of being brought to the margin. There are no summary tables to help you out here either. For example, in the July/August 2006 issue there is an article titled "New Releases from Australia." Approximately 825 wines are reviewed, which is a phenomenal achievement, and the individual reviews seem excellent, but if you want to know which wine was the best you have to wade through 825 wines to find that it is the Penfolds 2004 Block 42 Cab Kalimna Barossa ($425) score 98 (unless I missed a higher rated wine). By the time you find it your favorite shop may have sold their tiny allotment to a faster reader.

Connoisseur's Guide to California Wines

This highly regarded newsletter was begun 30 years ago by Charles Olken. He and associate Stephen Eliot presumably do all the tasting, which should offer consistency. The *Guide* only reviews wines from California. If your tastes are eclectic then this will not be your only subscription. If you are big on California wines then Connoisseur's is nevertheless a must-get because of the extensive coverage and second opinion it offers. No other newsletter covers California with near the breadth and frequency offered. It is not unusual to find reviews of over 100 wines on a theme, and all the major varietals are reviewed – frequently. There are excellent introductory articles to each review, and the 100-point scale score is conveniently placed at the margin. They also use a cookie-scale with the best wines getting one to three cookies. The cookies are helpful if you want to scan quickly for the best wines. The type is larger than the competition uses, and the reviews are not crammed together, which makes for comfortable reading. On the back cover you will find a summary table listing all the wines reviewed in the issue, and it is three-hole punched, ready for your binder. $60 paper, $80 web, $112 combined. cgcw.com.

California Grapevine

Once a week or so the publisher Nicholas A. Ponomareff gets together in San Diego with his expert panel of tasters and they taste a dozen or so wines of a theme. The 20-point scale scores are averaged and listed from best to worst, with averaged score, Nick's score, and equivalent 100-point score following a brief assembled tasting note. This format has not changed for 32 years. Six times a year these tasting reports are printed and mailed to the subscribers. No matter that the same theme may be reviewed the next week, each session is reported on its own. The problem here is that hardly any wine category except a one-property vertical can be covered adequately these days with a review of only a dozen wines. The best part of this publication is the extensive series of wine book reviews. $38 Calgrapevine.com

Wine shop newsletters

Most wine shops maintain a mailing list. At regular or irregular intervals, you'll receive invitations to store sponsored tastings, notices of regional wine events, recipes, reviews of recent arrivals, futures sales, specials of the month, inventories, tasting results, and even descriptions of the owner's wine country travels. There's no charge. The reviews of the wines available for purchase must be taken in context. These publications are store advertisements. By all means get on several mailing lists to keep abreast of tastings, prices, and availability. Some shops offer specials to their mailing list or email customers before they advertise them in the newspaper. Beware any wine that is "the Lafite of California." You'd probably be disappointed. I was.

Wine tasting Web sites

There are several free websites that feature tasting notes, either by the web master or contributed. In no particular order here are just a few of them: Wineloverspage.com, Thewinedoctor.com, Yakshaya.com, and Winereviewonline.com. If you Google "wine" you can probably find many more. The plus here is that you will not be competing with the subscription list of *The Wine Advocate*.

Winery newsletters

Many domestic wineries keep a mailing list. Some merely keep the faithful posted on the wine maker's tasting notes. Others announce release-day parties where you drive out to the winery, taste the new wines, picnic to the strains of a jazz band, and fill your trunk. The mailing list is often the vehicle for a U.P.S.-direct sales program, in some cases the only way for East Coasters to obtain the wine. Most are leaning towards website and email communications. Check out your favorite winery on the internet. The newsletters usually give the web addresses following their reviews.

Auction house mailings

Older wines are regularly auctioned off in Chicago, New York, San Francisco, Los Angeles, London, Geneva, and Amsterdam. You can attend the auction in person, including the fabulous pre-sale tasting, or leave your high bid with the auctioneer for shipping or delayed pick up. Get on the mailing list for dates and detailed instructions. Auctions are the only legal way for private American collectors to sell their wines: Morrell's for New York (Morrellwineauctions.com), Christie's for Chicago, Los Angeles, London and Amsterdam (Christies.com). The seller pays a commission of 15% of the hammer price to the auctioneer and the buyer pays 10% over the hammer price (plus shipping).

Wine Spectator and Decanter

These slick, advertisement-filled, large-circulation magazines are *the* source of wine news, focusing respectively on the US and

Europe. Browse through one at your local wine merchant and by all means take out a subscription, but rely on your newsletters for purchasing advice. These publications do have extensive tasting notes, and many do rely on them for purchasing advice. Both are $50 a year (Winespectator.com and Decanter.com). The *Wine Spectator* also has a web version for $50 or $75 combined. The *Wine Enthusiast* (Winemag.com.), which started out as only a wine accessory catalog now publishes a magazine that mirrors the format of the *Wine Spectator.*

Food and Wine Magazine

This magazine covers mostly food with a relatively useless wine article or two in the back of each issue.

The Wine Price File

This unique publication tracks the auction and store prices of fine wines. Its best use would seem to be for the trade and upscale restaurants that want to frequently re-price rare and older wines. For the private collector who is not trying to sell his wine, this publication has little value. Wineprices.com $50/year.

Chapter 18

KEEPING TRACK OF YOUR INVENTORY

When I was younger and owned only three cases of wine, my memory easily kept track of my stock. My brain is now older and loaded with decades of trivia, and my wine stock is greatly expanded. I knew that it was time to get organized when I couldn't put my hands on the two bottles of 1970 Latour that I was positive I bought 30 years previous, and certainly would have remembered opening.

A bookkeeping system must be simple to install and maintain. It must, at minimum, tell you what you have and where it is. It would be nice to also know what the experts have to say about it and its expected years of drinkability.

Computer inventories

Specialized wine inventory software is advertised, but I have no personal experience with it.

Supermarkets and large wine shops stay on line continuously. When stock arrives it's entered into the computer. Bar code stickers are printed and applied – if they're not already on the label. The bar codes automatically adjust inventory and ring up your purchases as they cross the check-out counter. The manager can have a daily printout of his inventory. When you call to find out if he has any 2000 Pichon Lalande left and the current price, he can respond instantly.

On line systems would be ridiculous for a home cellar where days often intervene between entries. With a home computer you must turn it on, call up the program, and manually type in every entry. When you arrive home with a mixed case, the logging in operation can easily stretch to 20 minutes. Once you fall behind on your entries, it's all over.

If you already have the software, and the determination to keep up with it, then please let me know how long you really kept up with it. My computer is fabulous for writing and editing manuscripts, but maintaining an electronic wine inventory doesn't seem worth the effort.

File card inventories

File cards are less expensive than computers and are easier to arrange and maintain. Use one file card for each property. List the vintages that you own and the number of bottles – in pencil – and the bin number (e.g. Latour: bin 3 '70 - 2; '75 - 1; '82 - 3; '86 - 2; '90 - 6). Add, if you wish, the Parker score and range of drinkability years. As you add or consume, adjust the pencil entries. All of the Bordeaux cards go together alphabetically in one section of your card box. Use dividers with write on tabs to identify the sections.

On the newsletter

In many newsletters, vintage reviews are accompanied by a table that lists and scores all of the wines reviewed. If this is a vintage that you plan to patronize in a major way, then keep a running pencil notation of your holdings directly on that table, and your log will be bound together with the relevant reviews. *The Wine Advocate* regularly publishes property-specific vintage charts for all of the major wine regions. Simply circle the entries for the wines that you own.

Label notation

Label notations are simply pencil notations directly on the bottle label of purchase date, source, and price. When your heirs open the

'86 Lafite, they will marvel at its relatively low purchase price; just as we marvel today at the low release price of the '61 Petrus.

Bin organization

In case you're beginning to feel guilty about the casual organization of your cellar, let me hasten to note that the vast majority of cellar masters don't bother with any of the four systems just described. Most have pretty good memories of what they own, and far more important things in life to keep track of. However, an organized bin arrangement is essential. I recommend a geographical organization. If you have only a dozen Bordeaux, collect them all in one bin. If you have more, sort them by right bank versus left bank, or by commune, or, finally, by property. When I have a half-dozen or so from each of several properties, I let two properties share a bin, one on the left, the other on the right. Prepare a file card for each bin, as described above, but hang it by a tea cup hook or roofing nail screwed or nailed in to the top or bottom of each bin.

The alternative to this geographical approach is a chronological arrangement with a bin for each vintage. Each Bordeaux or California Cab. or Burgundy vintage gets its own bin or bins. I use a geographical arrangement, but have a few special chronological bins for, for example, my small collection of '74 California Cabs. I also have a future horizontal tasting bin with one each of a dozen '87 California Cabs, and another with a dozen unready '82 Bordeaux. A diagonal string across the front signals "**tasting bin, keep out**." Put all your reds on one wall, whites of another, or use one wall for American wines, another for Europeans. Finally, I have a "**ready bin**" containing wines that I'm anxious to try or that are in danger of decline. I can safely delegate a guest to select from that bin without risking my '75 Latour.

Chapter 19

※※※※※※※※※※※※※※※※※※※※※※

PLANNING AHEAD

Many enophiles have no conscious purchasing strategy. Once a week they stop at their favorite wine shop, perhaps drawn by the camaraderie at the Friday afternoon, free store tasting. Every Friday they acquire another mixed case in order to qualify for the 5% mixed case discount. If you own this haphazard approach, then in the long run you'll regret it. Serious wines often require long term cellaring. Your selections should integrate anticipated maturity with anticipated need.

How, I hear you wonder, does Dr. Gold expect me to anticipate my vinous desires 15 years in advance? The appeal of a home wine cellar is to have mature wine on hand whenever an occasion arises. You can't predict your daily drinking rate 15 years in advance, but you can predict your averaged needs. To aid your prognostication, I offer a catalog of the occasions in anticipation of which you may wish to lay away fine wine. By the end of this process, a 1,000 to 2,000 bottle cellar may evolve into a reasonable goal.

(a) Weddings

On such an important occasion you serve the same wine or wines to the entire assemblage. Estimate one bottle of Champagne or equivalent for every six adults. You can purchase the Champagne at the last minute, so no cellar space is required. If the only other wine is a red dinner wine, estimate one 750 ml bottle for every three adults that drink wine, which comes to one case of red for every 36 people – three cases per hundred. Magnums are especially impressive, mature more slowly, hold their maturity longer against uncertain wedding dates, serve the typical banquet table of six to eight people, and halve the amount of double decanting should there be sediment. For large families six cases of red for 200 guests is about right. This assumes they all drink wine. Discount for children, teetotalers, and those that favor beer and distilled spirits, so given the typical American palate maybe a bottle for every six adults is more realistic.

If the wedding reception is held at your home, the site of your wine cellar, then a mature red with sediment can show to its potential. If an uncooperative child or in-law demands a wedding at a distant location, then the logistics of sedimented reds could be daunting. The location of a future wedding can be predicted at birth. The traditional arrangement is for the bride's father to pay for the wedding, including the alcohol, and to hold the affair in the bride's home town. The groom's father is only responsible for the wedding rehearsal dinner, which is held the night before the wedding and is attended only by the wedding party. Therefore, cellar enough red wine for the entire wedding for girls, but only a few bottles for boys. If you're currently unmarried, or plan to be soon, then don't forget to anticipate your own first, second, or third wedding. The quality of the wedding wine should relate to the sophistication of the guests and your desire to impress them. In some families a first growth Bordeaux would be wasted, while other families would notice. If this occasion doesn't call out the Lafite, what will?

You must have an adequate supply of each wine. If you were to serve one wine to some tables and another to other tables it would lead observant guests to suspect that you were serving two qualities of wine to two classes of guest. This would be an unpardonable breach of etiquette. The head table must drink exactly what everyone else gets. If you place bottles of the same two competing red wines at every table, you'll avoid the first gaffe, but will invite instead the criticism that you're turning your child's wedding into a wine tasting seminar, which is probably precisely your secret intention. You would also need extra wine glasses. To avoid the need for six cases of Lafite, serve four wines sequentially – Champagne for the toast, White Burgundy with the appetizer, Lafite with the entree, and Vintage Port with dessert.

If the wedding is being catered at a commercial establishment, be certain that your bringing of the wine and their supplying of the glasses are agreed to in advance, in writing, before you sign a contract. Ask to see samples of the glasses they will use. (No, you may not use plastic cups.) Caterers rely on liquor mark-up for a major share of their profit, so be prepared for a substantial corkage fee. There probably will be a bar with bartender in addition to wine poured at table. You can leave single bottles of unusual wines with the bartender.

(b) Other special occasions

For birthdays, anniversaries, and holiday gatherings you might predict four events per year times three bottles, usually red, for a total of one case per year. You'll want wines that are sure to please, which means top quality wines that you've recently tasted and enjoyed.

(c) Dinner parties in your home

Proceeding to smaller events, a typical expectation is to have four guests over to dinner once a month. Three bottles of dry wine should be sufficient, plus a half-bottle of dessert wine. At these events you can experiment with wines you've not recently tasted, as you will have back-up alternates waiting below.

When dinner guests bring nugacious wine

Dinner guests will occasionally arrive at your door with what they consider the obligatory bottle of undistinguished $10 plonk that they picked up on the way over. What does the consummate host do when the 1945 Mouton is ready to open and the well meaning guests walk in with a bottle of 2005 Mouton Cadet? If you don't open the Cadet the guests will be insulted. If you do and serve both wines side by side, won't they be embarrassed at the contrast?

Figure 19-1. Four guests over for dinner once a month.

Go ahead and serve the two wines side by side – first wine versus tertiary. Serve them blind, hiding the labels inside numbered bags. If the brought wine is a poor match and you've got a more appropriate contrast in your cellar, switch *your* wine – e.g. if a regular '96 Mondavi Cab walks in the door, fetch the same vintage of Mondavi Reserve Cab from your cellar. Whatever you do, you must open and graciously serve the brought bottle. No exceptions. Never ask the guest if you really have to serve his wine. He'll always give you permission to pass, but will be grievously insulted nevertheless.

Buying by the case

You can be spared unpleasant surprises when the boss comes to dinner if you purchase by the solid case. The bottles within a case of wine are all from the same lot and share common shipping and storage experiences. Bottles from one case will evolve over time, but not precipitously. With a good wine, gustatory boredom won't set in if you serve it but once or twice a year. *Au contraire!* You'll be overcome by the pleasant anticipation of revisiting a past pleasure. The wine that you serve to the boss should, above all, be predictable.

If you stock up with scores of solo bottles, then whatever you select to drink will be the last of its kind, leaving you reluctant to open anything. What scares most people from purchasing 12 bottles of one wine is the fear that it will turn out poorly. They hedge their bets by buying one of everything. The fear of getting 12 identical dogs is nevertheless quite valid. Advice from unimpeachable sources or, better, personal comparative tasting is *de rigueur*.

The long-term cellaring of one bottle lots is a no-win situation. If your now irreplaceable 20-year-stored single proves a winner, you'll chastise yourself for not having bought more when you could. If it turns out to be yuk, you won't be happy either.

The one-of-this-and-one-of-that approach also insures that many of the wines will be opened too early or too late. You'll be forever frustrated trying to decide when each wine is ready to drink. Another motive for solo rather than case cellaring is to have greater variety available. Unfortunately, 1,000 different labels are nearly impossible to keep track of without elaborate inventory systems. Solo purchases for cellaring are a good idea only when you're collecting specific labels or vintages for future vertical or horizontal tastings. Solo purchases also freeze you out of the futures market where the purchase of half-case or full-case lots is required.

Magnums

With dinner parties it's usually fun to serve two contrasting wines rather than two identical bottles or a single magnum. If this is your pattern, then avoid magnums. They're pretty to look at and fun to fondle, but except for really big affairs you'll rarely have an occasion to open one – and they usually bear a premium price tag.

(d) Dinner at their house

As the reputation of your cellar grows you may be expected to bring wine more often than dessert when invited to a friend's home for dinner. A reasonable expectation would be to bring one bottle to another's home each month. When the dinner is across the street it's easy enough to go for a replacement should the bottle bomb, or should you discover twice as many guests as you were led to expect. However, if you've traveled an hour, you're stuck.

The opposite problem arises when you bring a cellar treasure and discover everyone swilling palate-numbing cocktails or beer before dinner or that the main entree is hot dogs with barbecue sauce served on the lawn.

The ice chest solution

The only safe way to travel to dinner at "their" house is with a cellar assortment in an insulated ice chest. Discretely park it near the coat closet when you arrive – not in the hot trunk of your car. The easy-to-carry, one-handled Igloo Playmate works nicely and holds up to eight bottles. A 12" interior length to match the length of a wine bottle is the critical dimension to seek. See Chapter 20 for additional details.

(e) Brown bagging at restaurants

As your palate and wine cellar mature you may find dissatisfaction with the selection and pricing of restaurant wine lists. This becomes a serious problem if you love your wine but hate to cook. You'll be reduced to the prospect of '96 Ridge Monte Bello with hamburgers at home and NV vin rouge ordinaire with truffles at the Hilton. To survive, restaurateurs must protect their profit margin, much of which comes from liquor sales. If they're permitted to serve liquor, they are therefore loath to set a BYO precedent. New restaurants that don't yet have liquor licenses welcome BYO's, but the policy changes as soon as the license is granted. An occasional enlightened restaurateur with a liquor license will discretely permit brown bagging. Expect a corkage fee.

Figure 19-2. Obtain in advance an empty bottle of the cheapest wine on the restaurant's wine list, perhaps by rummaging in their trash barrel.

Try to get prior approval, in private, personal face-to-face consultation with the manager or owner. Over the phone rarely succeeds. This usually means patronizing the restaurant at least once before asking for BYO privileges. Your best chance is at an unpopular restaurant on a slow night. You might not be allowed in the main dining room with your own wine, but a large party in a private dining room that is not legally considered part of the restaurant is usually viewed more benevolently. You can check for BYO places on ERobertparker.com's free Bulletin Board which has a section reserved for BYO info.

If your most heartfelt supplications are rebuffed, there's still a one-shot, non-recommended, deceitful technique that I describe only for its amusement value. The key is to present a fait accompli. Transport the bottle, corkscrew, and even wine glasses discretely, in a shopping bag or large purse. Get your party seated in a prominent location, use the water glasses and bread dishes, and order lavishly. When the waiter is otherwise engaged, quickly uncork the bottle and place it and your glasses boldly on the table as if they really belonged there. Pour and enjoy. It's then up to the management to create a fuss in the midst of their main dining room, disturbing other guests and risking a walk-out that would leave an unused reservation, soiled place settings, and half-cooked meals, all with no compensation for the wait staff or management. When faced with this effrontery most restaurateurs will merely admonish you never to do it again, to which you plead ignorance of the rules and humbly promise to be good the next time.

If management's objection is more spirited, you could inquire as to just what you're supposed to do with an opened $500 bottle of '82 Pichon Lalande that will die of oxygen poisoning within the hour if not consumed. The manager may cite state or local ordinances to bolster his BYO ban. He's often correct. He will nevertheless often bend the rules to keep the peace.

Once, when asked to re-cork and store their bottle in the coat room at a posh out-of-town restaurant, one daunting reader threatened to lead her boisterous party out to chug the wine in the parking lot while awaiting the food. They all arose from the table, giving the impression that they were actually going to execute their daring plan. The manager quickly decided to grant a one-time exemption to his state's liquor control laws.

A more devious subterfuge that has never to my direct knowledge been implemented, and is not recommended because it's probably illegal, would be to obtain in advance an empty bottle of the cheapest plonk on the restaurant's wine list, either by rummaging in their trash barrels, or by purchase at a wine shop. Decant your cellar treasure into the decoy bottle in a convenient bathroom close by or even within the restaurant. Sneak the loosely re-corked bottle into the restaurant in a large shopping bag or purse. Order the cheap wine and instruct the waiter to open it but then let it breathe on your table prior to pouring. When no one is looking, switch bottles.

Even the hypothetical discussion of such ploys may not be appreciated by some of your friends, while others may find their execution to be the high point of the evening. The archaic liquor control laws deserve some bashing, perhaps even civil disobedience. A fair corkage fee would increase restaurant patronage by enophiles.

When dealing with your favorite local eatery a friendly approach to the management, an offer of a modest corkage fee, and a glass of wine for the owner is recommended. The management might also find comfort if you offer to bring the bottle by in the afternoon before the restaurant opens, and will be more flexible if you have chosen an off day for your dinner, and promise to also order something off the wine list.

(f) Dinner at home for one or two

At midweek intimate dinners for two, and especially for those who dine alone, a full 750 ml bottle may be excessive if you wish to avoid obliterating the rest of the evening. Upon opening you could immediately pour half the bottle into an empty 375 ml bottle, cork, and refrigerator-store until the next night. You could also use a nitrogen system to keep oxygen away from the unused wine for a few days. Nevertheless, it's safer and simpler to have an assortment of chateau-filled half (375 ml) bottles in your cellar. Most top producers bottle some of their wine that way. The surcharge for the smaller format is surprisingly modest. If this consumption pattern fits, then it's well worth the extra trouble to ferret out half bottles. Some shops specialize in odd sizes. Some do not but will special order for you. I've cellared some of my favorite wines in both half and full bottle formats.

(g) Wine tastings

Many serious students of wine consume more of it at tastings than at all other venues combined. With foresight you can prepare your cellar for your turns as tasting host.

A horizontal tasting compares similar wines from one vintage year. Imagine how exciting it would be if you could now arrange from your cellar a horizontal tasting of the legendary '61 Bordeaux. Most of these wines are, unfortunately, consumed. The rare bottle that shows up in a shop or at auction is prohibitively priced and has probably come from a private cellar where it has been stored beyond your control for more than 40 years. It's already difficult to find the best of the great '82 or '90 Bordeaux. Even some top California and Oregon wines from anything but the most recent release are impossible to locate.

In anticipation of the horizontal tastings that you'll want to sponsor, wait for the next great year, and then collect 18 of the best wines. Some of the most highly rated or hardest to find should be bought in half or full case lots. The most common mistake is to collect only one bottle of each wine. Horizontal tastings of great vintages can be repeated with increasing pleasure. Once you've gone to the trouble of selecting and locating the wines, grab at least three. Unless the theme's already been served by your wine merchant, arrange, on first release, a private tasting of those highly rated wines from the vintage that are available in the marketplace. The knockouts at the tasting can then be stocked in case lots. Save the second and third bottles for horizontal tastings at roughly ten year intervals. Husband the tasting notes and guest list from each decadal tasting, and bring them out for the group to update. What better excuse for a reunion of wine associates? These tastings will also give you updates on the progress of the wines which you bought by the case.

A vertical tasting compares wines of one property from a series of vintages. Vertical tastings of a property are generally once-in-a-lifetime affairs, so you only need single bottles. In anticipation of verticals, collect a single bottle of every decent or near decent vintage of your favorite properties. Go back as far as availability and your budget will allow. As each new vintage is released, update your holdings. The prime time to schedule the event is when the property releases a real winner but some is still available for purchase. Segregate the bottles for the vertical into isolation chambers (i.e. dedicated bins with don't touch labels). As I mentioned before, I use a string tied diagonally across the front of the bin.

(h) Selling wine

It doesn't make a lot of sense to buy at retail with the intention of selling at wholesale. Yet, despite the best intentions, the vicissitudes of life sometimes force a sale. Death, illness, divorce, and business failure are the most common reasons. This is the moment when your relationship with your wine merchant is put to the test. It's currently illegal in the United States for private parties to sell wine to one another. Nevertheless, whole cellars occasionally change hands, albeit discretely. The only legal way to sell your wine is at auction, by which venue you'll collect about 75% of what the high bidder pays. Lots of wine is also offered by individuals on internet sites, EBay.com being the biggest.

(i) Friendly storage

Sooner or later a friend still in the nomadic stage of life or having to abandon his cellar but not his wine following marital discord, will want to store his wine in your cellar. You surely don't want a lack of cellar space to stand in the way at such a desperate time, although a written disclaimer of liability for expensive caches is not a bad idea.

(j) Gifting wine

Mature wines make great gifts for weddings, housewarmings, birthdays, Christmas, and of course cellar christenings. For major gifts a full case in its original wooden crate is sure to impress.

(k) Your wake

Wouldn't you like to share a final wine experience with your friends should you die before depleting your cellar? An assortment of those cellar treasures that are ready at the time would be a fitting send-off to serve with the food at your wake, to be followed by your finest dessert wine and vintage port. A wake should be a gala affair that celebrates the life of the departed. Make your wishes known to those who are likely to be making the arrangements, and attach this paragraph to your last will and testament. Fearing non compliance, and unwilling to miss the party, I hosted my own pre-wake on my 60th birthday, and plan to repeat on my 70th etc.

Your wine cellar legacy

While considering endings, instructions might also be left for the disposition of your cellar lest a court-appointed executor bring in a callous wine merchant who will snap up your rare wines at 40% of their retail value. Surely someone in the family, perhaps your grandchildren, will in time come to appreciate what will by then be irreplaceable treasures. This may be the only way that your grandchildren will remember you.

Summing up

If you've been keeping score, then you likely have reached an annual total consumption of around 10 cases, or 2.5 bottles per week. For devotees of cellar-worthy red Bordeaux, 15 years of storage is not excessive. Ten cases x 15 years yields a 150 case, 1,800 bottle cellar. To convert 150 cases to cellar dimensions in feet or meters, refer back to the simple calculations of Chapter 11.

Figure 19-3. The wake. Sharing a final (or semi-final) wine cellar experience with your friends.

Chapter 20

❊❊❊❊❊❊❊❊❊❊❊❊❊❊❊❊❊❊❊❊❊❊❊❊

WINE ACCESSORIES

When an enophile receives a bottle of wine as a gift, he either consumes it in short order, or adds it to untasted tiers in the cellar. In either case it's soon out of sight and out of mind. But when an enophile receives a new and useful wine accessory, such as a Screwpull corkscrew, it's pressed into frequent, appreciative service.

Wine accessories can be found in most wine shops and upscale housewares shops. Several mail order firms deal exclusively with wine accessories. When buying by catalog you select on the basis of a picture and a carefully crafted text. No all of the items that appear useful actually are so. These reviews are offered to help you discriminate between the useful and the merely decorative.

Wine accessory catalogs

Two U.S. firms sell wine accessories out of attractive mail order catalogs. They are both reputable, and they both want to hear from you. Their mailing lists are their life blood. Catalogs alone are modest gifts, but enophiles who have never perused one typically greet them with enthusiasm. Tell them I sent you. They are:

International Wine Accessories, IWAwine.com, and
Wine Enthusiast, Wineenthusiast.com.

Wine videos

Watch it once, with a yawn, and then it gathers dust. Just as with movie videos, it makes little sense to purchase one that you'll never want to watch a second time. They're generally low budget and a poor substitute for actual travel and tasting in wine country.

Wine newsletters

Enophiles who have not yet discovered the newsletters react with jubilation upon discovering a good one. Subscription information can be difficult to obtain from wine shops because they don't want all their customers chasing the same few 100-point wines. Reviews and ordering information can be found in Chapter 17. Most serious enophiles already subscribe to a newsletter, so unless you check in advance with a spouse, a gift subscription could prove redundant. The subscription department of the newsletter should be able to check the subscription list for you as well. For those who already subscribe to one newsletter, a competing publication provides a welcomed second opinion.

Three-ring binder for newsletters

Most of the newsletters come pre-punched for a 3-ring binder. The binder keeps the issues together and in proper sequence, which facilitates use of the annual index. A fat binder is also more difficult to misplace than single issues. This item is found in stationery stores. If you're gifting a newsletter subscription before the first issue arrives, then present an empty binder with the name of the newsletter printed on the spine.

Wine books

The book you are reading can be sent directly as a gift.

There are some excellent books that evaluate wines, but the information becomes dated too quickly for me to meaningfully review the market in this book. Start with the shelves at your local bookseller, where the selection is modest but you can examine actual copies.

The *Wine Spectator* has an active publishing and direct sales program for the books that it publishes, and Robert Parker's books are available through his *Wine Advocate* newsletter or web site ERobertParker.com. Several wine books are also offered in wine-accessory catalogs.

In addition, there is one specialized wine book seller:

The Wine Appreciation Guild (Wineappreciation.com), which publishes this book, is primarily wholesale, but may serve individuals in exceptional cases.

Amazon.com has a good selection of wine books as well.

Temperature controlled wine locker

This is the big splurge item that every apartment or hot climate dwelling enophile dreams about. The wine accessory catalogs devote many pages to them and are eager to provide telephonic consultation. You can also get a more modest 20 to 50 bottle wine refrigerator at the Home Depot or from a wine accessory catalog at little more than $10 per bottle capacity.

Cellar logbook

I favor a blank bound book for my temperature logs. For inventory notations I use file cards. Fancy wine cellar logbooks are merely decorative.

Thermometer

To maintain a meaningful cellar temperature record, it's necessary to assign at least one thermometer to permanent cellar duty. Place it once and never move it. Do not get a recording thermometer because it records too much, generating 52 inked charts per year. Record the temperature (and humidity) in your cellar logbook a few times each month. The best thermometers use mercury in glass. This is a good gift for someone who is contemplating wine cellar construction.

Thermobottle

The air temperature in a cellar or refrigerated locker can change quickly when you open the door. A thermometer inside a water-filled wine bottle damps those air temperature shifts, giving an accurate reading of the temperature of your wine. Drill a hole in a cork. Insert the cork into a water-filled wine bottle, and slide the thermometer in, using Vaseline to ease the passage. Make sure that the range of the thermometer scale that you'll be reading is not obscured by the cork. Pick a bottle with relatively clear read through-able glass.

Hygrometer

It measures humidity. Every cellar master must have one. They are available from hardware stores and through wine-accessory catalogs. Some may need high end calibration (see Chapter 8).

Passive wine cellar humidifier

This is the least glamorous and cheapest looking gift of all. It consists of a rectangular, plastic washbasin and a small bath towel. A complete description and diagram appear at the end of Chapter 8. To avoid confusion, provide a Xeroxed copy of the end of Chapter 8. Don't upgrade to an ultrasonic humidifier because of the risk that the humidistat will get stuck in the on mode.

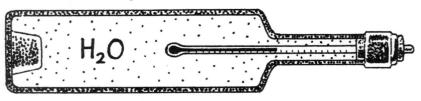

Wine rack

The little racks with 12 slots are designed to display wine in kitchens and dining rooms, which are terrible places to store wine. For your cellar, you need bins and shelves that store more than 12 bottles.

Ice chest & wine transporter

No, it isn't just for picnics. The ice chest is used to transport wine to tastings, to a friend's home for dinner, and from distant wine merchants. It's especially useful in the summer. Put in a re-freezable, phase-change pack and it will keep your wine cool for hours. The phase-change packs with soda-can sized indentations will fit best in the spaces between your bottle necks. Keep the phase-change packs in your freezer between excursions and you're always ready to go. If caught out shopping without your phase-change packs, you can substitute a bag of regular ice, but keep it bagged to protect your labels. Note – When re-warming excessively chilled bottles, keep them upright to prevent weeping. A one-handled carrier is the most convenient as it leaves your other hand free for door knobs and your glasses. The critical feature is to match the 12-inch length of a wine bottle with a 12-inch long interior.

If you prefer to carry your wine-sedimented bottles vertically, the wine accessory catalogs offer both 2-bottle and 6-bottle capacity wine luggage with Styrofoam insulation. Some come with a compartment for a re-freezable phase change "Blue Ice" pack, a desirable feature.

Decanting cradle

If you stand up an old red to uncork it, you'll be disturbing the sediment. Instead, from horizontal storage set it into a stand at a 30° angle above horizontal. Set it into the stand as much as a week before serving in order to concentrate the sediment at one corner of the bottom. Screwpull the cork (see below) and decant without ever raising the bottle to the upright. Clear plastic cradles are featured in wine accessory catalogs as a way to display wine, but they are actually functional. You can also build a less-pretty one from wood.

Decanting machine

Decanting by hand works just fine, and requires no fancy equipment. Brass decanting machines work too. To get every last sediment-free drop out of your 1899 Lafite, set it for a week at a 30° above-horizontal angle in your decanting cradle (see preceding entry). Screwpull the cork from the still-cradled bottle, and transfer the opened bottle without reorienting to a decanting machine. Turn the crank to smoothly tip the bottle, decanting into a decanter. Stop cranking when sediment appears in the neck as revealed by your candle or high-intensity flashlight. I always have trouble deciding when to stop, so decant the last ounce into a glass. Practice with lesser wines. The decanting machines in the catalogs are quite expensive and pretentious. Decanting by hand works fine.

Foilcutter

With only a twist of the wrist, four miniature pizza-cutter-style wheels neatly zip the foil or plastic capsule off the bottle just below the rim. Most foil or lead capsules peel off quite easily without this device, thank you. The Foilcutter usually saves you but a few seconds per bottle. However, some plastic capsules put up stiffer resistance, making this item actually useful. This inexpensive item makes a nice novelty gift, but if you use it for blind wine tastings you may leave enough distinctive capsule visible to identify the wine.

Corkscrews

The straight pull-type corkscrew with a dull, pointed, solid shank screw is a cork-chewing, arm-wrenching, cork-pushing dinosaur. Air pump cork removers are occasionally advertised. You

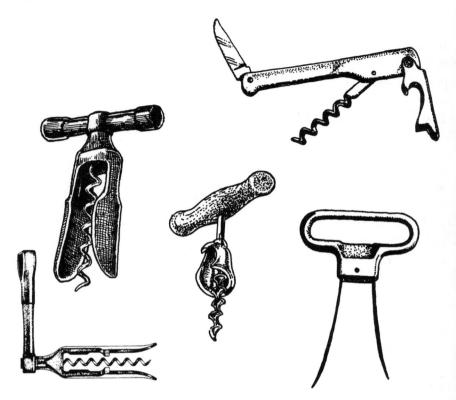

press a needle through the cork and pump in a cork-popping head of pressure. I've never invested in one because everyone I know who has, has been disappointed. The Ah-So has two flat blades that you slide in alongside the cork using a rocking motion. You then rotate to remove the cork. Since the cork is never pierced, the Ah-So never dislodges bits of cork into your wine, though it does occasionally push an entire loose cork into the bottle. This unusual device intrigues first time users, is modestly priced, and actually works.

The waiter's corkscrew is a style, not a patented item. It's made by numerous firms, most of them Italian. The positioning of the fulcrum gives a threefold mechanical advantage over straight pull corkscrews. The lifting action nevertheless requires a bit of coordinated muscle power, making it unloved by the inexperienced and the out-of-shape, and the jolt when the cork lets go can disturb sediment if the bottle's not held firmly. Most waiters prefer them because they're quick and reliable, can be used while standing in the aisle, and make for a showy performance. Look for one with a sharp-pointed, slender, five-turn worm. Worm refers to the lack of a solid shank.

The Screwpull is a patented delight that comes in two styles (three table-models and one pocket-model) and used to come in two colors (red and black). The slender, sharp, Teflon coated worm glides into the cork. Once the worm is fully inserted you keep turning and the cork slides out of the bottle jolt-free. Due to this double-action, which requires 16 full rotations of the handle instead of the usual 8, your wrist can become fatigued at massive affairs. The first four rotations drive the screw into the cork. The second four draw the cork out of the bottle. Eight more rotations are required to get the cork off the worm. The original and still-available version is the Table Model which comes with a small, counter-cluttering stand. In recognition of the strain of all the twisting, the Pocket Model (also referred to as the Spinhandle) has a hole in the end of the handle into which you insert your index finger for rapid spinning in place of twisting. It quickly disassembles into a tiny package for pocket or drawer. Get the pocket model, and get the red color, if they ever reintroduce it, which is easier to locate than the black when misplaced. After a few thousand usages the Teflon will, I'm told by professionals, wear off the worm. I haven't gotten there yet, but I have had one of the originals where the plastic area holding the worm cracked with advanced age. The Screwpull line also includes a massive and very expensive space-hogging lever-model that is intended for big professional operations, and works beautifully, and a new more slender table model. My choice is still the spinhandle aka pocket model. They also make an inexpensive Champagne star that grips and controls champagne corks, facilitating their extraction and avoiding expensive lawsuits from guests injured by flying corks. A Champagne key, which is not a Screwpull product, serves the same function, as does the traditional waiter's towel.

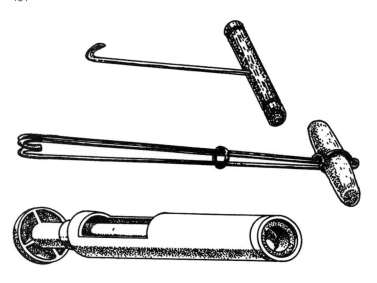

Cork retriever

On very rare occasions a corkscrew pushes a loose cork into the bottle instead of grabbing it. The person with the corkscrew can then go into a panic, especially if the bottle is expensive and rare. When this happens you must instantly take command. Whip out the cork retriever that you've been carrying around for thirty-five years awaiting just this occasion. This device grabs the cork and allows you to extract it. The single-hook and triple-hook varieties both work.

Don't allow anyone to first try to pour the wine because they will only succeed in pouring a few ounces before the cork blocks the pour, after which the floating cork will retreat beyond the reach of the retriever. Once the cork is safely removed, you are at the optimal moment in life to gift the cork retriever which you will probably never again have occasion to use anyway. If you have lacked the foresight to acquire one of these items, then you can probably fashion one on the spur of the moment from a wire coat hanger. Straighten the wire and then bend a very short hook on the end.

(Re)Corker

I've tried in vain to convince the wine accessory catalog people that there's an untapped flood of orders awaiting this item. It is currently only available through wine-making shops, but special requests might succeed in getting them from wine accessory firms. I use my corker to re-insert the original or a replacement cork into a half-emptied bottle of wine after displacing the air with nitrogen from a spray can. You can also use it after transferring half the contents of a 750 ml bottle into a 375 ml bottle. Do not reverse the cork, as the outer end is full of bacteria. Moisten the cork and corker barrel with water to lubricate the insertion. A few sharp raps with the heel of your hand drive the cork home. The most modest and inexpensive plastic corkers are quite adequate and take up little space in your kitchen drawer.

High-intensity flashlight

The krypton bulb projects an intense beam that will pierce even the darkest bottle to reveal the degree of ullage and the amount of sediment. It also makes an excellent decanting light if the base is broad and flat enough to safely stand it on end and in that use is preferable to the traditional candle.

Port tongs

Heat the business end red hot in an open fire, clamp it briefly onto the neck of a brittle-corked old bottle of vintage port just above the shoulder, remove, apply a wet towel to the heated area, and the corked neck cracks cleanly off. This ancient approach to bottle opening actually works and predates Teflon worms by several generations. However, it does take a fire, several minutes to heat the tongs, and they will not fit into your kitchen drawer. Nevertheless, consider giving this unique gift to your port and drama-loving friends.

Champagne stopper

This device seals in the bubbles between servings. It really works, but I never use it because my thirsty guests drink the champagne so quickly that there are plenty of bubbles left even on the last pour. However, if you serve single bottles of champagne at intimate dinners for one or two as both aperitif and dinner wine, then get one to hold the bubbles between courses.

Wine brick & ice bucket

There are many ways to keep your white wine chilled to proper serving temperature, but they are not all alike. An ice bucket requires a supply of ice and gets your labels soggy, but it works. Allow 20 minutes to chill Champagne. Putting your loosely recorked bottle back in the refrigerator works too, but running to the kitchen every time you want to refill a glass is inconvenient and socially awkward. The wine brick is a fragile, porous, red ceramic pot that holds one bottle. You first soak the brick in water for several minutes to fill the pores. Evaporative cooling of the absorbed water slows the warming of pre-chilled wine. Marble chillers work through pre-cooling the stone in the refrigerator. Double-walled clear glass or plastic wine buckets provide an insulating air chamber between the doubled walls that slows warming. The phase-change chillers are best. They come in two styles. The rigid plastic bucket version has four slim removable phase-change inserts that you store in your freezer until needed. The flexible chiller version folds up and stores in your freezer until needed. You unfold it and wrap your bottle. The Velcro closure adapts to any bottle size. Phase-change chillers keep wine cool for hours. They also chill warm bottles, and do it just as quickly as ice buckets.

Nitrogen dispenser

Nitrogen makes up 80% of air, but the 20% of oxygen that makes up most of the balance quickly destroys unconsumed wine. A variety of techniques are available to substitute inert 100% nitrogen for the air in contact with opened wine.

The simplest and least expensive is a pressurized spray can with a plastic hose called Private Preserve. You open your bottle, pour off as much as you want to consume, and immediately spray nitrogen into the air space in the bottle and recork or stopper. Since air and nitrogen are both colorless, there's no way to judge when you've sprayed enough to displace all of the oxygen.

All of the other nitrogen systems involve gas tanks, regulators, and special fittings, and handle from one to a dozen bottles, the latter being for by-the-glass wine bars. They all have the advantage that air never contacts the wine, as the wine is pumped out of the bottle by the introduction of pressurized nitrogen. The nitrogen systems work very well indeed, but are only as good as their fittings. A tiny leak can drain your nitrogen tank in a few days, and a loose fitting on a bottle will admit oxygen. The tiny amount of wine that sits within the plastic or metal plumbing during storage *may* acquire a taste, in which case you'd want to discard the first 1/4 ounce when you serve after a delay. The safest tack is to disconnect from the tank after serving, and to consume wine preserved under nitrogen within a few days.

Vacu-vin

Instead or replacing the air in a partly consumed bottle, you can now evacuate part of it by pumping it out. You pour what you want to consume, insert the special rubber cork, apply the plastic pump, and pull, pull, pull. You won't get all the air out, but it's better than nothing. One theoretical disadvantage is that the vacuum will pull aromatic compounds out of solution.

Decanters

For multi-bottle tastings the easiest serving vessel is the bottle that the wine came in. If there's sediment or if you want to aerate the wine, then you need a decanter for the first pour. You then rinse the sediment out of the bottle with chlorine free water and pour the wine back into its bottle, using a funnel. The requirements for a double-decanting decanter are that it pour without dribbling, be easy to clean, easy to handle, and be large enough. If you can get your hand into the bottom, it will be easy to clean. If not, it will be difficult to clean. A one-quart Pyrex measuring cup meets all of these criteria for 750 ml bottles of wine. You can also serve at tastings from numbered decanters, if you have enough of them, but if you get your decoding notes mixed up you will be in big trouble.

For dining, serving-decanters are more refined. As with wine glasses, there's some concern with the high lead content of so called lead crystal glass which is 24% lead. The lead is probably safely bound into the glass, but there's no apparent advantage to high lead content glass.

The criteria for serving decanters are clear glass so you can see the wine, pleasant appearance, adequate capacity, easy cleaning, pouring without dribbling, and having a stopper.

It's rare to find a wine decanter into which you can get your hand for cleaning, but the narrower the opening the tougher it will be to get even a flexible wire cleaning-brush into all the corners, and the harder it will be to get it to air dry after cleaning. When the decanter is filled with 750 ml. of wine the air-to-liquid surface should be large to permit aeration inside the decanter, but there should also be a stopper to retain aromatics. The largest air-to-wine interface is obtained with what are called ship's decanters so called because they resist toppling when the ship's dining room is rocked by waves. If you're serving more than one wine, then contrasting shapes will avert confusion. With any new decanter, test for dribbling by pouring water from a 750 ml bottle into wine glasses. If you own any magnums you'll need at least one decanter large enough to hold 1.5 liters of wine and pour without dribbling from a 1.5 L fill. As with wine glasses, rinse vigorously at least six times after cleaning with detergent.

Funnels

When double decanting, it takes a steady, sober, and brave hand - or a funnel – for phase two. Since you will not meet all of the former criteria when decanting for the last flight, get a funnel. Why risk a $100 bottle by the lack of a $2 funnel?

Inert, unbreakable nylon or Teflon funnels are best and are available in supermarkets, hardware stores, and from laboratory supply houses. Bring an empty bottle to the store with you to insure a fit. Get the largest opening that will still fit loosely into the bottle. Remember that air must escape around the outside of the funnel as the wine goes in. Glass is fine too if you're careful.

Fancier and much more expensive pewter funnels with screens to catch sediment are advertised. If only stray specks of sediment escape the bottle, then the screen is a fine idea – but if you rely too heavily on the screen it will clog, and your funnel will overflow.

According to my dictionary, "pewter is an alloy in which tin is the chief constituent, originally tin and lead". One of the theories of the fall of the Roman Empire was that lead poisoning from pewter wine jugs and goblets dulled the wits of the ruling class. There may be no lead in modern pewter, and the contact time in a funnel may be negligible, but until I get definitive word otherwise, I say better plastic than sorry.

Silver plated funnels with screens are also advertised, and they contain no lead. Some have a bent tip to direct the wine to run down the interior side of the bottle instead of free falling, possibly an advantage with very old wines where you might want to minimize the aeration.

Wine glasses

Wine glasses come in a confusing array of shapes and sizes. Clear glass and a stem are *de rigueur*, though the only purpose of the stem seems to be as a transition from the round bowl to a flat foot that won't tip over, and secondarily to keep your hot hands away from the wine.

The shape and size of the bowl makes a tremendous difference, especially in the smell department. I once brought a white wine impitoyable brand (no longer available) stem to a white wine weekend and detected aromas from nearly every wine that much younger participants completely missed from their hotel ware. Nevertheless, the profusion of separate, special sizes for every color and type of wine strains credulity. Basically you need a wide bowl with a narrow mouth to permit safe swirling, and enough capacity for about three times as much wine as you'll be pouring.

The most expensive glasses are made of very thin 24% lead crystal, and ring beautifully when you tap their edges. The use of such a high lead content is controversial, as ingested lead causes

brain damage. The greatest concern, however, is leaching from high lead decanters when they're used to store cognac for several months, in which case the lead level in the cognac does increase perceptibly.

Your wine does not stay in the glass very long, so it's probably quite safe. Lead in the glass of wine bottles or from grapes grown next to a busy highway that was once used by vehicles using leaded gas would be of much greater concern. Nevertheless, the lead in the wine glass serves no readily apparent useful purpose. Perhaps it imparts strength, clarity, or ductility during manufacturing. Since the shape of the glass does appear to make a big difference, my advice is to invest in a variety of styles and experiment. Finally, after washing wine glasses with soap or detergent you *must* rinse them thoroughly with hot water a minimum of six times. The aroma of a dried out detergent residue that has been liberated by wine is simply awful.

There is a new breed of wine glasses made with magnesium or titanium fused into glass instead of lead. They are supposed to be much stronger than lead crystal glasses. They cost the same. I tried a set of four and they have not broken (yet). The Wine Enthusiast, wineenthusiast.com, sells and distributes the magnesium glasses as their "fusion" line, and International Wine Accessories iwa.com carries the titanium glasses. They are usually also available at fine wine shops.

Watch glass wine glass covers

The watch glass is put on top of a just-poured glass of wine as a cover. It should slow the loss of aromatics into the room. The wine reacts with the oxygen picked up during decanting and pouring and present in the bowl of the glass, no additional oxygen from the room being required. Over several minutes after the wine is poured, aromatics escape the wine into the bowl where the cover traps them. You lift the covered glass, swirl with your index finger securing the cover, and then lift the cover off and sniff the heavenly, concentrated, trapped-for-you aroma. Watch glass covers also keep the occasional fly out of your wine. None of the wine accessory catalogs carry this item, so you would have to go to a scientific supply house.

Wine tasting tablecloth

Wine tasters get sloppy as the evening progresses. Dried out red wine stains are wicked impossible to remove, especially from the white tablecloths that are *sine qua non* for the viewing of wine color. There are two solutions to this dilemma.

The first solution is a clear-plastic tablecloth cover that protects the fine linen. It's slippery, tacky, and hard to keep the linen flat underneath.

The second solution is inexpensive disposable white paper table-cloths with plastic liners that are on sale in the paper plate depart-ment of your variety store or supermarket. For a large table you might need two. While you're shopping, pick up two more to pass to the next host.

Table salt and New Liquid Tide

If you insist on real cloth white table covers when serving red wine, then have these items handy as your third solution. When red wine spills, immediately pour on a pile of dry table salt. The salt will osmotically draw out the pigment. After the guests depart and the table is cleared, pour full strength New Liquid Tide onto the stain and throw the tablecloth into your clothes washer. When Consumer Reports magazine rated laundry detergents, they gave New Liquid Tide high marks for the removal of grape juice stains.

Tastevin

This item is a silver-plated giant teaspoon with bumps. It comes on either a chain or a sash and is worn around the sommelier's neck. When he decants your wine in his candlelit wine cellar he steals the first few drops into his tastevin to determine whether it's a good bottle. He checks its color by reflected candlelight, the shiny silver acting as a mirror. The bumps are supposed to facilitate the visual evaluation of tiny amounts of wine. He then tastes it, hence the name of the device which is French for "wine taster." There is considerable tradition behind this item in Burgundy, going back several centuries. Members of an ancient and very exclusive wine society, the Confrerie du Tastevin, use the tastevin around the neck as a membership badge. The domestic version is called The Knights of the Vine. Enophiles who are deadly serious about their Burgundies consider tastevin possession as an honorary membership. Others consider them to be ridiculous and utterly useless puffery.

Breathalyzer

A breathalyzer is a gift for those you truly love. It really works. Don't allow your guests to drive off until they get the green light. Bring this item out no less than ten minutes after the last wine is consumed, as alcohol from the lining of the mouth gives false high estimates of blood alcohol.

Section 5 * CONSUMING

Chapter 21 * BREATHING, AROMA & TASTE

Breathing

In 1979, in honor of a 24-year old guest's birthday, I served my solo bottle of the '55 Clos de la Vigne au Saint. Because of its age, I poured this Cote d'Or Burgundy directly upon uncorking into outstretched glasses. There was hardly any aroma and the taste was insipid. The polite guests turned the discussion elsewhere. Only my final smell and sip some 30 minutes later revealed the terrific bouquet and gustatory nuances the wine had had to offer, but we had missed them through inadequate breathing. I was most embarrassed by my inept service.

The next time I served a red wine with some age, I opened it as the guests began to arrive. I proudly set the just opened and doubly decanted magnum of '66 Giscours out beside some glasses for a 30-minute breathe and went to fetch the Champagne. When I returned a few minutes later I was aghast to find that my thirsty friends had served themselves as aperitif what was to have been the centerpiece of the dinner. I was barely able to salvage an unready ounce for myself. No matter how proud you are of the visual display created by the vessel you'll be serving from, never leave an opened bottle or filled decanter on display to breathe amongst the guests without your constant surveillance.d detected nuances in nearly every wine presented, which much younger palates in the seminar failed to detect from their clunky hotel ware.

As a rule of thumb, old wines need less breathing time than young wines, tannic reds more than fruity whites. Over an hour or so of breathing, young reds complete an oxygen-dependent maturation that parallels, but does not equal, the years of maturation that takes place within corked bottles. Even half-emptied bottles of tannic young reds occasionally improve if left loosely corked overnight. Mature wines can peak and decline within 5 minutes of being opened, but they too need some air

Many of the chemicals responsible for aroma and taste form during the breathing or oxygenation that occurs after wine is exposed to air. The goal of breathing is to introduce oxygen while retaining the volatile aromatic compounds. Since many of the aromatics are formed during the breathing, they would be lost into the room if the wine were poured off the sediment after the breathing was completed. It follows that if decanting is desired, do it immediately after the bottle is opened.

To decant a wine but still serve it from its own labeled bottle you double decant, into a pitcher and back, after rinsing out the sediment, into the original bottle. Besides getting rid of the sediment, double decanting also increases the air contact. With older wines you can avoid the possibly excessive aeration of double decanting by decanting into a decanter from which you serve, or into an empty wine bottle. Always use a plastic funnel when pouring into a wine bottle. Avoid pewter as it may contain lead.

The surface area exposed to air influences the rate of oxygenation. The wine in a bottle that is simply uncorked will receive oxygen slowly, whereas decanting will briefly expose a large surface during the pour, plus a large surface in the decanter. Some go so far as to pour the young wine back and forth several times to thoroughly aerate it. I've never had the audacity to experiment with this non-traditional concept.

After decanting, wine should be stored in a loosely recorked bottle or stoppered decanter while the absorbed oxygen does its work. If the wine is to be consumed very soon after decanting, and you want more aeration, then choose a wide bellied decanter to maximize the wine to air surface. The pour into glasses should be delayed until the guests are ready to drink.

If your cellar is cooler than the desired serving temperature, then warm the wine after decanting, not before. Warming wine prior to decanting, unnecessarily releases aromatics during decanting, as warm molecules move faster than cool ones. Warming typically involves no more than bringing the decanted wine up into the house for the half hour or so of breathing time.

Serving ancient wines

Old wines have in a sense breathed before they're opened, which means that decanting to eliminate sediment may dissipate already formed aromatics. If the amount of sediment is modest and seems well compacted, then carry the venerable old bottle gently around the room, always at a tilt, and pour directly from the bottle into each person's glass. This non-decanting is traditional for Burgundies. Warn your guests to sample their aerating-in-glass wine in low gear lest they finish it before it's ready to drink. If there's significant sediment, then decant into a decanter and serve immediately, but with the same go-slow caveat. The maestros at wine tastings who hire pseudo-sommeliers to pour at a distant table and then distribute from a tray of wide mouthed filled glasses do your nose no favors, as aromatics are lost by the air currents while the wine is en route.

An untested concept is to chill the ancient bottle in your refrigerator for several hours prior to opening and double decanting. If time is limited, freezer time for rapid chilling is two minutes per degree F, four minutes per degree C. This should discourage the loss of aromatics during decanting. However, consider the notion that the thermal shock of chilling shuts wine down for an extended time. One reader reports that wine from his cellar at its annual low is relatively dumb. I suspect that these anecdotal tales are related more to slowed breathing and low serving temperature than to any effect that persists after re-warming, but I have no comparative tasting experiences to support this explanation.

Aroma etc.

Aroma-producing chemicals (aromatic compounds) evaporate from wine into the air. If they reach the olfactory area high in the nose in sufficient concentration and stay there long enough, they elicit the sensations we call aroma, stink, bouquet, smell, nose, etc. Aroma and bouquet connote pleasant sensations while smell, odor, and stink have unpleasant associations, though there are many devotees of the barnyard stink of certain French wines. Some authorities make a distinction between aroma and bouquet, the former being fruity and represented by apple, pear, cassis, plum, currant, raspberry, strawberry, and perhaps coffee, hazelnut, and chocolate, the latter being perfumey as from a bouquet of flowers and represented by violets, eucalyptus, mint, cassis, cloves, tea, licorice, cinnamon, cedar, and perhaps smoke. In many cases the categorization between aroma and bouquet is arbitrary, the two terms being used interchangeably. The pseudo distinctions merely serve to intimidate the beginner who detects a particular smell and describes the aroma only to be corrected by the expert at the podium who labels the identical olfactory sensation as bouquet.

Nose is a totally neutral way to refer to olfactory sensations. For me, the worst nose a wine can have is none at all. I'd prefer even the stench of goat cheese. Incidentally, the questionable practice of assigning anatomical features and functions to wine goes well below the nose and the breathing. Wines are said to have body (concentration) and legs (glycerin rivulets on the inside of the glass). They were once described as manly (robust) or feminine (delicate), terms which are no longer politically correct. Wines are also given personalities such as brooding, and intelligence ratings such as precocious and dumb. Don't be intimidated by the hyperbole.

Never fill a wine glass. Leave a large space in the glass above the wine. The space collects heavier than air aromatics as they evaporate from the wine in anticipation of your olfactory pleasure. The concentration of aromatics is greatest a few minutes after a properly breathed wine is poured. If everything has been timed perfectly then the final dose of oxygen needed by the wine is acquired during the pour. It can take a minute for that final dose of oxygen to do its chemical thing. The wine then releases aromatics from its surface. Swirling the wine in the glass changes the surface layer which facilitates the release of aromatics. With further passage of time the aromatics spread into the room where they become too dilute to detect. The wine can continue to release aromatics for a time, but the rate of release quickly declines. Repeated swirling accelerates the decline and gives diminishing returns. Within minutes the aromatics are undetectable, leaving an odorless and relatively tasteless fluid that I am reluctant to call wine. I say tasteless because a big part of taste is accomplished by the stimulation of smell detectors that are stimulated by aromatics that are released in the mouth and travel from the back of the throat up into the nose. The blockage of this route is what makes food less tasty when your nose is clogged. If the aromatics have dissipated by the time you taste the wine, then your taste of the wine will be impaired just as if your nose were stuffed up.

Wine glasses with enormous bowls but tiny mouths have taken favor in recent years. The large bowl maximizes the wine to air surface and provides a large air space for aromatics to collect. The narrow opening keeps the wine and the aromatics in the glass during swirling. The opening is left just big enough for smelling and tasting. The only problems using such glasses at tastings are their cost, transporting the bulky and fragile glasses, and getting a big enough pour. Some glass manufacturers offer a unique glass shape for every imaginable type of wine, hoping to fill your glass cabinet and thin your wallet. Some of it may be hype, some tradition, but the shape of the glass does make a tremendous difference. I once brought an Impitoyable brand (not currently available) white wine glass to a white wine weekend and detected nuances in nearly every wine presented, which much younger palates in the seminar failed to detect from their clunky hotel ware.

Fast sniffing Vs slow sniffing

Smell is a notoriously adapting sense. When an odor is encountered you notice it for less than a minute. The aromatic chemical may still be around, but you no longer sense it. Thus, it should come as no surprise that the first smell of a breathed wine, or even the first in a series of very similar wines, is the most intensely experienced.

Nevertheless, from a much shorter time frame, aromatics require more than fleeting contact with the nasal detectors. Therefore, you smell more when you sniff slowly. With a slow sniff the aromatics don't rush past the sensory endings. A fast sniff takes a second. Try to stretch your sniff. The most intense sensations seem to come two seconds into the sniff. The large volume of inhaled air needed to sustain a long sniff requires both abdominal and thoracic breathing. If your stomach sucks in instead of out when you sniff wine, then you are only using thoracic breathing. It's easy to break the habit.

People who are relaxed sniff their wine slowly. When anxious or harried they unconsciously sniff more rapidly. When an anxious enophile then suspects that his nose is failing he becomes even more agitated, and sniffs even more abruptly, exacerbating the problem.

Swirling

Swirling wine in the glass releases aromatics into the top of the glass. However, swirling can also create air currents that spill aromatics out of the glass. To avoid this risk, you wouldn't swirl. You would leave your just poured glass of wine untouched for a minute before sniffing, preferably with a watch glass cover in place. If you choose to swirl, do so with a tight arc so the glass scarcely changes position. The wine will still swirl, but more of the released aromatics should remain in the bowl. One or two swirls only please. Excessive swirling is counterproductive, blowing away what you have just released. After swirling, sniff immediately, without first putting your glass down.

Swirlers and waiters alike should raise their glasses to their respective noses gently and slowly, preferably meeting them halfway, as if they were filled to the brim, which in a sense they are. Air currents that disperse aromatics can also be created if you wave your arms near the glass, or if the air in the room is moved by air conditioning, fans, or forced hot air heating. Air currents are the reason why you shouldn't do serious tasting outdoors.

Air-quality control

Between sniffs, and between wines, clean room air gives your nose a chance to revive. Extraneous odors can interfere with this recovery and can compete with wine odors. Cooking odors, cigarette smoke, scented candles, smoke from a fireplace or wood stove, dried flowers, the musty aroma of mold, used kitty litter, body odor, and body perfume can all interfere with the detection of wine odors. Some experienced tasters take the precaution of discretely sniffing strange ladies for perfume before selecting their seats.

Tasting

In addition to aromatics, breathing produces less volatile chemicals that contribute to taste. With taste, as with smell, the first is often the best. The first taste should therefore be a bold encounter. Take enough into your mouth to engage all surfaces. Slosh the wine around within your mouth. Inhale air bubbles through the intra-oral wine. This repeatedly interrupts and renews contact between the wine and the taste buds, while adding extra oxygen for a final in-the-mouth burst of oxidation. Practice the technique privately with water lest you drool.

Between tastes saliva bathes the taste buds, re-establishing a neutral environment. Recovery to full sensory acuity is slow. The more leisurely the pace of a tasting, the more your senses will recover between wines, and therefore the more you'll smell and taste.

Sip and spit

Alcohol in the brain impairs the senses, including smell and taste. There are only two reasons for swallowing during a wine tasting. The first is to achieve the mild level of intoxication that enhances the overall pleasure of the event. The second is to experience the finish that is attributed to the stimulation of taste buds in the back of the throat and upper esophagus, which are only reachable during swallowing.

Finish is the taste sensation that lingers after wine is swallowed. There's no finish after spitting. Experienced tasters often spit the swill, which promises no finish, but swallow the spectacular. Receptors for sweetness predominate in the throat. As a result, wines that are swallowed appear sweeter than wines that are spit. The field testing for New Coke used sip-and-spit testing, which understates sweetness. The testing produced a formula that was ideal for sip and spitting, but too sweet to swallow. New Coke was a commercial disaster.

Not being as sweet as New Coke, most wines profit from being swallowed. Swallowing also displaces air upwards from the throat into the nose where the wine is smelled again as it is being swallowed. Wines that you sip and spit are thus not as intensely experienced as those that you swallow. It appears that to ensure that nutrients reach the stomach, evolution has withheld some of the pleasures associated with ingestion until the final consummatory act of swallowing.

It is nevertheless perfectly acceptable, indeed is general practice among professionals, to spit after tasting and always to dump any wine left in glass after it has been evaluated. The practice of tasting and spiting is second cousin to the behavior of bulimics who ingest enormous meals and then purge themselves to keep slim. The purging is done secretly in the bathroom. Tasting and spitting is acceptable at wine tastings, but never at dinner parties. Most wine tasting hosts neglect to provide spit cups, so bring your own. A discrete opaque cup should be brought to use as a spittoon, as wine mixed with saliva is a disgusting sight. The spitting process, especially if saliva hangs on your lips, can be pretty disgusting to watch as well. Spit discretely and quietly. Neophytes who observe your behavior may assume that you have terminal liver failure and are spitting under strict doctor's orders. At Bordeaux chateaux sawdust-filled spittoons or sawdust covered floors are sometimes provided. I have visited many winery tasting rooms in the US, but have yet to encounter a spitter or a spittoon. When, as designated driver, I've inquired, I've been told that spitting is not permitted in the tasting room. I wandered outside with my glass, but felt awfully self-conscious.

Chapter 22 * HOW TO ORGANIZE A WINE TASTING GROUP

Have you religiously acquired on release every vintage of Mondavi Reserve Cabernet going back to the now fading but once fabulous '74? There must be a dozen folks living nearby who would be delighted to share the cost of opening them all for a spectacular vertical tasting. Did you buy fifteen different cases of the 2000 Bordeaux but have not had the opportunity to taste them? Surely a bunch of the other collectors in town who stocked up on that five star vintage would want to join you in a horizontal tasting to see how they're doing. Beware. You may find it difficult to fill the chairs around your tasting table.

Join an existing private tasting group

The easiest solution is not to organize a new group, but rather to join an ongoing private tasting clique. If you can wangle a one-time invitation, perhaps as an alternate, then offer your home and theme for a subsequent meeting. There's no surer way to attain permanent group membership. There may however not be a private tasting band in your area. Even when there is one, it's likely to be at capacity. Wine tasting cadres tend to stabilize, being limited by personal ties and by the number of tasters that can comfortably be served from one bottle. Openings for new members rarely occur, and are filled selectively.

Form your own private tasting group

If you're not satisfied with the local wine shop's tastings, cannot coax an invitation from an ongoing private corps, have a suitable site, and are willing to do some organizing, then you could form a new private group. Not everyone who would like to participate in private tastings is willing to organize them. There may be a pool of unattached enophiles in your region sufficient for the formation of a new

Figure 22-1. The easiest solution is not to organize a new group, but rather to join an ongoing private tasting clique.

group. The new force might even attract members of established groups who would double up in order to taste more frequently.

This chapter is my Guide to the Art of Organizing a Wine Tasting Troupe. Once initial start-up is completed, others may be willing to share the organizational and hosting duties.

Themes

Tastings can be vertical (wines of many vintages from one property; for example, 15 vintages of Chateau Latour going back to 1961); tandem vertical (wines from two properties over a series of vintages; for example, Haut Brion versus La Mission Haut Brion both from a series of 6 to 9 vintages); or horizontal (wines of many properties but all from the same vintage, for example, 15 different 1982 Bordeaux); varietal (one grape or one grape versus another – for example, 18 different Zinfandels or Cabs versus Merlots); geographical (wines from one country or region–for example, a survey of the wines of Australia, or between regions such as California Cabs versus French Bordeaux); or financial (great cheap wines or, at the other extreme, cellar treasures).

The host assembles the wines. BYO can be disastrous, unless carefully orchestrated, being rather the exception among serious tasters. Only in a well established group can you pull off a theme like Bring Your Own Cellar Treasure, and even then only as a one-time novelty.

Selecting the wines

Try to include at least one sample of the most famous. For vertical Bordeaux tastings that still means a legendary '45, '59, '61, '70, or '82, even when as a drink it's not worth the price. For horizontal tastings, select a vin-de-garde year (literally wine-to-keep) and include as your show stopper one or more of the most famous properties such as Lafite Rothschild or Screaming Eagle. Even if those stars don't turn out to be the brightest of the evening, you'll at least know that you've sampled the very best that tradition and the newsletters say the theme has to offer. It's a mistake to limit your tasting to a narrow price range in the interest of fairness. A narrow price range within a strict theme often results in too much taste uniformity. Part of the interest in contrasting Petrus with Trotanoy is to decide for yourself whether the Petrus is worth its price. Another relatively boring theme is a vertical from a property that is very consistent year to year.

Provide variety

You can improve the sensory pleasures of a wine tasting by selecting wines that are sure to provide variety. If the newsletter that you're using to guide your selections describes unusual features but gives only an average rating, it still might be an excellent choice for your affair. One wine could have mouth-searing tannin, another overwhelming mint, while a third has a powerful mineral taste. Yet another could be excellent but overpriced, an opinion that your guests might like to test against their own palates at the cost of a taste rather than a full bottle. Petrus is the wine that most often comes to mind in this category.

A ringer is often inserted. A single California Cab mystery wine slipped into a Bordeaux vertical is often a most pleasant sensory surprise, and vice versa. Similarly, a top Oregon Pinot Noir can be slipped into a red Burgundy tasting. A first growth tasting suggests a wine from a less famous contiguous property, or perhaps an example of their second label. Chateau Musar from Lebanon is my personal favorite ringer.

Avoid a theme that's likely to be unpleasant, as can occur when trying to taste tannic monsters such as 2005 Bordeaux before their time. One or two such wines add interest to a vertical tasting, but hold off on the horizontal until they're closer to maturity.

Finding the people

Before you announce your nascent group's first tasting, you need a list of the names, email addresses and telephone numbers of at least 20 wine enthusiasts whom you have met personally and who have expressed an interest in tasting. A good place to generate this list is at a store tasting or, even better, a multi-session wine appreciation class. So arrive early, sit with and befriend strangers, and ask those who seem likely to fit into your plans to join your tasting group. When you call to invite them to a private tasting they'll be responding to an anticipated call from someone remembered. Try not to be too obvious about the name collecting. If you send a sign-up sheet around the room, the brew master running the show will rightly conclude that you're attempting to borrow his best customers.

Your local wine merchant has, over the years, generated a clientele of hundreds of customers and is in the store every day to greet and serve them. When a tasting is announced through the store's mailing list, only a tiny percentage of those contacted actually attend, and partly in response to recollections of a personable and helpful wine merchant.

You will occasionally find a wine tasting prospect in the aisles of a wine shop. It's easy to distinguish serious neo-enophiles by their shopping style. They frequent the serious aisles, agonize over mixed case selections, and consult vintage charts, newsletters, often Xeroxed because they haven't yet taken out their own subscription, or Robert Parker's Palm Pilot. After a few helpful suggestions, most neo-enophiles will gladly divulge name, email, and telephone number for your list of tasters.

The internet wine chat rooms have become a good source of tasting buddies. The Wine Bulletin Board at ERobertParker.com is one such place. They have a separate section for people who want to get together to taste. No membership fee is required.

If your theme is a vertical then try contacting the property, the importer, and the regional distributor, both for possible attendees and for hard-to-find and not-yet-released vintages. The contact info is often on the bottle. In most cases you should be able to Google a website.

Up to this point you've worked at filling your tasting group with total strangers. Surely some of your friends, acquaintances, and work associates would be interested in wine tasting. With "regular" friends great caution is advised. Asking friends to attend a pay-at-the-door function is an excellent way to destroy friendships. Just mention that you're interested in wine, or invite friends to accompany you to a store tasting where someone else will be collecting their money.

While you're still generating a list of wine tasting enthusiasts you might, for practice, throw a free tasting for your "regular" friends. Ask everyone to bring their favorite wine under $10, or provide the wines gratis. For this event the socializing would be the primary attraction for most guests. Those in the group interested in moving up to more serious tasting will identify themselves via animated wine talk.

Acquiring the wines

The first thing to do for any tasting is to get the wines into your very own cellar. This admonition applies equally to the trade. I once attended a vertical tasting of Gressier Grand Poujeaux, (a minor Bordeaux) sponsored by the local distributor and attended by the Count de Saint-Afrique himself. The advertised center piece of the tasting was a double magnum of his chateau stored 1899. Many in the crowd that gathered that evening were eagerly anticipating their first, and probably only, opportunity to experience a 19th century wine. Imagine the disappointment when it was announced, after everyone had paid and assembled, that the 1899 failed to arrive due to pilferage on the shipping dock in Bordeaux. On another occasion the wine consultant at a major Massachusetts outlet had to scramble all over New England to borrow wines for a tasting that was to feature the contents of an overdue container from France. To repeat: Get the wines into your cellar before advertising the wine list or the date. You surely don't want to spend the week prior to the event scrambling for key wines.

If any of the wines are coming from a guest's cellar, or are to be brought by a wine merchant guest, then it is possible that those wines and that person will never arrive, or arrive late, or with wine that is too warm, too cold, badly ullaged, with disturbed sediment, or opened and decanted for you last night.

I once arrived a few minutes late for a horizontal tasting of '83 Bordeaux with my carefully transported Chateau Margaux contribution from my cool cellar carefully packed in Styrofoam. A few minutes later the wine was correctly identified in the first flight because it was colder than the others. Just as with the wines that you supply, get contributed wines into your cellar weeks in advance, even at the inconvenience of picking them up personally. Besides, with new acquaintances it's a good excuse to visit their home and cellar. I didn't say that hosting was going to be easy!

Getting ready to invite

There are several predictable queries that you'd best be prepared to answer when telephone, instant-message, or Email inviting. I have at one time or another been caught short by each one of these.

(1) **How much will it cost?** Fix the cost per person. After the group is established, members may assume that the wine selections will be inspired but not extravagant. Initially, however, be prepared with a fixed price.

(2) **What wines are you serving?** Make a written wine list. Even better, note the Parker scores.

(3) **Where and when?** Write down the date, time, and location lest you inadvertently direct a guest to arrive on the wrong day, hour,

or at the wrong address, and be prepared with travel directions from all compass points.

(4) Who else is coming? Have an up-to-date confirmed guest list in hand. If the first or second person you invite asks who's coming, simply flatter him by his placement at the head of your list.

Nailing down the key guest

The first person to contact is the key guest such as a wine merchant, wholesaler, or someone with a fabulous cellar. Set the date and time to suit the key person, and adjust the wine list to accommodate the wines that the key guest suggests or offers to bring. Even famous people will be flattered when you tailor your event to ensure their participation. Drop the key guest's name when inviting.

Wine merchants have the proper patter to accompany the evaluation of wine, and can advise you on breathing times and service sequence. The merchant will be tied down at the store at the time you're most likely to consider ideal, that is Friday or Saturday night, so be prepared for Sunday afternoon or a weekday evening. For entry-level tastings a wine merchant will come as an extension of his job. For advanced tastings such as a first growth vertical don't hesitate to invite two or more professionals. They'll enjoy vying with one another to identify the vintages and label the nuances, and as regular members of the group can locate key hard-to-find wines for future tastings.

The art of the telephone or email invitation

Once you have the wines, key person, date, and time firmly set, you're ready to begin serious inviting. Start two – or, better, three – weeks in advance. If you think you might fill up before getting to the end of your list, then set priorities. People with friendly demeanors, deep cellars, idyllic settings for future tastings, exquisitely educated palates, or wholesale wine contacts are valuable assets to any tasting group. Cellar owners will vary in their willingness to supply wines for tastings. Those who share are the best to invite, but most hoarders eventually loosen up as friendships develop within the group.

Many invitees will not give a definite "yes" or "no" when you first call or email, but will promise to get back to you. Don't get flustered by this apparent put off. Have a positive, cheerful response prepared such as "I sincerely hope you'll be able to participate. We would be exalted by your participation." The surest turnoff is the hard sell such as "I'll probably fill all the seats within the next 37 minutes, so you had better decide quickly or you'll miss out on the tasting of the century". Even if it's true, don't say it. Some people really do have to check with their spouse or misplaced calendar, or want a few private minutes to research the theme or consult with their astrologist. Others have no intention of participating, but have trouble giving a direct no. Most who want to come will remember to get back. Those who have no such intention will rarely do so, even though they promised to. Therefore, treat all "will-get-backs" as nos until you hear otherwise. Keep right on inviting without pause until you've filled all your chairs with definite yeses. When you reach an answering machine or human message taker, leave only name and number. Some spouses resent their partner's love of wine and can't be trusted to pass on an invitation.

If you dial, Instant Message, or Email through your entire list without filling, then wait one or, at most, two days and re-dial or re-mail the I'll-get-backs and those for whom you only left a message. The odd one will have been distracted or merely ambivalent, your recall being the necessary expression of interest to elicit a yes. If the response is negative, seize the moment, while they're at the zenith of guilt about not having gotten back as promised, to ask for the names, emails, and numbers of others who might like to participate.

The regional wine merchants, after you've invited them, may seem ideal sources of names to fill out a tasting. Try them, but don't expect much. They ardently wish you success, and will happily attend your affair, but they want your group to succeed independently. If you absorb members from established groups you won't be expanding their customer base. They want fresh meat. Sometimes the merchant's assistant, being naive to such matters, is a better source of names. Telephone him directly. He'll be flattered. Some wine merchants are reluctant to pass invitations along to their assistants because of the resulting expectation that the store finance the assistant's participation.

Keep and preserve a meticulous record of the names email addresses and telephone numbers of everyone you contact along with notes on their responses. Those who express interest but cannot make a particular date, or who are not keen on a particular theme, should be kept on file until the wines are more appealing. Ten years have passed, but I still anguish over the loss of the name and number of the gentleman from Connecticut who brought the 1945 to our La Mission vertical.

The telephone approach to inviting will take hours the first time around - time filled with friendly chatter, a discussion of the theme, wines, date and price, busy signals, not-homes, and will-call-backs. Email is probably a lot more efficient since you won't get busy signals or answering machines. Cell phone invitations can put people on the spot when they are busy. Wine shops announce their tastings more efficiently by newspaper advertisement or mailing list. Newspaper ads would bring legal headaches to your door. The mail approach requires full addresses and extra lead time. Both approaches are too impersonal for private tasting groups. I once tried the snail mail approach with an established group, sending a friendly form letter instead of calling. The replies came back painfully slowly, all but one in response to a chance personal encounter or unrelated telephone contact. Even the most dependable members required a follow-up telephone call in order to elicit a response. As the group becomes established you'll weed out the chronic nos, no-shows, and will-get-backs, leaving a short efficient list of dedicated responsive regulars and a few less-reliable back-ups. As a last resort go back to the people who are already committed and ask if they know of a couple who might like the last two seats.

The number of tasters

The number of people that you envision for your tasting need only be an approximation, not a rigid quota. If you end up with one or two fewer people than anticipated, don't panic. Eliminate a few of the wines and enjoy the larger portions and the elbow room. Conversely, you can usually squeeze one more person around the table, add a side table in the kitchen, add additional wines, and reduce the serving size when the odd will-call-back or no unexpectedly requests a last-minute seat. The anticipation of a few extra but accommodatable guests is a nice buffer against a last minute cancellation or the unpardonable but occasional no-show. The airlines do it all the time. If you do have to use a side table, make sure that it flies first class, with at least four tasters, including a major knowledgeable participant such as yourself, and gets first pour half the time.

While on the topic of no-shows, there are three ways to reduce the likelihood of unexpectedly empty seats. The first is to require a non-refundable payment or contributed wine collected in advance. Such stern remedies are best reserved for unreliable types who have reneged in the past. One of the great moral dilemmas of wine tasting-dom is whether the pre-collected irreplaceable '61 Petrus should be opened if the donor cancels out an hour before the event.

The second, and more diplomatic, approach is to place reminder calls during the days immediately preceding the event. If you're more comfortable with a pretext for the reminder call, discuss the theme, date, or site for the subsequent meeting; solicit recommendations concerning breathing times or flight sequencing; remind the guest to bring the appropriate number and type of glasses; request bread, cheese, chlorine free mineral water, flowers, or paper wine bags; or ask to borrow a breathalyzer, newsletter, extra chair or folding table. Deftly executed reminder calls subtly remind the guests while determining whether it is still their intention to attend. Reminder calls are especially critical for couples, where two seats are at stake. You might even go so far as to invent a reason to speak directly to the spouse for whom a second seat has been reserved, perhaps concerning a culinary matter, during the course of your reminder call. Some people come to depend on the reminder calls, but it's still an essential step.

The third way to reduce the likelihood of empty seats is to overbook if you know that some of your invitees are unreliable or untested. If the crowd becomes unbearable you and your spouse can always drop out of the tasting and enjoy the hosting aspects of the event.

There's nothing more depressing than a half-empty tasting table. My worst turnout occurred when I deliberately omitted reminder calls to compensate for overbooking, and two first-time couples and a single failed to materialize. In such situations the best tactic is to cut your losses. Gather together around one end of the table, relax, drop the last flight, and enjoy the ample servings and the intimate gathering.

For rare or very expensive wines you'll probably want to spread the cost and the pleasure as much as possible. The largest number you can stretch one bottle to serve, and still give each person barely enough to smell and taste, is 24 if there's no sediment or ullage. This would give each person only one ounce of wine. Most tasters appreciate, indeed expect and deserve, considerably larger portions, ideally to have some left in the bottle for a reprise. Couples at tiny-portion tastings would do well to pool their shares in one glass to intensify the aroma. When too many people are served from a fading giant, the best smell is usually afforded the person with the corkscrew. I always volunteer.

If you served 24 wines to 24 people, each would get the equivalent of a whole bottle, which, if they swallow, is excessive. Most people go into palate fatigue and drunken stupor by the time they reach #24. A more reasonable balance between variety and volume is to serve 12 to 18 wines to no more than 15 people. Besides, it's difficult enough to fit even 15 around a dining room table. To extend your dining room table, folding bridge-tables can be pressed into service.

Practice your shot glass technique in advance so that you can demonstrate flawlessly when the first wines are poured. Try to get two ounce shot glasses rather than the standard one ounce variety, as the standard pour is just shy of two ounces. After a bit of experience most groups do away with the shot glasses.

Exercise

Vigorous exercise before a tasting can heighten the appetite, sensitize the palate, calm the nerves, and clear the sinuses. I always try to get a run and a shower in before a tasting. To engage your entire tasting group beyond the trivial exercise of glass lifting, a brisk group walk around the block should precede the mid-tasting food course. Moderate exercise and modest alcohol intake both tend to raise the blood levels of High Density Lipoproteins (HDLs). High HDLs predict a long healthy life free of cardiovascular disease.

Smoking policy

Cigarette smoke lowers HDLs and also irritates the hell out of non-smokers. As wine tasting host you may have to deal with this issue. Nowadays the vast majority of enophiles don't smoke, but there are exceptions. Some are still brazen enough to light up, especially at the conclusion of a tasting. They seem to assume that the only valid objection to their noxious behavior is when it interferes with wine appreciation. They wait until the last wine has been downed, but remain oblivious that people are still breathing. Distinguished European guests are the most likely offenders and present the greatest diplomatic challenge. The Count de Saint-Afrique mentioned earlier was such a one. My objection to his behavior netted me a stern rebuke in the hallway from his inebriated host.

Violent, group-destroying altercations can erupt between inebriated smokers and non-smokers. My preference is to ban smoking entirely at, following, or in the vicinity of a tasting.

Six with one blow

Plan the groupings of the wines (the flights), and their sequence, in advance. The wines can be served one at a time, but flights of two, three, four, or more wines at one time offer more opportunities to compare and time to observe changes as the wines develop in the glass. The only difficulty with six wines in a flight is that 90 glasses on one crowded table of imbibers is a bit dangerous. Flights of two, three, or four wines are the norm. It's easiest on the host to have the guests bring their own glasses, but have a few in reserve for those who forget.

A classic technique in sensory psychology for testing the ability to detect differences is to present three solutions, two of the three being identical. The subject is asked to identify which solution is different from the others. You could do the same thing at a tasting, making two of the three wines in a flight identical, but it reduces the number of wines served. An adaptation of this technique for wine tastings is to have two wines of one region, grape, or vintage contrasted with one of a different region, grape, or vintage. For example, in a Bordeaux Vs California cabernet tasting you could announce that each flight of three wines contains two from one country and one from the other, the guests being asked to identify which one of the three is different, and only then, whether the odd one is a Bordelais or a Californian. The more advanced guests then try to identify the individual wines.

Orchestration

The progression of palate fatigue (generalized sensory adaptation) and intoxication dictate the progression of wines during a tasting from a delicate and refined first flight towards a full-bodied and tannic finale. A proper tasting is like a symphony with three movements: a prelude or introduction, a longer middle section, and a stirring conclusion. With a vertical tasting the prelude can be a flight of the few oldest wines that may be fading, requiring a rested palate. The larger middle flight or flights would be the mature, but still-robust, middle-aged vintages, and the finale would be the vintages still available at reasonable price for cellaring, but too tannic for current enjoyment.

However, the traditional approach for vertical tastings, and one that I have seen done with great success, is to start with the youngest wine and work backwards chronologically, one at a time, ending with the oldest – and presumably best and rarest.

For a regional tasting such as a survey of Italian wines, start with dry whites, then go to the main group of reds, and finish with dessert wines with fruit or pastry. Dry wines show poorly following sweet.

Arranging the flights

Wines are usually served blind in numbered paper bags. Adjust the information level so your guests are challenged but not confused. For example, in a vertical tasting of a Bordeaux chateau, a flight consisting of the '61, '75, & '80 as one identified group would be too easy. All of the guests would quickly identify the browning complex ethereal '61, the tannic fruitless '75, and the light washed out '80. However, if the years were '61, '66, & '70, a more closely spaced trio of classic years, or '81, '82, & '83, or '88, '89, & '90, then the task would be more challenging.

To further increase the challenge, list the contents of all the flights on a handout, but not the sequencing of flights. Thus, at each flight the guests would be asked to identify which of the several flights was being served, and only then which wine within the flight was which. More difficult, and the most common approach, is a chronological list of all the wines for the tasting, with no clue as to the groupings; and, the most difficult, and not recommended, is to announce only the theme.

A sample tasting

As a sample of the application of these notions, retrace with me my planning for a vertical tasting of Chateau Leoville Las Cases, a highly regarded and generally consistent second growth St. Julien. The event was held in 1982. The first 8 wines were easy to select, being sanely priced and including all of the best recent vintages. Those were the '66, '67, '70, '71, '75, '76, '78, & '79. The '79 was the most recent vintage available at the time. I had all of the recent "big" vintages ('66, '70, '75, '78), and enough of the others to provide plenty of contrast.

To give the tasting a first-class image I added two budget busters, the legendary '61 and the highly regarded '62. No additional older vintages were needed. Anything older than the '59 might merely have demonstrated, at great expense, that wine does not live forever. (Indeed it turned out that the '61 and '62, perhaps through sub-optimal storage, sadly demonstrated this point to the disappointed group.) I was nevertheless reluctant to stop at only 10 wines, so I added the two most recent and therefore moderately priced years of the neighboring property, Leoville Barton.

To provide additional sensory contrast and as a token to even older vintages, I added the 1920 Federico Paternia Gran Reserva, a Bordeaux style Rioja that I had purchased inexpensively from a tiny uncooled shop in Madrid. It was likely to be vinegar, but I was dying to try it, and surely even the trades-people attending had never tasted that one. For contrast with the 1920 Paternia and with the '61 Las Cases, I served one of the great successes of Federico Paternia, the '61 Gran Reserva, kindly donated by a guest when he heard about the '20.

At the end of the tasting I served some food and then two aged dessert wines from the Loire with elegant French pastry that my wife created. The dessert wines were relatively expensive, but considerably less so than a single older vintage of Las Cases or a Sauternes would have been. The arrangement of the wines into flights was described in the handout that I gave the guests as they arrived, which follows.

Vertical Tasting of Chateau Leoville Las Cases

(March, 1982)

"The wines will be served blind in pairs. The wines that will be paired together are revealed, as follows, but not which is which within each pair, nor the sequence in which the pairs will be presented.

A	Leoville Las Cases	1961,	1962
B	Leoville Las Cases	1966,	1967
C	Leoville Las Cases	1970,	1971
D	Leoville Las Cases	1975,	1976
E	Leoville Las Cases	1978,	1979
F	Leoville Barton	1978,	1979
G	Federico Paternia	1920,	1961 Grand Reserva

After the meal, with pastry:

Moulin Touchais (Anjou)	1959
Quarts de Chaume	1964"

The consecutive pairs of vintages I had chosen suggested the flights of only two wines. The first two flights served were both Las Cases to give everyone a fix on the characteristics of the property. I led off with flight A which, if fading in old age, might be easier to appreciate on a fresh palate. The interlopers, flights F and G, were placed third and sixth as taste breaks. The two Bartons fit right in taste-wise. One guest suggested that the radically different Riojas were disturbing. I welcomed the contrast. It drove home for me the point that the Leovilles have commonality. Several guests with more limited tasting experience volunteered that the '61 Paternia, which had an intriguing peanut butter taste, was the best wine they had ever met. Palate fatigue to the St. Juliens may have contributed to that impression.

As soon as each flight of wines was tasted and guessed at, the bottles were undressed to permit the association of fresh sensory

220

memories with the identities of the wines. Many then took a last taste of the identified wines while awaiting the next flight. The only time you wouldn't reveal identities until the end of an event is during a formal competition. Since I'd given the guests a list of all the wines, as the evening progressed the choices became fewer and the identifying easier – but the numbing effects of palate fatigue and advancing intoxication were an effective counterpoint.

The discussion leader

You may want someone to lead the discussion. This is needed only with neophytes. The leadership role must be arranged in advance to give the person time to prepare. Since you'll be fetching and decanting, and since you'll know which flight is which, you might want to ask the wine merchant to lead the discussion. Alternately, arrange to have someone else do the decanting. Groups of sophisticated tasters typically dispense with formal discussion leaders. This leaves newcomers to an established group insufficiently tutored. To counter this problem, it is best to seat the neophytes alongside the most gregarious and knowledgeable member of the group.

The caterer

Try to recruit one of the guests, or better still a non-drinking spouse - to take charge of final preparation and service of the food. An outside caterer or hired hand is a modest investment compared with the value of the wines that you might otherwise not have time to enjoy. Recruit a second guest to keep the bread basket and water pitchers full, but don't casually delegate the potentially disastrous task of emptying the dump buckets. The first guest to arrive should be corralled to admit and greet subsequent arrivals while you continue your subterranean decanting. Unless it is a well-established group you will need a guest list for your greeter. A set of pre-labeled stick on name tags will provide a running attendance. When all the tags are gone it means everyone has arrived. Running everything yourself keeps you away from the tasting table, and the stress of responsibility can impair your sensory acuity. Your exhilaration at your organizational success will otherwise be dampened by the apparent deterioration of your palate.

Decanting and breathing

Most wine needs time to breathe before serving. The amount of time required will vary with the wine, its temperature, with the amount of air contact that it receives upon and after being opened, and with the pace of the tasting. If the pace of the tasting is relaxed, then the wine will have time to blossom in the glass. If the schedule is torrid, insufficiently breathed wines will reach their zenith in the dump bucket. At a dinner party I sometimes open, decant, and immediately serve several tannic and relatively young reds as the soup bowls are being cleared. The guests then follow the blossoming and declining of the wine during the hour or so it takes for final preparation, service, and consumption of the entree.

With a wine tasting you're on a much tighter schedule. Older wines, lighter years, and white wines need considerably less than one hour of breathing. With these more fragile wines, I serve without delay. Highly tannic wines of recent vintage can improve for hours, even days. If the corks are merely removed, breathing is slow. Some swear by this practice. They uncork hours in advance and then decant just before serving. If the wines are poured into a decanter they will pick up oxygen during the pour and from the greater surface area in the decanter. Ship decanters with wide bases offer the greatest surface area. It is perfectly acceptable to serve the wine directly from decanters, assuming you have enough of them. The other option is double decanting. The bottles are rinsed (with chlorine free distilled water) and the wines are poured back into them.

To insure against the disaster of mixing up the identity of the wines, the Golden Rule is to double decant to reconnect with the label, and to completely double decant and bag only one wine at a time. That way it's almost impossible for the semi-inebriated sommelier, which is what you will be, to get the wines confused during decanting.

The traditional candle is still a good way to get a bright spot of light under the neck of a bottle during decanting so as to detect the approach of the sediment, but a flashlight standing on its heel, especially the high intensity variety, works just as well.

Practice decanting in advance using water to be sure that with the decanter you've selected you'll be able to pour back into the narrow opening of the wine bottle. Some decanters have the nasty habit of pouring in too wide a stream, or of inducing the most slowly poured wine to slide down their outer surface onto the table. (The most expensive wines are usually the most slowly poured.) I've found that an ugly, squat, one-quart Pyrex kitchen measure makes the safest, strongest, and least expensive vessel to use when double decanting 750 ml bottles. The modest investment in a plastic funnel – Teflon being the most inert – that goes into the bottle for the second transfer can save valuable wines from dribbling onto the table. Take an empty bottle with you when funnel shopping to ensure correct sizing. (If you use a funnel with a screen be careful. The screen can clog with sediment and overflow.)

As a guestimate, assume that the first flight will be poured 20 minutes after the announced starting time, and that the second flight will be poured 10 minutes per wine after that (e.g. 20 minutes for a two wine flight, 30 for a three wine flight). You'll be decanting between flights, usually two flights prior to serving. With this schedule you double-decant flight three while flight one is being poured.

It should be obvious by now that in order to adjust breathing times, someone at the table has to know which wines are in each flight. That someone will probably be you. You can, however, avoid knowing which wine is which within each flight by having someone other than yourself number the bagged bottles as they arrive at the table.

Scoring schemes

It can be fun to engage the group as a body in scoring the wines within the tasting. The 100-point scale is pretty familiar to every serious collector. At the end you can, by show of hands, determine the first, second, third, and last choices.

How to keep the group going

Once you've had a successful tasting, you'll have an easier time assembling participants for a reprise. The participants from tasting #1 will fill most of the seats, especially if the theme, site, and date were selected by the group at the debut. With an ongoing group, the best moment to begin discussion of the next theme and site is when you're reminder calling prior to a tasting. The best time at that tasting to broach the subject is before the first wine is poured, perhaps while waiting for stragglers to arrive. At that time everyone is comfortable, focused, and mentally sharp. Bringing it up later in the evening never seems to elicit much of a response as some are preoccupied with the current tasting, others are too mellow, and the rest are late getting home. If you've laid the groundwork, then at least one person will be prepared with a theme and offer of a site. Many couples need to consult in privacy before offering their home for such a major undertaking. Have some backup suggestion in mind lest embarrassing silence follow your query. Or, the theme and site of the next tasting can be left for email discussion at a later date.

A good way to establish the continuity of a group is to find a permanent schedule, such as the first Tuesday of every even numbered month, or settle into a permanent day of the week, usually Sunday if some of your members are in the trade.

A ceremonial passing of the tasting supplies on to the new host can symbolically effect the commitment and add a bit of tradition to the group – though I've had no personal success with the notion.

A well stocked host's kit would contain a name list, funnel, paper wine bags, paper tablecloth, breathalyzer, and a copy of this chapter.

When the flesh rebels

The most enjoyable tastings can have the most unpleasant aftermaths. When the wines are all excellent, in ample quantity, develop in the glass to encourage repeated sipping, and are sufficiently varied to invite multiple between-flight comparisons, you'll be tempted to consume to excess. A drive home or to a restaurant following the tasting, followed by food odors, can be just enough added stimulation to trigger vomiting. Food odors and rhythmic movements compound the effects of alcohol. Motion sickness and food poisoning, of which excessive alcohol consumption is an example, share the same neural circuitry. They complement one another in a most unappetizing manner. A dinner that you walk to after the tasting is usually a delight. A dinner that you must drive to can be a disaster. Most veteran tasters have had one, and only one, such experience. Note how little they now swallow at tastings.

Multiple dump buckets within easy reach and a plastic spit cup for every guest encourage spitting rather than swallowing. At the least, readily accessible dump buckets make it just as easy to dump as to gulp to empty the glasses when the next flight is passed. Extra glasses encourage saving over swallowing, which puts off the swallow versus dump decision to a time when a dump impulse is more likely to rule. Maintain a leisurely tasting pace to allow time for the liver to metabolize the alcohol from the first flight before the alcohol from the last flight enters the bloodstream.

Chapter 23 * THE PSYCHOLOGY OF WINE TASTINGS

Knowledge of the goals that motivate people to attend wine tastings should help you to orchestrate successful tastings. It may also help you to better understand your own behavior. I detect twelve, often complementary, goals that motivate people to attend wine tastings.

1 - Palate Education
2 - The Pleasant Taste of Wine
3 - Evaluation for Current Consumption
4 - Evaluation for Cellaring
5 - Socialization
6 - Companion Tending
7 - Philanthropic Zeal
8 - Modest Cost
9 - Business Contacts
10 - Exploration
11 - Culinary Delight
12 - An Excuse to Get Drunk

(1) Palate Education

Palate education is the process of learning to identify the various aromas and tastes of wine. A person with an educated palate enjoys wine more fully than someone who experiences but cannot identify the visual, gustatory, and olfactory components.

The base untutored protoplasm that palate education builds upon - the ability to smell and taste – varies between individuals and deteriorates with age, especially after age 60. Those most liberally endowed have the potential to discriminate quite reliably as to grape, vintage, region, and property, but even the least endowed among us has the right to enjoy trying.

For the palate education of beginners, experts are needed to provide verbal labels that the less experienced can attach to their taste and aroma sensations. Newsletter descriptions by experts help, but wine changes so dramatically with age and aeration and often bottle to bottle that an expert in the flesh is best.

When only one expert is present, tastings can become tutorials or lectures, and the group becomes dependent on the availability of Herr Professor. Unfortunately, experts who don't themselves learn from the group tend to drop out. In contrast, two well-educated palates can generate a delightful and educational intercourse. The educated palates should be seated close enough to one another to allow communication, but far enough apart to require full voice. Seating two experts opposite one another at mid-table is best. This way they cannot help but provide, through their interchanges, a spontaneous seminar. One of the most frustrating of life's experiences is to attend a tasting at which the experts assemble at the other end of the table and whisper among themselves. Getting the experts to cooperate with your seating plan is no easy task.

(2) The Pleasant Taste of Wine

Some of the wines at a tasting can be delightful, but you get very little of each wine. If one's goal is to drink good tasting wine with your friends, wouldn't one fine magnum and a-half-dozen friends suffice? Do you really do any more at a tasting than decide that you would or wouldn't enjoy a particular wine if more were available?

The answers to those questions are, respectfully, no and yes. One fine bottle is not as nice as samples from a carefully orchestrated variety, and tasters do enjoy the modest servings. When you visit an art gallery you could spend the entire visit admiring and analyzing one canvas, but it's usually more pleasant to view a variety of paintings.

When an organizer presents a tasting theme of young, high-acid brutally tannic, low-fruit wines that have no current charm, the pleasant taste motive is not appeased. Such was my reaction to the '75,

'81 and again the '86 Bordeaux at tastings held soon after their release, so I bought none of them. To date the evolution of these vintages has not led me to regret my decision. This is also the problem with some vertical tastings when the property is consistent vintage to vintage. You get some variation due to age, but overall it can get pretty boring even with a great property.

(3) Evaluation for Current Consumption

This motive refers to the question most asked of wine merchants: "What should I buy in the ten to twenty-dollar price range for tonight's dinner?" Tastings that address this query stick to currently available, ready-to-drink, moderately priced wines – the typical fare at introductory store tastings. People in the trade must evaluate and dispense these wines every day in the course of their trade. How could they relish repeating the experience for their supposed recreation by attending your "great cheap wine" event? This theme is strictly for beginners, and it's probably already adequately served by the weekly Saturday afternoon store tasting.

(4) Evaluation for Cellaring

Once you've experienced mature first-quality Cabs and Bordeaux, and have created suitable storage, you'll be on the prowl for cellar-worthy wines. The discussants at tastings should always address potential versus current appeal. I still remember the first serious tasting that I attended in 1978. It was a tandem horizontal – recently released '75 Bordeaux against '75 California Cabs. The Californians were all more attractive. No one announced to the uninitiated such as myself that the '75 Bordeaux were heralded in the wine press as having great potential - the best since the '70 - but lacking in current charm. The experts huddled together at the far end of the table. I ignorantly passed up most of the '75 Bordeaux, and the shop that sponsored the tasting lost a potentially big sale. (As it turned out, my palate was accurate. Most of the '75 Bordeaux never went anywhere.)

(5) Socialization

At introductory wine tastings, socialization is the main draw, the wine serving primarily to lubricate the conversation and, at store tastings, the wallet. At advanced tastings, socialization is less dominant, but still essential. A greeter as guests arrive is good form. A comfortable spot away from the tasting room for gathering as the members arrive is also nice – for once at the sit down table everyone is locked into seats, which prevents contact with the friendly faces at the other end of the room. The consummate host periodically circumnavigates the periphery of the table and engages anyone who's being neglected. A relaxed tasting-pace affords time for conversation beyond the business at hand, as does a get-up-and-serve-yourself food break. You should also provide an after-tasting lingering opportunity away from the tasting table, and join the lingering, leaving the clean up for the morning after.

(6) Companion Tending

This can be a dominant motive for one member of a couple. Companions accompany their wine-loving loved ones, but personally are only passingly interested in wine. They are along to be with and watch over their companions, and for motives such as socialization and food, and to serve as designated driver. Some companions eventually develop a passion for wine - usually not. The bug bites or it doesn't.

Some companions might prefer to withdraw during the formal tasting to a separate room. When you suspect that a companion is so inclined you can tactfully offer the option of attending the food part of the event without paying for or tasting any of the wines. If you suspect that your very own spouse is a tender, don't fight it. Tenders are especially appreciative of personalized conversation on topics other than wine, and can often be recruited to host wine dinners at their home. When the companion theme is neglected, those for whom it is the dominant motive are likely to nix the next invitation, and will keep their wine-loving associate otherwise engaged as well.

While on the topic of companions, a related issue, seat sharing, comes to mind. Seat sharing is when two people try to share the cost of one seat at a tasting. Since they actually occupy two seats at your already crowded table and consume as much food and wine as two, seat sharing is actually a euphemism for too-cheap-to-pay. As host you're damned by the sharing couple if you protest, and damned by the rest of the group if you don't. NO SHARING is the way to go.

(7) Philanthropic Zeal

Pricey charity tastings have become quite popular. The government co-sponsors these events. Although it may not appear quite kosher, the full, liberally estimated current retail value of the donated wine is tax deductible for the donor, as is the admission fee for the rest of the guests. Both the wine donors and the paying guests get to taste great wines under full protection of the philanthropic umbrella from any risk of being labeled wine snobs. If the wines have appreciated considerably since purchase, that appreciation is never taxed. This is the only way outside the auction market that private individuals can legally "sell" wine. Where the charity is a worthwhile enterprise to which you would donate anyway, the tasting is free. Everyone comes out ahead.

Many educational TV stations have an annual auction of donated merchandise. They often have a special wine section. You get a tax deduction for the liberally estimated retail value of your wine. You can also donate for auction seats at a tasting of great wines. Participation in the tasting is a secondary benefit for the donor.

(8) Modest Cost

A well-paid professional acquaintance of mine could be counted on to attend tastings where the cost was under $35, but he predictably passed whenever the tab exceeded $40. He remained at this balance point for a few years, and then dropped out when the group's advancing appetite consistently exceeded his arbitrary financial threshold. More often, though, a wine taster's threshold for cost and quality advance with experience. Within a few years of acquiring a taste for fine wine, many would pounce on the opportunity to taste 2005 First Growths for $200 a head.

The offerings in private tasting groups typically climb the quality-and-cost ladder in step with the interests of the majority of the members: those whose passion or budget lag or leap, drop out. It's inevitable and unavoidable. The best you can do is to please yourself while keeping pace with a solid core of members, and recruit replacements for the drop outs.

(9) Business Contacts

For introductory tastings the fellow from the local wine shop will be there as part of his job, and will be satisfied if he finds that you're serving wines that are currently available on his shelves. He'll be quite pleased if everyone notices and comments favorably on the wine that he has contributed. He'll be delighted if he gets to make a few astute comments that demonstrate his expertise, and will be ecstatic if a couple of your guests who were not previously among his clientele patronize his shop. There's nothing sinister about this. In most cases it's done graciously and with apparent social pleasure. The wine merchant's potential gain will be greatest on the initial visit, so the business theme alone may not bring him back as a regular.

The wine merchant will not be the only guest drawn by business motives. The dentist, lawyer, realtor, building contractor, psychologist and mortician are all interested in the wines and the camaraderie, but they also know that social networking is a critical part of their trade. To serve the business motive, invite no more than one of each type of non-wine professional, mention their trade on occasion, and structure time for socialization.

Despite the various business interests at play, a non-business atmosphere is essential to set private tastings apart from store-sponsored events. It should be obvious to all that everyone, including the host, pays their share, that there's absolutely no expectation to buy anything from anyone, and that the wines are selected regardless of commercial availability, and are at or below current retail cost.

(10) Exploration

Everyone is curious about new places. Visiting a restaurant, hotel, or home that you've never been to, serves the need to explore. Rotate the tasting site, even within one house. Repeating endlessly in one room is boring. You needn't be limited to private homes. A museum lobby after hours, the private room in a famous restaurant on an off night, a golf course club house, riverboat, panoramic lookout, or waterfall could be a special feature of a tasting. Visit the site before booking lest the management assign you to a windowless, basement function-room with a band blaring next door.

(11) Culinary Delight

It's always a relief to get up after an hour or more of sit-down tasting for a food break. If you're not inclined to cook there's always take-out, pot luck, or group members who'd be glad to host a tasting at their place, if you assemble the wines. Serve mildly seasoned food during an intermission. Hot chili, tangy barbecue sauce, or hot dogs laced with mustard are forbidden. Place the food intermission into the second half of the tasting – after three of five flights being typical. To break the rigid seating of the tasting, send the guests through a buffet-type food line.

A dinner with wines is a more elaborate matter which frequently brings out the spouses. It's not strictly a wine tasting, as the food tastes and odors interact with those of the wine. A fine restaurant is the easiest venue. A full-bore affair begins with a sparkling wine, usually champagne, followed by a seafood or pasta appetizer (with a white sauce) served with a pair of contrasting dry white wines. The main course follows accompanied by at least two matched red wines. A vintage port follows with blue veined cheese – an English Stilton being traditional. Finally, if you really must go all the way, a white dessert wine is served with fruity pastry. Some serve the white dessert wine before the port. The whole affair can take three to four leisurely hours, and is a welcome relief from straight tastings. Unlike straight tastings, larger portions of fewer wines seem to work best. Anywhere from six to ten diners work out nicely, or double that number with magnums.

After having participated in several gala wine dinners, I now prefer to omit the champagne and acidic salad dressing, and begin with an appetizer or soup with a single stunning white followed by the main attraction – the red wines. That way the palate is still fresh when the serious wine is poured. Up to four reds should be presented as one flight a few minutes before the main course arrives, to be tasted once without food, and reprised *ad libitum* with the food. I number the feet of the glasses with a waterproof felt marker. Separate glasses for a flight of four wines would exceed my supply of appropriate stemware. I get a bit of grumbling from wives when I ask couples to share four glasses with one another, but they usually go along. If a couple objects they're free to go two glasses per, and sample the wines sequentially. You can also marry a tasting to a dinner. I once worked a vertical tasting of 14 Conterno Monfortino Barolos around the courses of a three-hour, sit-down restaurant dinner, and no one complained.

(12) - An Excuse to Get Drunk

Alcoholics occasionally find their way to tastings, but they never repeat. They're probably disappointed by the modest servings. They quickly realize that vodka or Gallo are cheaper and quicker. This is not to say that alcohol on the brain is not an absolutely essential component of enophilia. Alcohol in moderation produces a pleasant high that is exponentially enhanced by the aromas, tastes, socialization, and other pleasures that this chapter is all about.

Chapter 24 * WINE COUNTRY TRAVEL

Many enophiles, including Robert Parker, can trace the birth of their passion to a romantic wine country vacation. My delivery took place in a sun-drenched Loire Valley guest house, midwifed by a bottle of, as I vividly recall, the latest vintage of the fruity local white wine. The midwife was assisted by bright sunshine, fresh French bread, my wife, and a pungent blue cheese.

Others travel to wine country at later stages of enophilia. If you've experienced the 1945 and 1982 Mouton, then a pilgrimage to the chateau that produced it – the very vats – the very vines – and a sample with the wine maker from the latest brew – could be a deeply moving experience.

I had expected my trip to Bordeaux to be like my earlier tour of the Napa Valley - open gates, guided tours on the half hour, and – shoulder-to-shoulder in the tasting room - after paying the modest tasting fee - at least six wines poured at every spontaneous stop, with the good stuff often available from under the counter for the asking. The newsletter authors glide from chateau to chateau, tasting all the way, don't they?

I was eager to visit the heralded wine museum and vast new cellar at Chateau Mouton Rothschild. When I arrived at midday without appointment, after driving a considerable distance, the iron gates were shut and locked. Margaux, Cos, Latour, and Petrus were locked as well. Yquem didn't even have a sign – just a vicious guard dog. The plowman at Rouget brusquely turned away and returned to his tractor. The man in the office at Giscours said they were closed for the day (it was after 4:30) – try Prieure Lichine up the road and come back tomorrow. At Prieure Lichine, Alexis Lichine was a wonderful host. He saved my vacation with a tour, a taste, and a chat in the parlor. But he's gone now and his son, Sacha, is, I'm told, not as welcoming.

A trip through wine country can be a delight or a disaster, the difference often resting on the possession of an up-to-date guidebook that tells you who's gates are open, and when, with locator maps, phone numbers, and the names of good hotels and restaurants. You may be too busy prior to your vacation to plan and reserve a detailed itinerary, or be willing to be tied down to one, but it takes only a few minutes to send for the guidebook; and once in wine country, plan as you go – calling one or two days in advance, and hitting the road early in the morning in plenty of time to get lost and still make the first stop by the typical 9:30 opening.

Professionally guided packaged tours of Bordeaux and its major chateaux are frequently advertised in *The Wine Spectator* and *Decanter* (the British equivalent of The American Wine Spectator) magazines, and on their, and many other, websites. They're not cheap, and they vitiate the spirit of independent adventure, but you're guaranteed your housing, your dining, your transport, your translator, and your reception at the chateaux listed in the brochure.

If you travel in Bordeaux on your own without a guide book, it will usually take you longer than you anticipate to get where you want to go, as you'll get lost in rush-hour traffic in the city of Bordeaux, and you'll not arrive at the property on the few days and hours when they receive visitors. Those Bordeaux chateaux that do give tours have very limited weekday-only hours. Most require appointments.

For example, the delightfully moldy cellar tour at Lafite is given only from 2–4:30 on Tuesday through Thursday but not in August or during the harvest. An appointment is required. The tour is in French, and there's no tasting. Only the latest vintage is on sale, by request, only in the 750 ml size, and at the equivalent of the full US retail price. Come at 4:35 or on Friday or in August and you're out of luck, even if your plane leaves from Paris in the morning. The other Medoc first-growths, and Petrus and Yquem, are even less accessible. They require appointments, arranged in advance, through your negotiant. My negotiant?

Try to avoid weekends as that's when the least is happening, the crush of visitors is heaviest, and the principals are absent, leaving the tasting room and the tours of the inactive winery in the care of part-timers who are not authorized to pour – or even to sell – the good stuff. The most exciting time to visit any winery is during the height of the crush in September or October. Provided they let you in, the winery will be buzzing with activity. The exact harvest dates vary with the weather, so call ahead. If you miss the harvest, go two years after a great vintage – for the tasting samples.

To get special treatment – tea in the parlor, barrel tastings, the opportunity to purchase rare old vintages from the winery's library, dinner reservations at the winery restaurant, or even admission to the winery, you must inquire in advance. Present yourself as distinct from the hordes – as a true connoisseur. Here's where the wine consultant at a big shop that you frequent might be able to pull some strings for you. Ideally, try to tag along when he next travels with his negotiant. If you're on your own you may have more success if you let it be known that you represent a tasting group containing major figures in the trade. In France, you must be able to communicate in French, however limited, or bring along someone who can, or join a professionally guided tour.

Obtain a wine country travel guide and a good highway map and don't forget to bring along a recent newsletter report on the wines of the region. The newsletter will be needed when you must decide whether to make an unscheduled stop at a winery with which you are not familiar and whose open gates suddenly appear as you motor along.

If you plan to buy, then rent a white car (to reflect the sunlight) with a no-see-in trunk. Tour in spring or fall to avoid crowds and wine-cooking heat. U.S. customs agents are very easy on wine. Buy all you can hand carry onto the airplane and declare it, but only if the current ban on liquids in the cabin is relaxed. The tax will be negligible. Never check wine as luggage into the hands of airport baggage handlers or, if it gets that far, un-pressurized airplane holds.

Sometimes all it takes is an earnest request for the opportunity to purchase a particular special vintage. At Quinta do Noval in Porto this approach earned me the opportunity to purchase a bottle of the 1963 National at a very reasonable price.

In contrast to the big wineries in Napa, California, which are mobbed by tourists in the summer, the nearby Oregon wineries, which specialize in Pinot Noir, are all small, and are not crowded with hundreds of visitors. Make your reservations in advance for dinner at Nick's in McMinville – a must stop. The countryside is rugged, rural, and scenic, and the natives are friendly. Spectacular Mt. Rainier is a few hours' drive to the northeast. (I'm told that travelers in Alsace receive the same friendly reception.)

France Wine Country Access

Here's a guide book aimed squarely at the traveling enophile. All the major French wine regions (Champagne, Alsace, Burgundy, Beaujolais, Rhone, Bordeaux, and Loire) are covered in moderate detail. Chateaux that are visitor friendly and interesting to visit, a few special restaurants, a few hotels, city maps, and regional museums and historic sites are all listed. The listings are by no means as exhaustive as you can find in the Michelin Guides, but then you'd need a suitcase full of Michelin guides to cover all the wine regions, and the Michelin Guides are not wine oriented. For the places listed, the critical visiting hours and telephone numbers for making appointments and reservations are given.

This guidebook is not exciting reading, but if you're already excited about visiting the French wine country you don't need a lot of hype. You need travel information, and that it does provide.

La Maison du Vin

There's one in Pauillac, one in St. Estephe, one in Margaux, one in the city of Bordeaux, one in Graves, one in St. Emillion, one in

Sauternes, and one in Barsac. They vary somewhat in their services and hours. Some offer tasting. Most have wine route maps, vineyard information, and someone who speaks a little English. They're some help with lodging and restaurant reservations. Some will arrange or lead chateau visits, and some sell new and/or old wines from the region. They're all listed in somewhat more detail in France Wine Country Access (see above). The Maisons du vin can rescue a wine country vacation in distress.

Regional websites

There are web travel-sites for virtually all wine travel regions. A few examples are NewYorkWines.org, WineCountry.com (California), Oregonwine.org, and terroir-france.com. If have not covered your destination, Google it. Go to the travel section of a major bookstore chain and also check the vast offerings on Amazon.com. Do not travel to a foreign language wine region and expect to find an English language guide book there.

Personal list of wine country superlatives

Best tasting at a winery: Symmington Brothers, Porto (I telephoned that morning from my hotel in Porto for the appointment. I tasted 7 then unreleased 1983 vintage ports plus a vertical of 10 wood ports.)

Best restaurants in wine country: Nick's in McMinville, Oregon and Les Crayeres, Reims, France (Champagne country).

Best hotel wines: Palace Hotel of Bucaco, near Luso, Portugal. Located 100 km south of Porto in a small palace in a spectacular forest setting. The private label wine is Bordeaux style from a tiny vineyard, and is only sold with lunch or dinner at the hotel. Vintages back to the 1920s are on the list, and are cellared beneath the palace. The old reds are magnificent and modestly priced, even the 375s. The old whites are less interesting. To book a room at the palace in season, advance reservations are required. If the rooms are all taken, stay in Luso at the bottom of the hill and bribe the head waiter in advance for a luncheon or dinner table (one seating only). Tell him that you've come half way around the world for the famous old wines.

Most scenic wine country: The Mosel (Germany) and Madeira (island off Portugal)

Most stunning highway travel near wine country: Route 1 along the California coast between San Francisco and Los Angeles. The views of the ocean and cliffs are breathtaking. When journeying in the Napa Valley, expand it by an automobile leg to the south.

Most spectacular winery setting: Ridge Montebello (California) and Cain (Napa, Ca.), and Quinto Do Noval (Douro Valley, Portugal)

Most primitive wine setting: Cinque Terres (Italy)

Best winery park: Cousino Macul (Santiago, Chile) and Ch. Lagrange (St. Julien, France)

Most unusual winery approach: Cable car to Sterling (Napa, Calif.)

Most ornate winery exterior: Cos d'Estournel (St., Estephe, France)

Most stunning architecture: Opus One and Clos Pegase (Napa, Ca.) King Estate, Eugene (Oregon), and Domecq (Jerez, Spain)

Most cordial treatment upon arriving after hours: Ch. Filhot (Sauternes, France), Lynch Bages (Pauilliac), and Haut Marbuzet (St. Estephe)

Prettiest gift shop: Beringer (Napa, California)

Best underground cave tour: Beringer (Napa, California) and Veuve Clicquot, (Reims, Champagne, France)

Best time to visit Bordeaux: In early April during *Portes Ouvertes* (open doors) weekend. Call Bordeaux's Office de Tourism 56-44-28-41 for the exact dates.

Most mold on a cellar tour: Lafite Rothschild (Pauilliac, France) and Pavie (St. Emilion, France)

Best self-guided winery tour: Sterling (Napa)

Most pleasant tasting room: Sterling (Napa)

Most luxurious, pricey, (and worth it) wine country resort: Stonepine (Carmel Valley, California)

Least expensive lodging: Motel 6, (Napa, Calif.- reserve ahead)

Most exciting winery visit: Wherever you happen to be at the peak of the harvest frenzy.

Best wine country boat ride: On the Rhine from Koblenz, Germany

Best winery art galleries: The Hess Collection (Napa) and Imagery Winery (Sonoma Valley).

Best antique car collection: Far Niente (Napa)

Best zoo near wine country: Royan, France. When traveling north by car from the Medoc towards Paris, avoid backtracking to and through the city of Bordeaux by taking the car ferry from Pointe-de- Grave to Royan, which also has excellent beaches and plenty of off season lodging vacancies. Plan on spending most of the day at the zoo.

Worst crowds: Napa Valley on a summer weekend.

Worst smog and worst traffic: Porto, Portugal

Most frustrating experience: Driving aimlessly in circles on unmarked roads in Pomerol and St. Emilion with neither map nor appointment.

Chapter 25 * MEDICAL MATTERS

I sometimes get so caught up in winelore that I forget that wine contains the drug alcohol. While the preponderance of wine connoisseurs are not fatty-liver alcoholics, some do run afoul of gastrointestinal difficulties that sabotage the fulfillment of their passion, while others are plagued by aroma-masking, allergic stuffy noses.

Wine as Medicine

Entire volumes and numerous research careers have been dedicated to the thesis that moderate alcohol consumption–or only wine–or only red wine–is good for your health. Some of this may be self-serving hype financed by the wine industry, but there are a lot of intriguing data. The French Paradox (there's even a book by that name) is that the French indulge in a glorious high-fat, high-choles-terol, low-exercise, hedonistic lifestyle which includes the consump-tion of a great deal of red wine. They also have a much lower incidence of heart attack than their wine-shunning American counter-parts. We could go on *ad nauseum* here trying to balance increased automobile deaths against increased quality of life, liver disease against clean arteries, more wife beating against less cancer, olive oil against margarine, and red wine against whiskey. Instead of getting into all that, let's just note that, both medically and societally, wine has redeeming virtues.

Nasal Congestion

No matter how well your Reidel concentrates the aromatic compounds, if your nasal passages are blocked the aromas will never reach your olfactory apparatus. For some unfortunates, even the slight mustiness in their passive wine cellar triggers an allergic reaction. Others have seasonal allergies from plant and tree pollens. What should you do when the date of the big tasting approaches, and your nasal passages are clogged? If only reputation were at stake, you could fake it, but that wouldn't be much fun. Modern pharmaceutical science offers many remedies for clogged plumbing.

One of the most potent unclogging agents is an over the counter that goes by the proprietary name Afrin. Afrin is a sympathomimetic nasal spray which clears clogged nasal passages and sinuses in less than an hour, permitting you to temporarily breathe nasally again. Frequent use is not recommended. In my experience, Afrin also temporarily anesthetizes the sense of smell.

For those who suffer from allergic nasal congestion, two types of prescription product can clear the nose without impairing smell. One type is a steroid in a metered dose nasal spray which supposedly is not significantly absorbed into the blood stream at the normal dose. The only drawback, aside from possible systemic effects, is that it may take a few days of use to obtain relief, so don't wait until the day before a major tasting to contact your physician for a prescription. The proprietary names for these steroid sprays include Nasalaid and Beconase.

The second type of nasal spray contains cromolyn sodium which blocks the H1 histamine receptors on the mast cells of the nose that are responsible for allergic reactions–very specific indeed, and no steroid risk. It goes by the proprietary name of Nasalcrom. As with the steroids, it's supposed to take a few days. I find that a squirt in each nostril a few hours before wine does the job nicely. I'm not a physician, so see your doctor before trying any of these items. Parker has mentioned the use of a nasal spray of physiological saline, available over the counter. Can't hurt.

Gastrointestinal Distress

A glass or two of wine with dinner is so diluted by the food that only the most exquisitely sensitive stomachs are disturbed.

A foodless, 20-wine-tasting orgy is a more serious challenge. Gastric irritation occurs when alcohol attacks the gut lining, allowing hydrochloric acid and pepsin, which are secreted by the stomach for the purpose of digesting protein, to begin to digest the stomach itself.

Esophagitis, or irritation of the esophagus, is believed to be associated with a weakness of the one-way valve that guards the entrance from the esophagus into the stomach. Gastric acid and pepsin leak back upwards, against gravity, into the lower esophagus where they cause chronic irritation of the esophageal lining, which is not equipped to deal with such challenges. When someone with an irritated esophagus swallows alcohol, he experiences a rapid burning sensation as the alcohol contacts his sensitized esophagus on route to the stomach. The more concentrated the alcohol, the more intense the burning, so whiskey is worse than beer or wine. By abstaining from straight shots of the more concentrated spirits, sensitive enophiles are usually able to continue to enjoy their wine.

Acid from the stomach travels forward into the first part of the small intestine, which is called the duodenum, along with the partially digested food. If the stomach secretes more acid than is needed, or continues to secrete acid after the food is gone, then, if additional risk factors are present, the duodenum can be irritated. Single episodes produce acute gastritis or duodenal inflammation. Chronic irritation leads to peptic ulceration, which means holes.

The risk factors that predispose to peptic ulceration, in addition to alcohol, include psychological stress, anti-inflammatory drugs including aspirin and Advil, steroid hormones such as cortisone (which are also naturally released during stress), ingredients in coffee which are not removed by decaffeination, acetic acid (vinegar), nicotine (from cigarettes), gastric infection with the bacterium *Helicobacter Pylori*, and, if it goes backwards into the stomach, bile (from the liver).

The nicotine from cigarettes relaxes the pyloric sphincter that guards the opening from the stomach into the duodenum. This allows bile to flow backwards from the duodenum into the stomach, where it can cause gastric ulcers by stripping off mucosal secretions that protect the lining of the stomach from acid and digestive enzymes. Smokers are therefore more prone to gastric ulcers, while non-smokers usually develop duodenal ulcers.

When wine consumption is combined with other risk factors, the likelihood of esophageal, gastric, and duodenal irritation are increased. By avoiding the non-vinous risk factors, you can increase the likelihood that your gut will be able to tolerate the continued arrival of your cellar treasures.

Wine and food together are usually safer than wine alone, as the food dilutes the alcohol and also slows its passage through the gut. In some individuals, however, protein snacks stimulate more gastric acid secretion than is required to digest the snack. Similarly, in some individuals fatty snacks, such as high fat cheeses served at tastings, stimulate bile secretion into the duodenum and can do more stimulating than diluting, leaving turned-on gastric and biliary secretions behind to collaborate with subsequently imbibed alcohol. Hourly, small portions of milk, once the backbone of peptic ulcer therapy, have the same draw-back. Chewing gum can also stimulate gastric secretion.

The traditional bread and water served at tastings are ideal. They provide carbohydrate and water to absorb and dilute the digestive juices and alcohol, and contain no protein or fat which would stimulate mucosa threatening secretions. Eat some bread and drink some water after every flight of wine at tastings.

When you take plain aspirin tablets, your stomach is temporarily faced with a high concentration of aspirin as the tablet breaks up and passes through the lining of your stomach. Buffered or enteric coated aspirin comes back to the stomach via the blood stream, but in a much lower concentration. Even enteric coated aspirin is best taken with food lest it reflux back into the stomach after the intestinal environment has removed the protective coating. Aspirin blocks the H+/Na+ exchange pump that puts acid (H+) into the stomach. If your stomach is already acidic when you take the aspirin, then the ion flow can reverse. The resulting high intracellular acid can digest the cells. Thus, aspirin taken with food, at which time the stomach's contents dilute the acid and the aspirin, is safer than aspirin taken on an empty stomach. If you swallow so much at tastings that you need aspirin to prevent a hangover, then you're swallowing too much.

The worst case scenario, and one which is not all that uncommon, is to take uncoated aspirin (to prevent a hangover), drink coffee (to wake up), and eat a quick hamburger (fat and protein), just prior to a tasting. At the tasting, which occurs at a time in your life when you're under personal stress, you forget to use a spit bucket, and finish up with more coffee and a cigarette in preparation for the drive home. Those who treasure wine consumption (and who else would be reading this) should avoid the contributing risk factors, no matter how robust their present health. People in the trade need to be specially wary, as a sensitive stomach rapidly leads to unemployment.

Theory on the cause and treatment of peptic ulcers has undergone a revolution. It has been shown that a major contributing factor for peptic ulcers is a bacterium named *Helicobacter pylori* that thrives in the acid environment of stomachs. Virtually all ulcer patients appear to harbor this bug. The infection is confirmed by a blood test for antibody to the bacterium. The treatment is a simple but specific course of antibiotics. This is great news for enophiles. If you have gastric symptoms when you drink, get tested. Perhaps you don't have to auction off your wine after all. A few years after the antibiotic treatment the antibodies will wear off and a repeat test should be negative.

Other problems such as gall stones, heart disease, and stomach cancer can mimic the symptoms of peptic ulcers. The ulcer diagnosis can only be confirmed by x-ray or gastroscopy, and simple non-ulcer gastritis (stomach irritation) is diagnosed by default after the more serious possibilities are ruled out.

Prior to the bacterial theory, the modern treatment of uncomplicated gastritis (stomach irritation) and peptic ulcer were drugs that blocked H_2 Histamine secretion. Cimetadine (Tagamet), famotidine (Pepcid), nizatidine (Axid), and ranitidine (Zantac) block the action of hormones that normally stimulate gastric secretion.

The Proton-Pump Inhibitors omeprazole (Prilosec) and lansoprazole (Prevacid) also very specifically and powerfully inhibit gastric acid secretion. They inactivate a specific enzyme responsible for the

Figure 25-1. The best remedy for an unstable enophile is to guide him to a comfortable couch to induce a nap. Your moral and legal responsibilities as host continue until your guest is safely home.

final step of acid release. A protective coating of the stomach lining is provided by sucralfate (Carafate), and antacids such as Tums, Mylanta, and Gelusil neutralize acid already within the stomach.

These drugs still have a place in the treatment of acute symptoms, but their role in long term management should now be greatly reduced.

Chapter 26 * THE DISCRETE CONNOISSEUR

Neoenophiliacs typically go through a phase of total immersion in their hobby. In time the symptoms subside, and a more balanced approach to life is restored. But while it lasts, the preoccupation with wine jeopardizes social position, status within the family, and respect at the workplace.

To introduce these risks, a few definitions are required.

Enologists are concerned with the production as opposed to the appreciation of wine, whereas **Enophiles** (wine lovers) are appreciators of wine. Besides tasting and enjoying it at all stages of development, enophiles love to talk about wine, and to visit and even invest in wine shops, vineyards and wineries. Two curious subspecies occasionally encountered are home winemakers and label collectors, but those folks go beyond the scope of this book.

In the early stages of enophilia most wine lovers go through a phase of compulsive browsing. **A Compulsive Browser** is an enophile drawn by an invisible tractor beam into every wine shop that crosses his path. The route and timing of his business and social travels are manipulated to bring the return leg of each trip past one of his favorite you-know-whats. As he approaches the shop he casually announces to his traveling companions that – since they're passing that way - he begs their indulgence for a few minutes while he checks out the new arrivals. He then meticulously examines the fine wine collection. Companions of compulsive browsers allow extra time for every excursion. They learn to amuse themselves by shopping, reading, or eating while the few minutes drag on towards closing time.

Astute wine merchants cater to the comforts of the companions of compulsive browsers, as contented companions are less likely to abort a big sale. Besides, companions are themselves a captive clientele. The merchant provides general merchandise racks and gourmet food departments, and locates adjacent to restaurants.

Companions of compulsive browsers can cure the affliction. Dr. Gold's prescription is to give gifts of wine books and newsletters. Gift copies of this book are an excellent example. These gifts convert compulsive browsers into **Compulsive Readers**. Compulsive reading is more educational than compulsive browsing, and can conveniently be done at home. Compulsive readers continue to buy wine, but usually place their orders by long-distance telephone and pay by credit card, wine pick-up often involving no more than a car-trunk exchange at the next tasting.

Being an enophile requires no proficiency. To acquire the label one merely pursues an interest in wine. When this pursuit leads to knowledge one merits the designation **Wine Connoisseur**.

Wine Snobs do many of the same things as enophiles and wine connoisseurs, but they also focus undue energy on trying to appear sophisticated. Wine snobs consider themselves, and perhaps a few internationally renowned experts, to be the only true wine connoisseurs. Occasionally they are knowledgeable, but mostly they are not. If they really were experts, then they wouldn't have to advertise. A Freudian might suggest that wine snobs are over-compensating for real or imagined inadequacy. They form exclusive tasting groups from which beginners (everyone less sophisticated than themselves) are pointedly excluded.

You are, I hope, a devoted enophile or connoisseur with no particular interest in impressing anyone. Some people will nevertheless think of you as a wine snob. These **Wine Derogateurs** are drawn from the uninitiated, who still constitute a majority of the adult population. They have never developed an appreciation for fine wines and cannot understand what all the fuss is about. By applying the label wine snob to everyone who consumes expensive wine, they convince themselves that they are not missing out on anything important.

Even blood relatives, indeed your own parents or children, may consider your wine cellar, wine library, wine glasses, and wine tastings to be the definitive expressions of wine snobbery. These persons consider all wines costing more than $10 to be rip offs, and view those who buy, taste, and cellar more expensive wines to be ostentatious fools and borderline alcoholics whose judgment in all matters is not to be trusted. Those who anticipate receiving an inheritance from you grieve over the lost revenue, while those from whom you anticipate receiving an inheritance interpret your profligate vinosity as an indication that you are not to be trusted with money.

Without a frank discussion of wine values, wine derogateurs, who in other respects can be quite reasonable, cannot be distinguished from the general population. They may even own liquor stores where they specialize in hard liquor and beer, and subject their wines to deplorable storage. Wine derogateurs also tend to intoxicate on martinis before dinner, which explains their lack of appreciation for any decent wine that might follow.

Some wine derogateurs can simply be ignored, but others are in positions where their opinions can be destructive. The best protection against wine derogateurs is to become a **Discrete Connoisseur**. Those who are unaware of your affection for Latour cannot denigrate you for it. Though not ashamed of his hobby, the discrete connoisseur is careful not to advertise.

Discrete connoisseurs have extensive wine libraries, and store them on bookshelves. Wine snobs buy the biggest coffeetable travels-in-wine-country picture books and leave them open at the first growth displays.

Discrete connoisseurs schedule their European vacations to coincide with the harvest in Bordeaux, the Rhinegau, or the Cinqueterre, where they vicariously join in the picking and the crushing, but when they return home they tell the relatives that were child-sitting for them about the view from the Eifel Tower and the Mona Lisa in the Louvre.

When entertaining employers, employees, and wealthy elderly relatives, discrete connoisseurs avoid ostentatious labels (such as Lafite Rothschild). When you serve wine to potential derogateurs you must remove the price tags, avoid ceremonial bottle opening and decanting, and refrain from comparative tasting seminars, all of which are reserved to be enjoyed in the company of other certified enophiliacs.

Wine snobs, in contrast, invest in $200 replicas of antique brass decanting machines. Fitted with the after-dinner port, the machine becomes the centerpiece at the dining room table. Everyone is supposed to be impressed by the turning of the gears while the dinner plates are being cleared. Decanting machines can be useful, especially for the feeble-handed, but their place is in the cellar or the pantry. Besides, vintage port, even 20 years after the harvest, demands several hours of breathing. This dictates decanting well before the dinner guests are scheduled to arrive.

Discrete connoisseurs seek out well-cellared restaurants where they pay more for the wine than for the food, but the next day they brag to their co-workers about the cuisine and the decor. Wine snobs visit the same restaurants and order the same wines, but subsequently name drop the $20,000 '31 Quinta de Noval that heads the list of vintage ports.

Discrete connoisseurs build passive wine cellars whose presence is undetectable by eye or ear. They do not offer to conduct wine cellar tours, leaving such extravaganzas to commercial wineries. When the existence of the wine cellar leaks out and they are probed by potential derogateurs, discrete connoisseurs casually note that the wine cellar came with the house, was converted from a fallout cellar, or was thrown together from left-over building materials. Wine snobs install illuminated directional signs and decorate the door to their wine cellar with branded end panels from Bordeaux crates.

Wine snobs indiscriminately tout their wine cellar and its contents, oblivious that people with no interest in wine storage will not appreciate their double walls, super-insulated doors, and polyethylene vapor barriers. Discrete connoisseurs do not go so far as to invent lame excuses, as is the practice at most restaurants, but cellar tours should be limited to board-certified enophiles who specifically request a visit.Cellar owners who impose cellar tours on all their dinner guests are correctly identified as wine snobs by the tourees. Worse, these amateur tour guides are occasionally visited by thieves who consider a well-stocked wine cellar to be a unique challenge, a sign of affluence, or an affront to their poverty. They apply a Robin Hood type of philosophy that anyone who can afford a wine cellar deserves to be robbed. Once in the house, thieves may not limit their attentions to the wines.

A discrete connoisseur need not sip in solitude. His circle of friends expands to include other aficionados in whose company he pursues his passion.

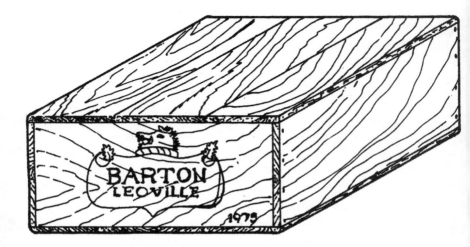

SUBJECT INDEX

****

The Wine Appreciation Guild has been an educational pioneer in our fascinating community.

—Robert Mondavi

Your opinion matters to us...
You may not think it, but customer input is important to the ultimate quality of any revised work or second edition. We invite and appreciate any comments you may have. And by registering your WAG book you are enrolled to receive prepublication discounts, special offers, or alerts to various wine events, only available to registered members.

As your first bonus for registering you will receive, free of charge, our bestselling, interactive GLOBAL ENCYCLOPEDIA OF WINE, on CD-ROM (a $29.95 value). This CD is compatible with PCs and Macs running Mac Classic. It has:

- Wine regions
- The process: from grapes to glass
- Enjoying wine: rituals and tasting
- Wine Guide, a fascinating database for choosing different wines
- Cellar Log Book, that will allow you to document your own wine collection.

You can register your book by phone: (800) 231-9463; Fax: (650) 866-3513; E-Mail: Info@WineAppreciation.com; or snail mail the form on the following page.

REGISTRATION CARD
for HOW AND WHY TO BUILD A WINE CELLAR

Name_____ Date_____
Professional Affiliation_____
Address_____
_____

City_____ State_____ Zip_____
E-Mail_____
· How did you discover this book?_____
· Where did you acquire this book?_____
· How many wine bottles do you intend to store? _____
· Where will your cellar be located? Basement?__ Out building?__Garage?__Spare room?__Other?_____
· Will this be new construction, or will you be remodeling existing space?_____
· What kind of wine racks are you considering? Red wood kits?__Pine kits?__X cubes?__Modular racks?__Custombuilt?__Other?_____
· Will you be needing temperature control equipment?__Split system?__Or in cellar Breezair or Whispercool?___
· When do you hope to complete your wine cellar? Immediately?__6 months?__1 year or more?__
· Would you like a free consultation on the planning and design of your cellar?_____
· Suggestions for this book:_____
_____
_____

· Comments_____
_____
_____

You can register your book by phone: (800) 231-9463;
Fax: (650) 866-3513; Email:
Info@WineAppreciation.com; or snail mail.

THE WINE APPRECIATION GUILD
360 Swift Avenue
South San Francisco, CA 94080

www.wineappreciation.com

Fold Here ▲

Tape Closed Here ▼